Senior International Officers

Essential Roles and Responsibilities

Senior
International
Officers

Essential Roles
and Responsibilities

EDITED BY **David L. Di Maria**

Edited by David L. Di Maria

NAFSA: Association of International Educators
1307 New York Avenue, NW
8th Floor
Washington, DC 20005-4715

NAFSA is the largest and most comprehensive association of professionals committed to advancing international higher education. Based in the United States, we provide programs, products, services, and a physical and virtual meeting space for the worldwide community of international educators. The association provides leadership to its diverse constituencies through establishing principles of good practice and providing professional development opportunities. NAFSA encourages networking among professionals, convenes conferences and collaborative dialogues, and promotes research and knowledge creation to strengthen and serve the field. We lead the way in advocating for a better world through international education.

Library of Congress Cataloging-in-Publication Data

Names: Di Maria, David L., 1981–, editor.
Title: Senior international officers: essential roles and responsibilities / edited by David L. Di Maria.
Description: First edition. | Washington, DC: NAFSA, Association of International Educators,
    [2019] | Includes bibliographical references.
Identifiers: LCCN 2019015194 (print) | LCCN 2019018564 (ebook) |
    ISBN 9781942719274 (EPUB) | ISBN 9781942719250 (alk. paper)
Subjects: LCSH: International education—United States—Administration. | Universities and
    colleges—United States—Administration. | Foreign study—United States—Administration.
Classification: LCC LB2376 (ebook) | LCC LB2376 .S38 2019 (print) | DDC 370.116—dc23
LC record available at https://lccn.loc.gov/2019015194

Edited by Natalie Ngo, NAFSA
Design and Layout by Kathleen Dyson

BULK PURCHASES
Quantity discounts are available for
workshops and staff development.
Call 1.866.538.1927 to order.

First edition, 2019
10 9 8 7 6 5 4 3 2 1

To the founding SIOs

upon whose shoulders we stand

and the emerging scholar-practitioners

of international higher education

who continue this work

and advance our knowledge

in areas previously undefined.

Contents

Acknowledgments

I have long been passionate about the professionalization of the post of senior international officer (SIO). Thus, when Martha Hawley-Bertsch, director of publishing services at NAFSA: Association of International Educators, approached me with the idea of developing a career book for SIOs, I immediately began working on a draft outline. Over a period of several months, Martha and her colleagues at NAFSA helped me to identify gaps in the existing literature and refine the focus of the book accordingly. I wish to thank Martha for providing me with this opportunity to contribute to the field and for granting me the leeway to explore important, but less developed topics, such as the SIO's role in supporting global operations and internationalization of research. Thank you for your confidence in me.

I am extremely grateful to Natalie Ngo, senior editor for publishing services at NAFSA, for her unwavering support throughout this project. From helping me to organize the chapters in a coherent way to providing detailed input on draft after draft after draft to helping me to resolve the tricky challenges that inevitably arise with such an ambitious project, this book would never have made it to publication without her. Thank you for everything!

To NAFSA's Deputy Executive Director of Knowledge Development Dorothea Antonio, Senior Director of Academic Affairs & Internationalization Mark Grace, and the 2018 leadership team of the International Education Leadership Knowledge Community, specifically Erich Dietrich (chair), Ivor Emmanuel, Jane Gatewood, Kate Jennings, Victoria Jones, Sonja Knutson,

Rick Lee, Samira Pardanani, and Christina Sanchez: thank you for endorsing and supporting this project.

To NAFSA's extremely knowledgeable and dedicated staff, including Senior Director of Education Abroad Services Caroline Donovan White and Senior Director of IEM-ISS Services Joann Ng Hartmann, who reviewed multiple drafts and provided valuable feedback related to the content, resources, and tone: thank you for helping to ensure this book serves a wide range of readers.

Thank you to all of the contributors to this book who volunteered their time, knowledge, and experiences. I especially wish to acknowledge Heather Housley, Victoria Jones, and Jesse Lutabingwa for writing quality chapters on such short notice.

Finally, I wish to thank my wife, Masha, for allowing me to work undisturbed on so many weekends, and my three-year-old son, Charlie, who late one evening said, "Daddy go to sleep; I go to work." I owe you both for your understanding, patience, and support.

Foreword

Ángel Cabrera

When I was president of Thunderbird School of Global Management (now part of Arizona State University), I had the honor of welcoming the Dalai Lama to our campus. During his presentation to a packed, and hushed, auditorium, His Holiness urged a class of future international business leaders to not define the world in terms of "us" versus "them." He said that the moment we understand that "our" well-being depends on "theirs," and that all our lives are inextricably interconnected, is when the interest of the "other" becomes our own.

Years later, at George Mason University, I recall those inspirational words often when contemplating the role that university leaders, including senior international officers (SIOs), and institutions must play to make students more globally aware and to embed global citizenship values into the educational experiences we offer and the research we conduct. In the case of George Mason University, as the largest and fastest-growing university in the state of Virginia, serving one of the most diverse student bodies in the nation, the question we face is how to ensure global education is not a privilege for the few, but a realistic expectation for all students.

Discussions of the internationalization of higher education tend to quickly jump into those types of "how" questions: how to send students abroad; how to attract students from abroad; how to convince faculty, deans, provosts, and presidents that they should care; and how to pay for it. It is not that these questions are unimportant—this book is an excellent example of how complex these questions can be and how crucial it is that we examine and exchange best practices. But a prerequisite to answering these questions is that we recognize that internationalization is not an attractive add-on, a luxury for a few, or a secondary concern among our already packed institutional priorities. Internationalization must be addressed as a core element of the mission of the university.

In other words, before we deal with the "how," we need to have a compelling answer to the question of "Why?"

We send students overseas because experiencing other cultural and economic realities is the most effective way to fully grasp the diversity of contexts in which human life unfolds and the interdependencies among all of us. We open our doors to students from other nations because we are committed to their own global learning and because their presence on our campus enriches the learning environment of students who do not study abroad. (Unfortunately, only about 10 percent of U.S. college students study abroad, even though studies have shown that more than 40 percent of first-year undergraduates intend to study abroad before graduation.) We organize international programs on our campuses in order to maximize interactions among students of different national origins and facilitate their collaborative learning. We engage in global research collaborations because, increasingly, in many disciplines, that is the only way to find the truth and new scientific breakthroughs.

Those of us in public universities have to make a compelling case to lawmakers and citizens who may rightfully ask why we should open our universities to international students, maintain operations overseas, or encourage our students to travel. We should be clear that our students' global competence is no longer an optional skill set, but one necessary for career success in a workforce environment dominated by global supply chains, global markets, and global partnerships. We should explain how the international talent that we attract helps power the United States's science, innovations, and entrepreneurship—and how the relationships forged with individuals and institutions overseas contribute priceless social capital that sustains U.S. business competitiveness.

Whatever our answers are to why global engagement matters, any institutional strategy of internationalization must be rooted in a firm, shared commitment to the idea that global education is quintessential to our mission.

This view of global education is increasingly shared by important international actors. In 2017, for example, the influential Programme for International Student Assessment (PISA) of the Organisation for Economic Co-operation and Development (OECD) incorporated "global competence" in its assessment framework. In its own words, "global competence is the capacity to examine local, global, and intercultural issues, to understand and appreciate the perspectives and world views of others, to engage in open, appropriate, and effective interactions with people from different cultures, and to act for collective well-being and sustainable development" (OECD PISA 2018, 7).

Once this shared commitment to global research and education has been achieved, we must recognize that internationalization is a multidimensional, adaptive, and never-ending process. It must be sustained by appropriate faculty policies and rewards, it must take real priority in the curriculum, it must be supported by appropriate administrative resources and capabilities, and it often entails a complex, evolving set of external partnerships.

When world leaders gathered at the United Nations Headquarters in New York in September 2015 to adopt a new set of global development priorities, the Sustainable Development Goals, the interdependencies between the well-being of peoples around the world were inescapable. In order to end poverty and hunger, to allow everyone to live dignified, productive, healthy, and peaceful lives while ensuring that our planet can sustain the lives of those who will come behind us, we must understand and address economic, social, geological, and biological dynamics that transcend national political realities. Only by recognizing the diverse realities around the world and the complex web of interdependencies among all our economies, cultures, and ecosystems can we begin to identify and apply solutions that may bring about improvements in quality of life for all of us.

There is no wall, figurative or physical, capable of withstanding the forces of international trade, global supply chains and finance, ocean freight, air travel, the internet, and the globally compounding effect of carbon emissions. While isolationist, nativist, and antiglobalization voices will continue to find echo chambers, the forces of freedom—of movement, of the exchange of goods and ideas—have been and will continue to be far stronger. We are bound together for the good and the bad, and only by ensuring that citizens around the world understand this reality will we be able to find reasonable paths forward. If we fail to educate citizens with some global outlook and understanding, we will be failing them personally and professionally and hurting our chances of building shared prosperity.

The ideas and wisdom contained in the following pages provide a valuable guide for SIOs to advance and promote the global impact that we must develop. There is much at stake in our ability to truly internationalize higher education—not just for our universities, but for the future of the world in which we live. Just as those budding business leaders learned in the auditorium that day from the Dalai Lama, this opportunity is "ours," not "theirs."

References

Organisation for Economic Co-operation and Development (OECD) Programme for International Student Assessment (PISA). 2018. *Preparing Our Youth for an Inclusive and Sustainable World: The OECD PISA Global Competence Framework*. Paris, France: Organisation for Economic Co-operation and Development Programme for International Student Assessment. http://www.oecd.org/pisa/Handbook-PISA-2018-Global-Competence.pdf.

Introduction

David L. Di Maria

International education leadership is still very much an emerging professional domain at most colleges and universities around the world. This is true despite the significant progress made over the past few decades by professional associations and graduate preparation programs in developing formal education and training programs designed to improve the specialized knowledge and skills of international education leaders. Thus, while the position of senior international officer (SIO) is far more common and prominent at colleges and universities today than in prior years (Helms and Brajkovic 2017), it is still more loosely defined than other senior administrative posts, such as chief financial officer and chief student affairs officer.

This book serves to advance the field of international education leadership by offering a broad overview of functional areas of responsibility for which SIOs are often directly or indirectly accountable. The chapters contained within this volume are written by a diverse array of experienced international education leaders mostly based within the SIO community. As such, this book is the most comprehensive and inclusive publication to date in terms of topics and perspectives. It serves a very broad audience that includes graduate students, faculty, aspiring international education leaders, experienced SIOs, search consultants, and senior administrators who are seeking qualified candidates to lead their institution's internationalization efforts.

Administration of Internationalization Programs and Activities

While the roles and responsibilities of SIOs may differ significantly from one institution to another, what all these positions tend to have in common is oversight of more than one program or activity designed to advance internationalization (Helms and Brajkovic 2017) in support of the mission, vision, values, and strategic direction of a given college or university.

According to Jane Knight (2015, 2), "internationalization at the national, sector, and institutional levels is defined as the process of integrating an international, intercultural, or global dimension into the purpose, functions or delivery of postsecondary education." Thus, internationalization represents transformative organizational change that requires genuine institutional commitment and prioritization if it is to be both effective and lasting. As presented in the framework of figure 1, the ability of SIOs to lead successful internationalization efforts may be conceptualized from two dimensions: strategy for internationalization and resources for internationalization.

- Strategy for internationalization. At some institutions, internationalization is a hobby enjoyed by a self-selected few. As a result, at these institutions, internationalization programs and activities are mostly restricted to one or more academic or administrative units where initiatives serve as a positive supplement to, but not an essential component of, the institution's overall mission. At other institutions, internationalization serves unique departmental interests and advances higher-level institutional goals and objectives under the leadership of a qualified SIO. Thus, in those instances, internationalization is an institutional imperative.

- Resources for internationalization. Some institutional leaders view international activities and programs as expensive accessories to be funded only after more essential needs are met. In this situation, internationalization initiatives often stall out as need outstrips resources, limiting the SIO's ability to implement effective internationalization initiatives. At other institutions, internationalization is understood to be a sound business plan requiring strategic investments of time, effort, and financial resources. In this instance, internationalization programs and activities are appropriately resourced for sustainable growth, and the SIO can promote an entrepreneurial culture that keeps the institution relevant in a rapidly changing and increasingly competitive global environment.

Figure 1. Framework for Administering Institutional Internationalization Activities

It is possible for various aspects of internationalization to place within different quadrants of the framework (figure 1). For instance, an institutional emphasis on applied learning may prioritize education abroad as an institutional investment, while a rudimentary understanding of international enrollment management may result in the treatment of international student recruitment as a departmental expense.

Five Factors Affecting Placement Within the Framework

A general assessment of approaches to administering internationalization programs and activities (see figure 1) can be achieved both in whole and in part by considering five basic factors that maintain importance across all institutional types. These factors are budget, SIO position, space, staffing, and work environment.

BUDGET

Regardless of rhetoric, institutional priorities are clearly represented by the allocation of funds. At institutions where internationalization is something other than institutional strategy, the SIO's budget may be heavily dependent on self-support activities, such as student fees. At institutions where the costs of internationalization are viewed as elective expenses as opposed to institutional investments, the SIO is likely to find himself or herself placed in a very difficult situation. A vision for internationalization devoid of adequate financial investment amounts to little more than fanciful thinking, which ultimately results in disappointment.

Considerations:

- What type of budget model does the institution employ?

- Is the SIO's budget scalable, or does funding remain flat despite program growth?

- What revenue streams contribute to the SIO's financial portfolio?

- What percentage of the operating budget is funded by the central administration?

- What level of discretionary authority does the SIO have in determining how to manage the financial resources?

- Is the SIO supported by internal accounting staff or a shared services accounting team?

- Does the SIO have access to reporting tools to assist with financial management and projections?

- Do other administrators view internationalization as a competing or complementary fiscal priority?

- Does the development office support the SIO in fundraising for internationalization?

- Is the SIO empowered to engage in entrepreneurial and grant-funded activities?

SIO POSITION

The most recent survey data collected by the Association of International Education Administrators indicate that 71 percent of SIOs report to a vice president/chancellor/provost of academic affairs, while another 11 percent report to a president/chancellor or chief executive officer (Kwai 2017). A 2017 report by the Association of Public and Land-grant Universities (APLU) cautions that progress toward internationalization is impeded when authority lines and reporting structures do not reflect a high prioritization of internationalization. Specifically, the report questions how "institutions plan to meet the global goals embedded in strategic plans if the SIO does not have a reporting line into the provost's or the president's office" (APLU 2017, 25).

Considerations:

- How does the SIO position fit within the institution's leadership structure?

- To whom does the SIO report?

- Who are the SIO's peers?

- For which programs, policies, and units does the SIO have administrative or academic oversight?

- Does the SIO have both the title and authority to represent the institution in international dealings?

- Does the campus community have a shared understanding and appreciation of the SIO position?

- Is the SIO supported by an appropriate advisory board?

- Is the SIO a full member of relevant committees and governance councils?

- Does the SIO have an appointment in one or more academic units?

- Is the SIO included in relevant meetings, events, and other functions?

SPACE

Facilities are physical manifestations of institutional vision and represent some of the most contested resources on any college campus. Just as effective internationalization programs and activities require sound strategy, so too do international offices require intentional placement and design.

Considerations:

- Does the space meet the basic legal, programmatic, and service needs (e.g., confidentiality)?

- Is the international office located in a high-traffic area, or is it hidden away in an odd or difficult to find location?

- Is the space located near complementary units?

- How is the space viewed by students, faculty, and other stakeholder groups?

- What cultural, political, and other messages does the space convey?

- How does the space reflect the institution's understanding and prioritization of international engagement?

- Does the space support campus and community programming, or is it purely utilitarian?

- Is the space an appropriate location for hosting international partners and foreign dignitaries, or must the SIO borrow more presentable space elsewhere on the campus?

- How does the space impact employee morale and productivity?

- What restrictions (e.g., catering or hours of operation) impact use of the space?

STAFFING

Regardless of the size or type of institution, the SIO requires adequate staffing support to manage core functions and achieve strategic goals related to internationalization. As more institutions create SIO positions (Helms and Brajkovic 2017), it is imperative not to overlook investment in the SIO's leadership and support team. After all, a leader is only as good as his or her followers, and an SIO who lacks adequate staffing to manage day-to-day operations is severely limited in his or her ability to move the institution's internationalization strategy forward. In environments where internationalization is highly centralized, adequate staffing may be achieved through additional funding for new positions. In more decentralized environments, this may simply require consolidation of existing positions scattered across various administrative units.

Considerations:

- How does staffing within the international office compare with that of peer institutions?

- Are position descriptions clearly written, and do they reflect current responsibilities?

- Are salary levels adequate to attract and retain qualified employees?

- How much bandwidth do the staff members have to support current and future initiatives?

- Do staff members have access to the basic tools (e.g., NAFSA's Adviser's Manual) to do their job effectively?

- What opportunities are available for professional development?

- Are staff members represented by unions?

- How are the staff members regarded by students, faculty, staff, and other stakeholders?

- Is the SIO expected to build, change, or maintain the current office culture?

- Is the employer supportive of work-life balance and personal well-being?

WORK ENVIRONMENT

According to Gallup (2018), 51 percent of employees are actively searching for new jobs or on the lookout for openings. Factors such as job fit, organizational culture, and relationship with one's supervisor are among the most common reasons given for leaving. Frequent turnover is not just a problem for entry-level and middle-management positions, but also for senior leaders, especially considering that nearly half of SIOs have served in their current position for less than 5 years (Kwai 2017) and the average tenure of a college president is just 6.5 years (Seltzer 2017). The SIO's work environment is a key factor in determining whether internationalization efforts will succeed. This is further complicated by the fact that while nearly all colleges and universities publicly commit to maintaining an equal opportunity work environment, SIOs can sometimes be targets for discrimination due to the specific nature of the institutional internationalization priorities. For instance, an institution focused on partnerships in the Middle East may prefer to employ a male SIO due to cultural customs surrounding gender roles, while an institution prioritizing connections in Asia may overlook younger SIO candidates based on the societal emphasis on age hierarchies. Finally, because many search committees for SIO positions include strong representation by members of the faculty, they may prefer a candidate with a strong background in teaching and research, even if the individual has never worked in an international office. Since the work of the SIO touches all aspects of the institution, this position is open to greater scrutiny than many other senior administrative posts.

Considerations:

- How do international and global themes fit within the institution's understanding and practice of diversity, equity, and inclusion?

- Do institutional policies, procedures, and systems help or hinder global engagement?

- What is the international profile of the institution and local community?

- What is the relationship between the administration, faculty, students, and local community leaders?

- How invested is senior leadership in the growth and success of the SIO and internationalization efforts in general?

- Is there an institutional bias (positive or negative) based on the SIO's academic background, age, ethnicity, race, national origin, gender, disability, political views, religion, veteran status, or other characteristics?

- Does the SIO have a clear understanding of performance goals?

- Does the employer hold the SIO harmless for critical events beyond the control of the SIO (e.g., economic recession and strained diplomatic relations)?

- Is the SIO granted flextime to recover from jet lag, account for missed holidays, etc.?

- Are members of the SIO's team supportive of each other and of the SIO?

While these are not the only factors that influence the administration of internationalization programs and activities, they tend to be common across most institutions and affect each role and responsibility covered by the chapters of this book.

Overview of Chapters

This book includes 20 chapters and two appendixes written by 26 experienced international education administrators representing institutions based in the United States and abroad. As such, it is arguably the most extensive contribution made to the professional literature to date. The chapters are organized into four sections: strategy, administration, faculty and academics, and partnerships and outreach. The authors represent different types of institutions, ranging from public to private, large to small, and community college to research intensive.

Chapter 1 presents a three-dimensional framework for understanding the roles of SIOs. The chapter describes functional areas of responsibility and provides an overview of the types of SIO positions found throughout the field. The author also examines current trends shaping the next generation of SIOs. The chapter is particularly useful for readers aspiring to SIO positions and for current SIOs considering a position at another institution.

Chapter 2 centers on the various types of stakeholders with whom SIOs interact. The author provides insights regarding stakeholder identification, analysis, and engagement. With broad application beyond the SIO position, the chapter is an excellent resource to supplement staff development and strategic planning initiatives.

In chapter 3, the author takes a critical look at SIOs' roles in risk management, crisis communications, and media relations. The chapter can be used as a reference in ongoing training and shared with other members on campus with whom SIOs collaborate in times of crisis. The content is highly relevant given the current geopolitical environment.

Chapter 4 focuses on key considerations for developing and executing an internationalization strategy. The author reviews the strategic planning process undertaken by the University of Calgary, an institution that has received both national and international awards for its integrated international programs and activities. The chapter is a useful resource for SIOs and other senior administrators wishing to move internationalization strategy from the departmental to the institutional level. Internationalization consultants as well as scholars of international higher education will find value in the chapter's detailed approach.

Chapter 5 is an essential resource written for aspiring, new, and experienced SIOs. The author covers the core aspects of applying, interviewing, and negotiating for employment contracts for SIO positions. The chapter also includes advice for newly hired SIOs with a focus on building cooperative networks to advance internationalization. The chapter concludes with a discussion of career progression for current and former SIOs.

Chapter 6 offers a high-level picture of the roles that SIOs play in managing budgets and finances. The author explains traditional sources of funding, analyzes key considerations for budget development, and shares innovative techniques for establishing new sources of revenue to support internationalization initiatives. The chapter is relevant for all SIOs, whether they are responsible for a modest operating budget or a vast financial portfolio.

In chapter 7, the author provides an overview of the field of education abroad. The chapter explores the historical development of education abroad programs, important business considerations, and essential findings from the research literature. This look into the policies and practices of learning abroad can be beneficial to SIOs who are tasked with expanding the business of education abroad.

Chapter 8 studies issues and trends related to the administration of intensive English programs (IEPs). The author touches on common administrative structures, challenges, and opportunities that SIOs today may face in working with IEPs. The chapter concludes with a proposed model to help improve the efficacy of IEPs.

Chapter 9 covers some of the central concepts that all SIOs should be aware of pertaining to the field of international enrollment management (IEM). The chapter is essential reading for SIOs who do not have prior professional experience in this area. While IEM may or may not be a primary responsibility of the position, all SIOs should understand this important field because healthy enrollment determines the overall success of other areas.

Chapter 10 describes the roles of SIOs in terms of immigration services and institutional compliance. The chapter imparts key administrative considerations, such as the need for appropriate adviser caseloads and the advantages of technology, as well as recommendations of fundamental immigration resources for SIOs.

In chapter 11, the author explores SIOs' coordinated efforts with other stakeholders, including academic deans, department chairs, and program directors, to ensure that internationalization is embedded into the academic offerings of the institution. The chapter contains an inspiring discussion of the ways by which the SIO at Kennesaw State University has advanced internationalization within academic affairs.

Chapter 12 dives further into the dynamic relationship between global learning and academic programs, with an emphasis on internationalization of the curriculum. The chapter includes a case study on Emerson College's highly innovative and effective Curriculum Internationalization Studio.

Chapter 13 reviews ways that entrepreneurial SIOs can strategically collaborate with continuing professional education units to advance internationalization. The authors describe the financial benefits resulting from these partnerships using a few case studies. The chapter is a useful read for SIOs seeking to expand revenue streams or those looking to support IEPs where the traditional student population is in decline.

Chapter 14 delves into the internationalization of research, a topic that receives too little attention within the field, particularly considering that the SIO position is most common at U.S. doctoral and master's institutions, where nearly 80 percent now have such an administrator on staff (Helms and Brajkovic 2017). The authors deliver strategies for success using the University of South Florida as a case study. The chapter is a handy resource for SIOs to share with their colleagues in divisions and departments that support faculty research, graduate education, and institutional effectiveness.

Chapter 15 continues the discussion on SIOs' roles in advancing the internationalization of research by highlighting a successful program for supporting faculty at Michigan State University. While this case study features the success made by one institution, it is easy to see how the program can be adapted elsewhere.

In chapter 16, the author outlines a strategic approach to managing international partnerships, contracts, and agreements. The chapter includes an overview of reasons for establishing international partnerships, as well as considerations for diplomacy, protocol, benchmarking, and assessment. A recent survey conducted by the Association of International Education Administrators found that 92 percent of SIOs consider international partnerships to be among their top three primary responsibilities (Kwai 2017).

Chapter 17 is a study of global operations—a term used to describe the business aspects of international engagement—a subfield that has received less attention than others. Some considerations for SIOs include the policies, procedures, and administrative support for hiring employees abroad; the registration of international programs and activities with legal presence; foreign taxation; property management; and much more. The chapter concludes with an overview of various models and methods for managing global operations, using the University of California Office of the President as a case study.

In chapter 18, the author uses a case study of Salisbury University to demonstrate the potential outcomes of relationships between SIOs and local government officials. Specifically, the author looks into the impact of aligning internationalization strategy with existing sister city and sister state initiatives.

Chapter 19 focuses on supporting international students' success through campus and community programming. The author shares novel initiatives undertaken at St. Cloud State University, where international students receive generous financial awards for demonstrating positive study habits and engagement with the local community.

Chapter 20 brings attention to SIOs' roles in engaging international alumni in institutional internationalization activities, such as student recruitment, networking, and fundraising. The author examines some common challenges and poses strategies for addressing them.

Appendix A provides a useful checklist for mapping immigration services at an institution to assist SIOs in supporting immigration-related matters.

Appendix B offers a list of resources that may be of value to SIOs and other international education leaders in their ongoing work. While the scope is not exhaustive, the list includes synopses of some of the most relevant professional associations, meetings, and tools used by a wide range of SIOs.

Conclusion

Senior International Officers: Essential Roles and Responsibilities is intended to serve as a practical resource for a broad audience, including graduate students and scholars of international higher education, aspiring and current SIOs, and executive officers seeking to hire an SIO to lead internationalization efforts at their college or university. The book provides insights and practical takeaways for SIOs of all types and backgrounds, ranging from a director leading a one-person office of international education to a vice president leading a global affairs division similar in scale to a multinational corporation with hundreds of employees spread across programs and facilities operating on every continent.

The chapters are written by a diverse and experienced group of international education leaders representing a wide range of positions, institutions, and countries. Each author provides a unique perspective based upon his or her personal experiences in the field of international education administration. Some of the chapters serve to highlight basic issues in more developed subfields, such as education abroad and international enrollment management, while other chapters focus on areas that have mostly been ignored, such as global operations and internationalization of research.

The content balances leadership considerations with managerial concerns and presents insights relevant to current trends, opportunities, and resources. The book offers a comprehensive look at SIOs' various charges, challenges, and strategic tools to ensure that all readers leave with new knowledge and ideas for their own career development as well as the advancement of the overall profession. With this guidance in hand, SIOs can continue to extend the reach of their efforts across their institution and beyond with strategic intention.

References

Association of Public and Land-grant Universities (APLU). 2017. *Pervasive Internationalization: A Call for Renewed Leadership.* Washington, DC: Association of Public and Land-grant Universities. http://www.aplu.org/library/pervasive-internationalization-a-call-for-renewed-leadership/file.

Gallop. 2018. *State of the American Workplace.* Washington, DC: Gallop. https://www.gallup.com/workplace/238085/state-american-workplace-report-2018.aspx.

Helms, Robin Matross, and Lucia Brajkovic. 2017. *Mapping Internationalization on U.S. Campuses: 2017 Edition.* Washington, DC: American Council on Education.

Knight, Jane. 2015. "Updating the Definition of Internationalization." *International Higher Education* 33, 6:2–3. https://ejournals.bc.edu/ojs/index.php/ihe/article/viewFile/7391/6588.

Kwai, C. K. 2017. "The SIO Profile: A Preliminary Analysis of the Survey on Senior International Education Officers, Their Institutions and Offices."

Durham, NC: Association of International Education Administrators. https://
www.aieaworld.org/assets/docs/Surveys/final-2017%20executive%20summary_
sio%20profile%20survey.pdf.

Seltzer, Rick. 2017. "The Slowly Diversifying Presidency." *Inside Higher Ed.*
June 20, 2017. https://www.insidehighered.com/news/2017/06/20/college-
presidents-diversifying-slowly-and-growing-older-study-finds.

PART 1
Strategy

1 Senior International Officer Roles and Responsibilities

David L. Di Maria

Over the past several years, there has been much effort placed into defining the positions of the most senior international education leaders. While titles and functions vary greatly across institutions and countries, there is something these leaders all have in common: a legitimate authority stemming from their positions, experiences, and expertise to shape one or all aspects of internationalization strategy.

In this chapter, the individuals holding these unique leadership positions are referred to as "senior international officers" (SIOs), a term that is mostly used in the United States. Yet, this unique position also encompasses pro vice chancellors (international), vice rectors, and other titles used around the world to classify the most senior international education leaders, in terms of authority, at institutions of higher education.

The actual titles of SIOs range from director to vice chancellor, but what 82 percent of these positions have in common is a direct reporting line to either the first (e.g., president, rector) or second (e.g., vice president, provost) highest ranked administrator at their institution (Kwai 2017). The appointment of SIOs as core members of institutional leadership teams has now become so commonplace that a recent report by the Association of Public and Land-grant Universities (APLU) calls into question the ability of institutions "to meet the global goals embedded in strategic plans if SIOs do not have a reporting line to the provost or president's office" (APLU 2017, 25).

While current definitions and profiles of SIOs published within the professional literature tend to focus on shared characteristics, this chapter explains the many ways in which SIO positions differ. The comparative frameworks and position types described in this chapter are intended to be of benefit to professionals seeking to acquire international education leadership positions, hiring officials aiming to fill such positions, and current leaders intending to accept a leadership position at a different institution.

A Multidimensional Framework for Understanding the Roles of SIOs

Just as approaches to internationalization vary significantly from institution to institution and country to country, so too do the roles of SIOs. How these positions fit within the organizational structure and the expectations that campus constituents have for them are often predetermined by institutional history, mission, and vision. For instance, consider how the role of the SIO would differ at an institution where internationalization is a core value and prominently embedded within the institution's strategic plan versus an institution only just beginning to establish a central international office. Similarly, how might the expectations for the SIO at an institution recently authorized to enroll international students vary from an SIO at an institution that has a long history of receiving major gifts from international alumni?

The multidimensional framework presented in this chapter is intended to provide a more nuanced understanding of the various ways in which SIO positions differ. The reader may best utilize this framework by first considering the role of the SIO along two dimensions. The first dimension reflects the level of alignment between internationalization and institutional strategy. The second dimension reflects the level of urgency with regard to international education leadership. Each dimension is divided among three levels: high, medium, and low.

Next, the reader should review the functional areas of responsibility to determine which apply to the SIO position in question. It is critical to identify the correct functional areas because they represent the scope of the SIO's work. The reader can then refer to the other chapters in this book to learn more about each area of responsibility.

Strategic Alignment

Strategy represents an intentional, high-level plan designed to achieve one or more overarching goals. Whereas, internationalization can serve as a rising tide that lifts all boats. It is critical for the work of the SIO to carefully align internationalization with the overarching strategy of the institution; failure to do so places the SIO and all internationalization efforts at risk for marginalization.

> One of the most important reasons why international education professionals are not given more importance on their campuses is precisely because they are perceived—and remain—at the technical level of functioning. While technical skills are very important, they don't prove to be very helpful on a higher level. (Mestenhauser and Ellingboe 2005, 39)

At institutions where there is a highly developed understanding of how internationalization relates to institutional strategy, the SIO tends to operate at the hub (see figure 1) of the institution's strategy wheel. In this case, internationalization represents a core value shared across multiple divisions and units. Institutional stakeholders appreciate and advance the international and global dimensions of their own academic disciplines and professional domains.

Figure 1. Placement Within the Institution's Strategy Wheel

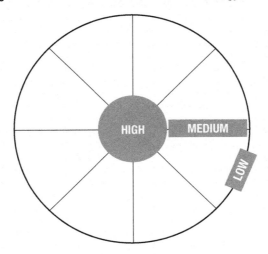

At institutions where there is a medium level of strategic alignment, the SIO operates as a spoke in the institution's strategy wheel (see figure 1). While still connected to the hub of the institution, internationalization represents one of many competing priorities. In this instance, institutional leaders recognize the importance of internationalization, but look to the SIO to elevate the conversation.

At institutions with a low level of strategic alignment, the SIO tends to operate on the felloes (i.e., periphery) of institutional strategy (see figure 1). In this case, internationalization is viewed as the responsibility of an individual or group of individuals who are mostly left to their own devices.

Urgency

Like the levels of strategic alignment, levels of urgency serve as useful measures of prioritization for internationalization. The key distinction within the context of the framework is that urgency is time sensitive. When institutional leaders ascribe a high level of urgency to the work of the SIO, it typically suggests there is both a desire and need to sustain something for which the institution does not wish to do without, fix something that is broken, or improve something that already exists. A medium level of urgency suggests certain internationalization programs and activities are prioritized above others, and the SIO is expected to address a particular need or achieve a particular result in relation to those priorities. A low level of urgency suggests the primary role of the SIO is to develop a long-term plan that aligns with future strategy, identify current challenges and opportunities that should inform future strategy, or simply fulfill the need for having an SIO.

Figure 2 is a multidimensional framework of the most common roles and responsibilities of SIOs, categorized according to the three levels of strategy and urgency. Each functional area of responsibility is discussed in further detail in the subsequent section.

Figure 2. Multidimensional Framework for Understanding SIO Positions

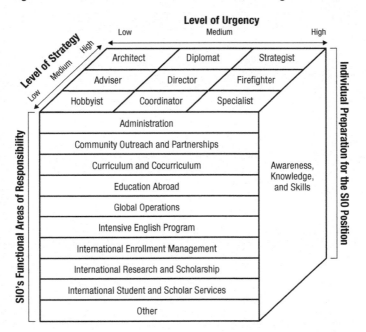

Functional Areas of Responsibility

According to the American Council on Education, the majority of higher education institutions in the United States centralize their international programs and activities under the leadership of a senior, full-time international education administrator (Helms and Brajkovic 2017). This means the responsibilities of SIOs increasingly include areas that extend well beyond inbound and outbound academic mobility. Table 1 presents some of the major tasks that SIOs perform within each of the most prevalent functional areas of responsibility. This list will continue to expand as greater numbers of campus leaders begin to understand that internationalization is not a stand-alone set of programs, but rather an essential strategy for achieving institutional goals and objectives.

Table 1. Functional Areas of Responsibility for SIOs

Responsibility Area	May Include...
Administration	Budgeting; ceremonies and events; facilities; fundraising and development; international alumni relations; leadership; management; mentorship; policy development and enforcement; staffing; and strategies
Community Outreach and Partnerships	Advocacy; civic, government, institutional, and private sector partnerships; hospitality and protocol; intercultural communication; international agreements; professional associations; public speaking; sister city programs; and World Affairs Councils
Curriculum and Cocurriculum	Accreditation; area and global studies programs; campus and community events; virtual exchanges; curriculum integration; foreign language programs; learning outcomes; residential learning communities; and student organizations
Education Abroad	Direct enroll; exchanges; dual-degree and joint-degree programs; faculty-led programs; internships; service learning; transfers of credits; and visas and stay permits
Global Operations	Foreign campuses, centers, and sites; counterintelligence; crisis response; foreign bank accounts; foreign licensing and registration; foreign offices; foreign workers; insurance; legal compliance at home and abroad; risk management; taxation; and transnational education
Intensive English Program	Accreditation; curriculum development; assessment; special programs; bridge programs; English for academic purposes; and English for specific purposes
International Enrollment Management	International admissions; international student recruitment; foreign credential evaluation; global brand management; international marketing and communications; and overseas advising and counseling
International Research and Scholarship	Contracts and grants; export controls; foreign licensing; global academic rankings; and performances
International Student and Scholar Services	Immigration compliance; nonresident alien taxation; predeparture and orientation programs; retention programs; and services for dependents
Other	Continuing education; Confucius Institutes; online education; and research centers and institutes

Types of SIO Positions

Returning to the framework's dimensions of strategic alignment and urgency (see figure 2), there are nine major types of SIO positions: architect, diplomat, strategist, adviser, director, firefighter, hobbyist, coordinator, and specialist. While the field of international education administration is constantly evolving and the roles of SIOs shift depending on institutional and government priorities, the following descriptions provide a broad snapshot of the various roles and expectations for SIOs.

THE ARCHITECT: HIGH LEVEL OF STRATEGY AND LOW LEVEL OF URGENCY

This type of SIO is hired to develop international programs at an institution where internationalization is a new or previously unattended priority. The architect's role mostly includes drafting initial plans for internationalization, benchmarking against peer institutions, and identifying necessary resources to complete the project. These SIOs must have the technical knowledge to perform duties for which there may be no other staff (e.g., budgeting and risk management), while also articulating and advancing a bold vision for the future.

THE DIPLOMAT: HIGH LEVEL OF STRATEGY AND MEDIUM LEVEL OF URGENCY

The role of the diplomat tends to be filled by highly distinguished academics, former ambassadors, and high-profile business and nonprofit leaders. These SIOs are mostly valued for their ability to obtain access to and interact effectively with high-level external stakeholders, such as multinational corporations, government ministries, and nongovernmental organizations. These individuals are highly valued for the gravitas they bring to their institution, and they often have an active role within the cabinet of their president or chancellor. Diplomats are often neither expected nor required to understand the inner workings of the international education units reporting to them because an experienced deputy (i.e., chief of staff) or team of high-level directors typically handle operational concerns.

This type of SIO position is most common at affluent and prestigious private universities as well as large public flagships. The position of the diplomat is almost exclusively externally facing, primarily serving as the dignified face of the institution in all international dealings. Other core responsibilities typically include alumni relations, development, and fundraising.

> While the words "development" and "fundraising" are often used interchangeably, they do represent different tasks in the higher education sphere. Development is a process through which strategic relationships are managed, while fundraising represents the act of generating revenue. It is important for SIOs to recognize and communicate these differences to campus, alumni, and partner constituents.

THE STRATEGIST: HIGH LEVEL OF STRATEGY AND HIGH LEVEL OF URGENCY

The strategist position is similar to the diplomat in terms of status and prestige, but these individuals are also expected to have a high-level understanding of international education administration. The role of the strategist tends to be filled by high-performing international education practitioners or scholars with a strong academic background related to international education. These SIOs typically hold sufficient academic and professional credentials to earn the respect of faculty, other senior administrators, and external constituents alike.

The key difference between the diplomat and the strategist is that while the former maintains an almost exclusively external focus, the latter serves to bridge both external strategy and internal execution. Therefore, SIOs serving as strategists tend to have significant experience and expertise in at least one functional area (e.g., education abroad, international enrollment management) within their portfolio of responsibilities.

THE ADVISER: MEDIUM LEVEL OF STRATEGY AND LOW LEVEL OF URGENCY

While the adviser position may lack authority over specific international programs and activities, these individuals serve to assist senior administrators with key considerations related to international opportunities and threats. These types of SIOs may carry the title of special assistant to the president or senior adviser to the provost. Advisers may hold a regular administrative appointment, be a faculty member who has received course release time to focus on internationalization strategy, or serve as an independent consultant on a fixed-term appointment.

THE DIRECTOR: MEDIUM LEVEL OF STRATEGY AND MEDIUM LEVEL OF URGENCY

Assuming a normal distribution, the director represents the most common SIO position across all types of institutions. The director leads a central administrative unit responsible for two or more functional areas of internationalization. At minimum, these responsibilities tend to include education abroad and immigration services for international students. While SIOs serving in this position direct key aspects of international education, these individuals may not necessarily hold the formal title of "director." The presence of this type of SIO position is most common at institutions where a strategic approach to internationalization is acknowledged but not necessarily a top priority, and where a medium level of urgency, usually due to the volume of inbound and outbound mobility, necessitates full-time administrative oversight.

THE FIREFIGHTER: MEDIUM LEVEL OF STRATEGY AND HIGH LEVEL OF URGENCY

Firefighters are usually hired to address an acute problem or crisis impacting the institution's internationalization initiatives. The decision to hire such an SIO may be predicated on a recent tragedy (e.g., death of a student overseas) or ongoing concern (e.g., declining international enrollment). These SIOs will often find a sufficient amount of support from institutional leadership to address the concerns, but they may encounter intense resistance to change among the staff in their own office, particularly when those staff members are partially or fully responsible for the development of the crisis in the first place.

This SIO position tends to involve both a high risk in terms of job security and high reward in terms of compensation and fringe benefits. The decision to accept an SIO position at a struggling institution or within a dysfunctional international education unit is one that should not be made lightly because even after all the major fires are extinguished, the SIO may find the position unsustainable.

THE HOBBYIST: LOW LEVEL OF STRATEGY AND LOW LEVEL OF URGENCY

In this scenario, the SIO position is most typically awarded to a current member of the faculty. The hobbyist role may include oversight of a central administrative unit, if one exists, or simply designation as the institution's official representative in international dealings. In some cases, the SIO role is added on to other responsibilities, such as teaching and research. Such SIO positions are most common at small liberal arts colleges, but the practice continues at other types of institutions as well. The hobbyist is typically a position created out of convenience more so than strategy or urgency.

THE COORDINATOR: LOW LEVEL OF STRATEGY AND MEDIUM LEVEL OF URGENCY

The coordinator position represents an early attempt to centralize certain international programs and activities. These SIOs may serve in a one-person office, oversee a small team with limited scope, or convene the meetings of faculty committees focused on international engagement. Coordinators are most commonly found at small rural colleges where internationalization is not yet viewed as an essential component of the institution's strategy.

THE SPECIALIST: LOW LEVEL OF STRATEGY AND HIGH LEVEL OF URGENCY

Specialists are appointed or hired for the specific knowledge and skills they hold. The need for this position is often present at institutions where one area of internationalization is valued above all others. An example is an institution where there is a presidential proclamation that education abroad participation will double in 5 years. This position requires a higher level of urgency in that the institution has identified and prioritized a specific functional area, but institutional planning is not yet systemic.

THE CHIEF OF STAFF

The various types of functions and responsibilities described above serve to map out the complexity of the SIO position. However, this chapter would be incomplete if it did not address a tenth type of international education leader, without whom many internationalization efforts would fail.

While not technically the SIO, and thus excluded from the framework (figure 2), the chief of staff may in fact have more influence over the strategic direction of the institution than the SIO to whom the chief of staff reports. These individuals may hold the titles of directors, executive directors, or even assistant provosts, and they are most likely to be found at large institutions where the SIO role is that of a diplomat or strategist.

The effectiveness of the chief of staff is based more on personal leadership than positional authority. As such, these individuals work behind the scenes to set unit budgets, coordinate institutional strategies, and otherwise allow high-profile SIOs to continue to shine. Chiefs of staff receive far too little credit for the contributions they make to their institutions and the field of international education. While chiefs of staff are often the backbone of successful internationalization efforts, they are frequently excluded from full participation in professional meetings, often unable to hold seats on important committees, and seldom invited to contribute to important projects focused on the field of international education. It is important that chiefs of staff be recognized for their ability to manage up, down, and across the institution. While SIO is a position (i.e., administrative designation), the international education leader is a person and the two are not always one and the same.

Not all of the functional areas of responsibility addressed in this book will fall under the purview of every SIO, and the types of SIO positions presented are not necessarily exclusive. Nonetheless, as international and global engagement grow in importance across all sectors of higher education, institutional leaders must regularly rethink their organizational structures if they are to remain relevant and competitive within the global century (Cleveland 1999; Kugler and Frost 2002; Association of American Colleges and Universities 2007).

Individual Preparation for the SIO Position

The profile of the SIO is rapidly changing, as is the field of international education. Since 1999, when the Association of International Education Administrators (AIEA) administered its first survey of what at the time were referred to as "chief international education administrators," the general profile of SIOs has shifted away from senior faculty members (Hoemeke et al. 2006; Lambert et al. 2007; Dessoff 2010) to international education professionals (Kwai 2017). One of the primary reasons for this change is the increased professionalization of the field, which has led to broader recognition that effective international education leaders require specialized education, knowledge, and skills.

Qualifications

A shift began to appear in the professional literature as early as 2006, with an article published in NAFSA: Association of International Educators's flagship magazine, *International Educator,* where one SIO, Joël A. Gallegos, observed, "for some of us, 15 years ago and earlier, we would just fall into it [the SIO position] through area studies or living abroad or the Peace Corps. Now, people are entering the workforce to specifically work in international education" (Dessoff 2006, 37).

In a guest column written for the *Chronicle of Higher Education*, Harvey Charles, former president of AIEA, and Darla K. Deardorff, AIEA's executive director, challenge the flawed logic used by many senior administrators when hiring SIOs. Charles and Deardorff (2014) argue that the reason why many colleges and universities fail in their internationalization efforts is because senior leaders do not understand that international education leadership is a maturing professional domain and SIOs require specialized knowledge and skills. As such, many search committees continue to apply superficial standards to the hiring process of SIOs in ways that would never be appropriate in the hiring of other senior administrators, such as chief human resource officers, chief financial officers, or chief technology officers.

> Individuals have been appointed, for example, because they teach languages other than English, because they are immigrants to the United States, because they served as U.S. ambassadors to other countries, or because they have an affinity for working with international students, among other rationales. In other cases, universities have specifically sought distinguished research scholars with extensive publications, believing that this kind of credibility can be leveraged to quickly transform their universities into significant global players. (Charles and Deardorff 2014)

These qualifications no longer reflect the necessary characteristics and qualifications of effective SIOs, particularly as more institutions centralize previously disparate offices, programs, and activities under the SIO's purview. Thus, successful SIOs today often have broad experience and unique expertise related to multiple areas within and around the institution's internationalization portfolio. (For more on aligning SIOs' competencies with institutional needs, see chapter 5.) While it is important not to diminish the contributions of earlier generations of SIOs, many of whom served as trailblazers who laid the very foundations upon which the profession now stands, it would be an oversight not to acknowledge how advances to the profession have reshaped the hiring practices for the SIO position. Figure 3 depicts the traditional career path for SIOs, and figure 4 displays an emerging career path.

Figure 3. Traditional Path to an SIO Position

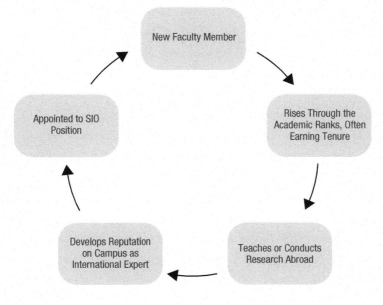

Figure 4. Emerging Path to an SIO Position

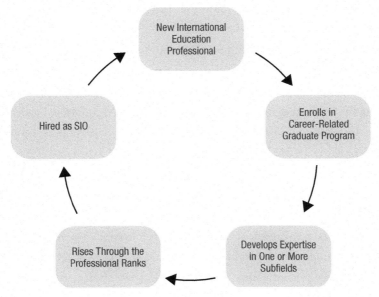

ESSENTIAL ATTRIBUTES

While there have been multiple attempts to identify the essential attributes of successful SIOs, much of the published literature (Lambert et al. 2007; Dessoff 2010; Koehn et al. 2011; Deschamps and Lee 2014; Merkx and Riall 2015; Kwai 2017) reflects only the views of SIOs. This is a serious gap in the literature, and the limitations of these studies raise concerns about the possibility of various forms of bias influencing their findings. Moreover, the current literature may also reinforce a preference for the traditional career path, skew understanding of essential attributes of SIOs, and, ultimately, perpetuate "less-than-ideal decisions regarding those hired or promoted to provide leadership in this area" (Charles and Deardorff 2014).

A smaller number of researchers have helped triangulate data by incorporating the views of non-SIOs. For instance, one study of subordinates' perceptions of the critical skills and knowledge of effective SIOs found communication, knowledge of the field of international education, and cross-cultural skills to be the highest ranked attributes, while research, fundraising skills, and academic background to be ranked the lowest (Turner 2013). Another study comparing SIOs and international education staff members found differences in perceptions of internationalization on their campus to be statistically significant (Poole 2012).

Professional associations such as AIEA and NAFSA have released their own publications on the most common qualities and capabilities that modern-day SIOs need to perform their job functions effectively. AIEA published its "Standards of Professional Practice for International Education Leaders and Senior International Officers" in 2016 to establish a common set of professional standards. In 2015, NAFSA released the *NAFSA International Education Professional Competencies*, a comprehensive listing of the necessary competencies for success in the field, across all international education domains.

As the field of international education administration continues to mature and international engagement initiatives further expand, a new model of the SIO is emerging. This individual is a prepared professional for whom international education represents a passion and career choice, as opposed to a hobby and career change. The professional SIO may not be a researcher in the traditional sense, but he or she is skilled at program assessment and is a respected scholar-practitioner in the field of international education. Such scholarship includes presenting peer-reviewed sessions and workshops at national and international conferences, serving in elected and appointed leadership positions with relevant professional associations, and contributing to the professional literature. In many cases, the professional SIO maintains his or her own carefully developed global brand and network that serve to raise the profile of the employing institution while also facilitating the execution of its global strategies.

Credentials

The professional SIO may hold a graduate degree, but not necessarily a terminal degree, in a field directly related to the work he or she is hired to perform. Graduate certificate, master's, and doctoral degree programs for SIOs tend to be applied and include specific coursework on internationalization strategy, education abroad administration, international research administration, international students, and other highly applicable topics.

In many cases, directors of these graduate programs prefer applicants to demonstrate professional experience in the field of international education or to hold current administrative positions at the time of admission. The students in these programs tend to focus their research on critical issues directly related to international education, which advances the field while also ensuring that future generations of SIOs are prepared to address the international education leadership challenges of tomorrow. The rise in such graduate preparation programs represents a major shift in the profession and one of the strongest catalysts for the changing SIO profile.

Conclusion

A sound strategy for internationalization and global engagement is required for colleges and universities to remain relevant within an increasingly competitive and collaborative global higher education landscape. Identifying and attracting the right type of SIO is essential to increasing the likelihood of success, but not all SIOs are appropriate for all situations.

The multidimensional framework presented in this chapter describes nine types of SIO positions based on different levels of strategic alignment and urgency. Each type of SIO position serves a purpose that meets institutional needs, priorities, and ambitions. This framework can be used to guide conversations with SIO search committees and hiring officers, as well as help prospective SIOs identify the types of institutions in which they would best fit.

Additional Resources

Association of International Education Administrators (AIEA). 2016. "Standards of Professional Practice for International Education Leaders and Senior International Officers." Durham, NC: Association of International Education Administrators. https://www.aieaworld.org/standards-of-professional-practice.

Association of International Education Administrators (AIEA). 2018. *Leading Internationalization: A Handbook for International Education Leaders.* Sterling, VA: Stylus Publishing.

NAFSA: Association of International Educators. 2015. *NAFSA International Education Professional Competencies.* Washington, DC: NAFSA: Association of International Educators. http://www.nafsa.org/competencies/.

NAFSA: Association of International Educators. 2018. *Hot Trends for Senior International Officers.* Washington, DC: NAFSA: Association of International Educators. https://www.nafsa.org/Professional_Resources/Browse_by_Interest/ Internationalizing_Higher_Education/Network_Resources/International_ Education_Leadership/Hot_Trends_for_Senior_International_Officers/.

References

Association of American Colleges and Universities. 2007. *College Learning for the New Global Century.* Washington, DC: Association of American Colleges and Universities. https://www.aacu.org/sites/default/files/files/LEAP/ GlobalCentury_final.pdf.

Association of Public and Land-grant Universities (APLU). 2017. *Pervasive Internationalization: A Call for Renewed Leadership.* Washington, DC: Association of Public and Land-grant Universities. http://www.aplu.org/ library/pervasive-internationalization-a-call-for-renewed-leadership/file.

Charles, Harvey, and Darla K. Deardorff. 2014. "A Failure to Capitalize on Globalization." *WorldWise* (blog), *Chronicle of Higher Education*. June 18, 2014. https://www.chronicle.com/blogs/worldwise/a-failure-to-capitalize-on-globalization/33965.

Cleveland, Harlan. 1999. "The Global Century." *Futures* 31, 9–10:887–895.

Deschamps, Eric and Jenny J. Lee. 2015. "Internationalization as Mergers and Acquisitions: Senior International Officers' Entrepreneurial Strategies and Activities in Public Universities." *Journal of Studies in International Education* 19, 2:122–139.

Dessoff, Alan. 2006. "A Key to Your Career." *International Educator* XV, 1:36–43.

Dessoff, Alan. 2010. "The Rise of Senior International Officers." *International Educator* XIX, 1:45–49.

Helms, Robin Matross, and Lucia Brajkovic. 2017. *Mapping Internationalization on U.S. Campuses: 2017 Edition*. Washington, DC: American Council on Education.

Hoemeke, Thomas H., Maria Krane, Judy Young, and Gerald Slavin. 2006. "A Survey on Chief International Education Administrators, Their Institutions and Offices." Durham, NC: Association of International Education Administrators Committee on Campus Administration and Programs. https://www.aieaworld.org/assets/docs/Surveys/ciea2006.pdf.

Koehn, Peter H., Darla K. Deardorff and Kerry D. Bolognese. 2011. "Enhancing International Research and Development-Project Activity on University Campuses: Insights from U.S. Senior International Officers." *Journal of Studies in International Education* 15, 4:332–350.

Kugler, Richard L. and Ellen L. Frost, eds. 2002. *The Global Century: Globalization and National Security*. Washington, DC: National Defense University Press.

Kwai, C. K. 2017. "The SIO Profile: A Preliminary Analysis of the Survey on Senior International Education Officers, Their Institutions and Offices." Durham, NC: Association of International Education Administrators. https://www.aieaworld.org/assets/docs/Surveys/final-2017%20executive%20summary_sio%20profile%20survey.pdf.

Lambert, Susan, Riall Nolan, Norman Peterson, and Deborah Pierce. 2007. *Critical Skills and Knowledge for Senior Campus International Leaders*. Washington, DC: NAFSA: Association of International Educators. https://www.nafsa.org/uploadedFiles/delphi.pdf?n=8208.

Merkx, Gilbert W. and Riall W. Nolan. 2015. *Internationalizing the Academy: Lessons of Leadership in Higher Education.* Cambridge, MA: Harvard Education Press.

Mestenhauser, Josef A., and Brenda J. Ellingboe. 2005. "Leadership Knowledge and International Education." *International Educator* XIV, 6:36–43.

Poole, Leigh Anne. 2012. "The Internationalization of U.S. Higher Education: Perceptions from International Educators and Senior International Officers." Athens, GA: University of Georgia. https://getd.libs.uga.edu/pdfs/poole_leigh_a_201212_phd.pdf.

Turner, Paaige. 2013. "Subordinates Perceptions of Critical Skills and Knowledge for Senior International Officers." Unpublished research presented at the Annual Conference of the Association of International Education Administrators, Washington, DC. https://www.aieaworld.org/assets/docs/Conference_Materials/2014/docstoupload2/managing%20the%20sio%20role%20presentation.pdf.

2 | Stakeholder Engagement

Erich Dietrich

Universities are very hierarchical organizations, sorting knowledge and ability and granting students with credits that add up to ranked degrees, from a bachelor's or first university degree up to the doctorate. Faculty and administrators also exist and are ranked within these hierarchies: assistant, associate, and full levels of professors, directors, deans, provosts, and presidents (and many other permutations). When it comes to institutional goals and priorities, stakeholders involved in any given initiative may come from several different levels of the various hierarchies. Stakeholders are individuals, groups, and institutions that have an interest in a project and can influence, or be influenced by, its outcomes. Their shared investment in the issue at hand can often promote a sense of shared responsibility, initiative, and promotion.

Identifying strategic goals is a process unto itself (see chapter 4) and, once in place, successful stakeholder engagement becomes the key to achieving those goals. One cannot successfully develop and carry out large, complex projects in higher education without communicating the importance of the project to a wide array of stakeholders; soliciting their thoughts, input, and, often, their actual work time; adjusting the project to incorporate their input when necessary; and keeping them apprised of project timelines, challenges, and outcomes.

Senior international officers (SIOs) must be able to effectively navigate up and down internal university hierarchies in order to accomplish the strategic goals of the office and institution. Compounding this internal complexity, SIOs, by definition, engage a variety of external stakeholders as well, many of whom may be based in other countries with very different academic cultures and a broad array of customs, communication styles, and strategic goals of their own. This chapter presents best practices in stakeholder identification, analysis, and engagement for SIOs.

Stakeholder Identification

The first step in successful stakeholder engagement is identifying the stakeholders themselves, whether internal or external. For a simple project or one that replicates similar work, identifying the stakeholders might be a fairly straightforward process, even though the list of stakeholders may be substantial. Take the example of the SIO working with enrollment management to develop an international student recruitment strategy. Most of the stakeholders will be internal to the institution and will be working in unison toward the strategic goal once it is agreed upon. Typical stakeholders in such a scenario would be the university leadership team (i.e., president, provost, and senior team), staff from the office of enrollment management who will develop tactics for outreach and metrics for success, staff from the office of international student services who will support additional incoming students, and staff from the student affairs division who will support student success. Of course, given the faculty governance structures in place at most universities, the faculty should also be considered a key stakeholder in all strategic goals and should be engaged through governance channels, such as the university senate and other committees, as well as through the university's hierarchy of deans, department chairs, and program directors. Depending on the university's location and its status as a public or private university, additional external stakeholders may include the state and local government, the chamber of commerce, and others in the community likely to be affected by an increased number of international students in the town or city.

Larger and more complex global projects will generally include a wider variety of stakeholders and will typically require not only top-down management by the SIO, but also consultation and persuasion to achieve buy-in to the goal. Consider the example of developing a new dual-degree program with an international university. The SIO will need to actively engage many of the same internal stakeholders mentioned above, plus several others, including department faculty and chairs of relevant departments who will develop and review curricula and manage ongoing program review and assessment; academic affairs committees where program review and approval will take place; and staff of external accreditation bodies and state offices of higher education who may also be involved in program review and approval.

Of course, in this example, the collaborating international university will need to be identified and agreed upon based on whatever criteria the SIO and the university leadership have developed, including reputation, rankings, revenue potential, and due attention to risk factors (for more information on international partnerships, see chapter 16). Once the two universities come to an initial agreement to collaborate, representatives from both institutions should work together to identify and educate each other on their key stakeholders. Working from the U.S. perspective, it is important to explain to the international partner the role of faculty, accreditation bodies, and state departments of education, which may all function very differently than in other countries. In turn, the SIO will need to actively learn about the international partner's stakeholder context. In this case, the universities become reciprocal stakeholders. The SIO will not only engage internal stakeholders and the international university as an external stakeholder, but he or she may also be called upon to help the partner university engage its stakeholders by helping to educate them on the value and potential rewards of the partnership.

Strategies for Stakeholder Identification

In this initial stage of stakeholder identification, it is important to identify all stakeholders. It is often easy to overlook key stakeholders or to mistakenly assume that some are so distant from the process or project goals as to be inconsequential. As one university asserts, "You can forget about stakeholders, but they won't forget about you" (University of Sussex 2018).

Possible questions that SIOs can use to identify the stakeholders may include:

- Who are the members of the governance body and administrative leadership?

- Who holds budget approval over this project?

- Whose criticism or disapproval would be damaging to, or even stop, the project's success?

- Whose influence could change, redirect, or reshape the intended outcome?

- Which stakeholders can influence other stakeholders?

- Which stakeholders may be able to influence the project's timeline?

- Which stakeholders will remain involved in the project over a long period of time?

- Who will "own" the project, including its risks and rewards, after the SIO has led the project from development to a full, steady state?

- Which stakeholders may be needed to support the next project or goal?

As projects come together, stakeholders who were not identified in the initial planning process may come forward and, often, with a heightened level of resistance to the project because they were not a part of the early consultation. For example, individual faculty members or groups of faculty often express surprise and dismay about a project if they are not consulted early in the process. As a result, achieving their buy-in after the project has begun may require much greater effort. Stakeholder identification should be an ongoing process because stakeholders may change over the life of a project, or their influence may grow or dissipate as the project develops.

Possible strategies that SIOs can use to effectively identify stakeholders may include:

- Making lists of stakeholders (as comprehensively as possible);

- Conducting stakeholder identification workshops wherein each participant makes a list of possible stakeholders and then the group compares and aggregates the names;

- Conducting focus groups by bringing together groups that map the scope of the project and asking participants to brainstorm all possible stakeholders; and

- Consulting regulations, compliance documents, legal frameworks, and governance documents.

Once the SIO and team have identified the key stakeholders for a given project, the next step is to conduct an analysis of the stakeholders' levels of influence and interest.

Stakeholder Analysis

The stakeholder analysis can help to inform the engagement process. A common and useful stakeholder management tool that many SIOs employ is Mendelow's Matrix (1991), also known as a "stakeholder analysis grid" (see figure 1). The tool is used to analyze and map an organization's stakeholders by determining the level of power and interest of each stakeholder. For any given project or strategic goal, the SIO should classify each stakeholder's relative level of influence and interest and engage with the individual or group accordingly.

Figure 1. Mendelow's Matrix for Stakeholder Analysis

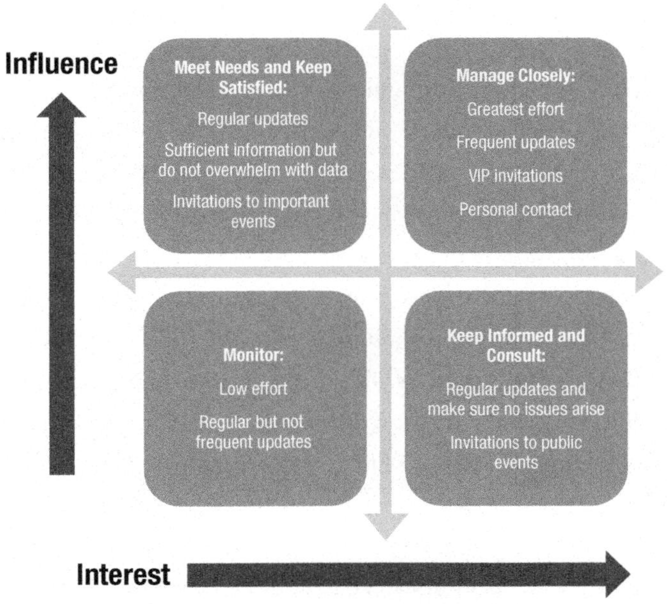

Influence

Meet Needs and Keep Satisfied:
Regular updates
Sufficient information but do not overwhelm with data
Invitations to important events

Manage Closely:
Greatest effort
Frequent updates
VIP invitations
Personal contact

Monitor:
Low effort
Regular but not frequent updates

Keep Informed and Consult:
Regular updates and make sure no issues arise
Invitations to public events

Interest

Source: Adapted from Mendelow (1991).

Possible questions that SIOs can use to help pinpoint the stakeholder's level of influence and interest may include:

- What is the stakeholder's formal position in the organization?

- What is the stakeholder likely to gain or lose as a result of change brought about by the project?

- What is the stakeholder's relationship to other stakeholders?

- How busy is the stakeholder?

- What is the stakeholder's readiness for change, or resistance to it?

- What is the stakeholder's level of confidence and trust in the SIO and the SIO's team?

Once the SIO has assessed the relative influence and interest of stakeholders, classifying and grouping them using Mendelow's Matrix (1991) will inform the plan of engagement. The stakeholders who fall into the top right quadrant of figure 1 are usually the most important to the project because they hold both a high level of influence and a high level of interest. Stakeholders in this quadrant will need frequent consultation and progress updates to satisfy their interest. Given that their influence is high, they may be able to help the SIO overcome obstacles, garner additional resources if and when necessary, and influence and reassure other stakeholders. If, however, these stakeholders find issues with the project or develop resistance to it, the SIO will need to take immediate action because their negative responses can derail or even stop the project completely. Stakeholders in this quadrant have an amplifying effect on others because they tend to have influence over not only the immediate project at hand but over various projects within and even outside the organization.

Stakeholders in the top left quadrant of figure 1 hold a high degree of influence but a low level of interest. Such stakeholders may be university budget officers, funders, government officials, and others whose approval is critical but who do not want to be deeply involved in the details of the project. They usually require less frequent updates and far fewer details of the project. These stakeholders need only assurance of a project's successful development and major milestones. They will appreciate positive recognition of their support, and the SIO must make sure to include them in special events where their support can be publicly acknowledged.

In the bottom right quadrant of figure 1 are the stakeholders who hold a high level of interest but a low level of influence. These individuals may be staff members who report to the SIO and whose work is integral to the project's fruition, faculty in the relevant academic areas, department chairs, peers and colleagues in the administration (other vice provosts), and student groups that may be affected by the project. These groups will need regular updates from the SIO and should be made aware of the project's timeline and milestones. They should also be duly recognized for their contributions at occasions commemorating the project's success.

Stakeholders who sit in the bottom left quadrant of figure 1 should not be underestimated. They, too, require regular, ongoing updates and a minimal level of consultation. Given the shared governance model of universities and the value placed on open debate, critical inquiry, and participatory consensus, stakeholders of seemingly low interest and influence can quickly, and sometimes surprisingly, raise objections that the SIO will need to take seriously.

In general, universities are busy, diffuse organizations that often resemble decentralized networks more than hub-and-spoke or top-down systems. Faculty are engaged in research, teaching, and service; students are engrossed in intellectual and social development; and administrators have many competing priorities. In such a context, most projects, even large-scale international partnerships and major internationalization initiatives, will go unnoticed by a majority of the university community members.

The best way to avoid obstacles and opposition to initiatives is to make sure to cast a very broad net when identifying the stakeholders in the first place, and then to keep them updated and informed of progress via push methods of communication such as emails, newsletters, and announcements at faculty meetings, student government meetings, and other venues. The SIO needs to monitor these various groups for positive and negative reactions to project updates.

Engagement Strategies

Once the stakeholders are identified and their levels of influence and interest classified, the SIO needs to develop a strategic plan of engagement. This should include:

1. A differentiated plan of engagement for each of the four stakeholder quadrants (see figure 1);

2. Further differentiation within each sector for particularly critical stakeholders;

3. Guidelines and talking points for staff who will interact with the various stakeholders;

4. Metrics for assessing stakeholder engagement; and

5. A feedback loop to the SIO, who will continue to refine the strategy at project milestones.

The SIO should engage key stakeholders early in the project development process, and their input should be considered genuinely. People generally do not like to be consulted after a project's outcome has already been determined. At the same time, the SIO should be clear with stakeholders from the start about which parts of a project are non-negotiable or beyond the scope of influence of any given stakeholder or group of stakeholders.

In international education, SIOs are often engaging stakeholders over great distances and with infrequent opportunities for live, face-to-face contact. This has always presented a particular challenge for SIOs working on complex international projects where clear, precise, and frequent communication is necessary. Technology has helped by expanding communication channels and, in many cases, reducing decisionmaking timelines. Videoconferencing, in particular, has been a tremendous boon to international educators, adding a visual communication dimension that feels far more personal than email or telephone (auditory only) contact. However, SIOs should continue to recognize the immense power of real, live contact through in-person visits and meetings, and they must effectively communicate this need to colleagues to make sure the international office has sufficient budget to allow for international travel and/or domestic travel to conferences where critical stakeholder engagement often takes place.

Assessment of Stakeholder Engagement

Once the stakeholders have been engaged initially, the SIO should build on the momentum and work to quickly incorporate feedback and circle back with updates. One way to assess stakeholder engagement is ranking both awareness and level of support, thereby rating the stakeholder's level of commitment to the project at any given moment. This information can be plotted on a spreadsheet and monitored over time. The ranking typically comprises the following categories:

1. Leading: These stakeholders are actively engaged, supportive, and can be called on to influence others.

2. Supportive: These stakeholders are aware of the project and have a positive regard and attitude toward it.

3. Neutral: These stakeholders are aware of the project and do not have a positive or negative attitude toward it.

4. Resistant: These stakeholders are aware of the project and oppose it.

5. Unaware: These stakeholders do not know about the project or its goals.

The SIO needs a majority of the stakeholders to be in the first two categories (leading and supportive), while recognizing that 100 percent positive commitment is not realistic. When a stakeholder's levels of awareness and support drop to other categories (neutral, resistant, or unaware), more engagement is clearly necessary. The SIO should put forth reasonable attempts to move neutral and unaware stakeholders to more positive and informed positions to avoid future pitfalls, including charges that they were not properly consulted.

It is tempting during the initial engagement stage to focus on only the positive feedback that reinforces the SIO's vision of the project's outcome, but negative feedback must be taken seriously and given proper attention. While never losing sight of proponents, the SIO or key team members should seek multiple avenues for engagement with resisters. Consider who may be the best person to circle back to a resister: the SIO or another, more supportive stakeholder? Often, engaging resisters one-on-one and in person, outside of emails or group meetings, can allow for building trust, even if the stakeholder remains opposed to the project or goal. In the end, there will always be resisters, and possibly even direct opponents, to large and complex initiatives, but so long as they have been properly and respectfully engaged, the project can move forward and the goal can be achieved.

Long-Term Progress

Stakeholders should be recognized, thanked, informed, and consulted on a continuous basis. Ongoing engagement includes sharing:

- Summaries of project outcomes;

- Project evaluations and data corresponding to the project's metrics of success;

- Newsletters and email updates;

- Personal updates by phone, videoconference, or in person;

- External recognitions of success, including awards, publications, and research citations; and

- Transformation narratives of personal impact.

Additionally, SIOs should solicit feedback from stakeholders on the engagement process and the project outcomes. How and to what extent were their needs met? What is their evaluation and feedback on the project itself? Among this feedback may be personal stories of transformation, which often lie at the core of international education and are important to building long-term stakeholder engagement in a higher education context.

Conclusion

Stakeholder engagement is about building relationships of trust to accomplish shared goals over a sustained period of time and across multiple initiatives.

While there may be some shuffling of the stakeholders who are critical to future projects or goals, these key individuals are rarely replaced with a completely new set of stakeholders. The SIO will likely need many of the same people and entities to support the next goal. Over time, the level of trust between the SIO and the stakeholders can grow, significantly aiding and accelerating future engagement.

Additional Resources

Freeman, R. Edward, Jeffrey S. Harrison, Andrew C. Wicks, Bidhan Parmar, and Simone de Colle. 2010. *Stakeholder Theory*. Cambridge, United Kingdom: Cambridge University Press.

West, Charlotte. 2012. *Engaging Stakeholders in Internationalization: Strategies for Collaboration*. Washington, DC: NAFSA: Association of International Educators.

References

Mendelow, Aubrey. 1991. Mendelow's Power Interest Grid. Kent, OH: Kent State University.

University of Sussex. 2018. "Planning, Governance and Compliance: Step 1: Identifying Stakeholders." Brighton, United Kingdom: University of Sussex. http://www.sussex.ac.uk/ogs/project-services/support/change/stakeholder/cmse1.

3 International Risk Management and Crisis Communication

Cheryl Matherly

The scope of the risks that senior international officers (SIOs) are expected to manage reflects the breadth of the international activities in which students, faculty, and staff are engaged, including study abroad, internships, service programs, university-sponsored tours, athletic competitions, global health activities, recruiting events, conferences, faculty research, and collaborations with international institutions and governments. Risk management is such a significant part of the SIO's role that it is often considered to be requisite expertise. In the Association for International Education Administrators (AIEA)'s "Standards of Professional Practice for International Education Leaders and Senior International Officers," standard 3 advises that the SIO has "an appreciation for the risks associated with global engagement for the institution and its faculty, staff and students, and works closely with the relevant others to minimize risk" (AIEA 2016). Additionally, NAFSA: Association of International Educators's *NAFSA International Education Professional Competencies* cites mitigating organizational risk as a key component for any strategy role in campus internationalization (NAFSA 2015).

For most institutions, managing international risk is predominantly equated with student travel and study abroad. However, as suggested by the wide scope of international activities in which institutions engage, SIOs are also often expected to navigate contractual, regulatory compliance, and legal risks that stem from activities beyond student mobility. This chapter considers the specific elements of an effective risk management strategy for international activities, including crisis communications and media relations. The recommendations assume these key principles:

- The SIO must share in the responsibility of establishing risk management policies for global programs with other risk officers on campus. The SIO must be part of the campus risk management team and must closely collaborate with other members of this team to appropriately protect the interests of the institution.

- The SIO must adapt to changes influenced by geopolitical developments and institutional activities. As such, risk management strategies are dynamic and must be regularly reviewed to ensure that they sufficiently address current activities.

- The SIO must help instill a culture of compliance among faculty, students, and staff who support and engage in global programs. In order for this to happen, the SIO must have the authority to make decisions and delegate and must communicate and collaborate with other institutional decisionmakers (McQuaid and Klahr 2018).

- The SIO must have a variety of resources available for mitigating global programs' inherent risks. These resources include support staff, institutional policies, insurance, financial resources, and access to relevant expertise.

Terminology

In this chapter, both risk management and crisis management are discussed, terms that are related but have different implications for practice. "Risk management" refers to the steps that an institution takes to prevent or minimize threats to an individual or to the institution itself. As an example, an institution's insurance policies or training programs for faculty leading programs abroad are part of a risk management strategy. In addition to the SIO, other members who serve on the risk management team may include representatives from the offices of the general counsel, institutional risk, communications, and student affairs.

"Crisis management" refers to the plan to respond to an actual emergency in real time, such as a natural disaster or medical emergency. The individuals involved with crisis management may include individuals outside of the risk management team who are part of the institution's overall crisis response plan, such as campus police or on-site program staff.

Risk Management for International Programs

Any discussion about managing institutional risk must first begin with an understanding of what constitutes "risk" and the level of institutional tolerance for this risk. All institutional activities come with some risk, and the SIO must help evaluate the likelihood of specific threats versus the merits of the proposed international activities. Such evaluation can be a challenge when the students or faculty involved with the activity have a different assessment of the relative risk than do other institutional decisionmakers.

This is why institutional culture is a significant, though infrequently discussed, factor affecting risk management strategies. An institution's experience with international programs, its history in dealing with crisis situations, its faculty and staff expertise, institutional mission, financial health, and the risk tolerance of its senior leadership are just a few factors that provide clues as to how an SIO should balance between the risks and benefits of the proposed activities.

The goal for a risk management plan is, of course, to make sufficient preparation so that threats are mitigated to acceptable levels. The most common causes of lawsuits filed against colleges and universities based on incidents related to international activities include sexual harassment or assault, personal injury and accidental death, unlawful discrimination, motor vehicle and pedestrian accidents, improper or negligent medical treatment, and lack of due process or unfair dismissal claims (Rhodes and Ludeman 2012). According to Lindeman et al. (2005), it is common for institutional risk management plans to focus on two approaches to preparing for risks:

- Design approach. Stakeholders identify and analyze hazards for specific activities and aim to manage possible risks in advance.

- Operations approach. Stakeholders implement specific strategies for each component of the program abroad should a problem arise over the course of the activity.

An accurate inventory of current and proposed international activities (see Lehigh University [2018] for example) is the key to ensuring that the institution has adequate policies, business practices, and insurance in place. Such an inventory may range from a listing of proposals, agreements, and activities manually tracked within a spreadsheet to commercially available international partnership management software that automatically pulls information from electronic travel request forms, faculty annual reports, and other relevant sources of data. Because institutional activities continually evolve, it is good practice for the SIO to review the scopes of current international programs and partnerships on a regular basis with other members of the risk management team.

Risk Management Policies

Most institutions seek to minimize risk through institutional policies designed to regulate international activities. For example, the policies for international travel involving students are typically focused on health and safety issues. At a minimum, these policies address the ways in which student travelers are identified and tracked, student eligibility for university travel, assessment of risk in a potential travel location, emergency response procedures, and training for participating faculty and staff leading the activity. Institutions must ensure that campus policies for responding to Title IX and Clery Act issues are also sufficient for incidents that occur abroad. The issues to which these policies (e.g., insurance) are responding are rarely the sole responsibility of the SIO and should, therefore, be developed with the risk management team, including legal counsel and student affairs staff.

Institutions may also develop policies for travel involving faculty and staff that are independent of the policies for students. The faculty policies are most typically developed with the business office and address potential issues related to institutional travel and financial practices. Many institutions have implemented travel tracking systems for faculty and staff. The highly decentralized nature of most academic departments, however, can make it difficult to ensure that all travel is captured in the system, unless travel registration is required in order to receive travel reimbursements or other benefits. (For more on the operational issues pertaining to travel, health, and safety abroad, see chapter 17.)

Finally, institutions may also develop risk management policies that are aimed at reducing technology vulnerabilities. For example, such policies may restrict the use of laptops and other equipment in high-risk countries. Given the ever-evolving innovations in technology and social media, it is imperative for the SIO and the rest of the risk management team to remain apprised of best practices for data management and record-keeping.

Crisis Management Plan

Institutions must take steps to mitigate risk during the planning and implementation of any activities. Part of this proactive planning is to have a well-developed and practiced crisis management plan that aligns with the emergency procedures already in place on campus. The plan generally includes the following features:

- Crisis management team. The crisis management team are those individuals who will be involved in responding to an actual emergency in real time. In addition to the SIO, the team typically consists of campus decisionmakers such as representatives from the provost's office, the business office, legal counsel, student affairs, health services, counseling services, campus security, and the communications office. Depending on the emergency, the crisis management team may choose to include in-country staff or partners.

- Definition of an emergency. A crisis management plan defines an emergency based on its severity in order to determine the appropriate institutional response. Minor emergencies can be resolved quickly with existing staff and limited university resources. For example, a minor emergency might involve a student losing his or her passport or a student going to a local doctor for a minor stomach illness.

Major emergencies can affect the safety and welfare of students, staff, faculty, or community members; impact the continuity of a program or activity; or create a public relations concern. For example, this may include a natural disaster or terrorist incident. Emergencies of this level activate the crisis management team and may require significant institutional resources to resolve.

- Procedures for responding to an emergency. The plan articulates specific steps for responding to the specific emergency, including the individuals to be contacted and the degree of their involvement. A clear delineation of steps and responsible parties helps to ensure a consistent and comprehensive response.

- Communication plan. A critical part of the plan is mapping out the appropriate and timely communications to the families, campus, and larger community. This process includes managing communications in compliance with applicable domestic and foreign data protection and privacy regulations, such as the Family Educational Rights and Privacy Act (FERPA) and the Health Insurance Portability and Accountability Act (HIPAA) within the United States and the General Data Protection Regulation (GDPR) within the European Union and European Economic Area.

A crisis management plan is only as effective as the team responsible for its implementation. It is important that the crisis management plan be regularly practiced so that everyone who is involved understands their roles and is familiar with what is expected during an emergency. Regular drills can help uncover weaknesses in the campus's readiness to respond to an emergency. A variety of international scenarios can be included as part of the training.

Possible questions that SIOs can use to assess their campus's level of readiness to respond to emergencies may include:

- Have the risks associated with international activities been identified?

- How and when were the identified risks assessed?

- What are the causes of the risks identified?

- What is the likelihood of these risks occurring?

- Is there a crisis management plan that addresses each of the risks identified?

- Do all parties involved in the plan understand their role and the roles of others?

Media Relations

An institution's crisis management plan should include a communication plan, which comprises a media plan. Even with the engagement of representatives from the communications office, the SIO, as the face of the university's international activities, may still serve as the primary contact for the media while responding to an international threat or emergency.

A media plan should align with the crisis management plan and be designed well in advance of an emergency. A media plan typically designates who will be the institutional spokesperson; steps for ensuring that the information shared is complete, accurate, and approved for public release; and a plan for how and when information will be released to the media.

The SIO should complete training with the university communications staff about media communications in the event of an emergency involving international programs, students, or scholars. Such trainings should serve to familiarize the SIO with preferred institutional approaches to media engagement, brief the SIO on the institution's prior interactions with specific reporters, and provide the SIO with practice responding to likely questions based on different scenarios. It is essential that the language used by the SIO when speaking with the media is in line with the institution's voice and historical approach.

The Impact of Social Media

The proliferation of social media in today's society uniquely affects the communication strategy in the event of an emergency. On the one hand, such technology is an important vehicle for communicating quickly with the campus community, domestic and abroad. For example, students can check in and confirm their well-being with the push of a button. On the other hand, these tools also make everyone a de facto reporter, and news of an emergency, real or imagined, can spread rapidly and be very difficult to manage by the institution.

When developing a media plan, it is wise for the SIO and the rest of the risk management team to consider social media separately and to specifically identify how communication will be managed via the university's website and social media platforms. It is also key to develop a strategy for monitoring social media chatter and to be aware of how news is spreading (Stoller 2015).

Conclusion

While an SIO has particular responsibilities for protecting students, faculty, staff, and the institution from risks associated with international activities, this is not a one-person job. Risk management activities happen within the larger institutional framework, and there should be a team of partners ready to help with developing policies, assessing risks, and managing actual emergencies. Additionally, there are significant professional resources, such as this book, that provide additional guidance on establishing, deploying, and evaluating effective plans.

Professional Resources

- The Forum on Education Abroad. The Forum is designated as the standards development organization for the field of education abroad. Its standards, developed by education abroad practitioners, provide guidance for most education abroad models.
  forumea.org/

- International SOS. International SOS provides medical assistance, travel security advice and information, emergency services, health care, and evacuation and repatriation services. The organization provides resources and consultations that help reduce exposure to and mitigate risks while traveling abroad.
  www.internationalsos.com/

- NAFSA: Association of International Educators. NAFSA produces resources that address the diversity of risk issues that SIOs will manage,

including those affecting the management of programs abroad, support for international students, and engagement with international governments.
www.nafsa.org/

- National Association of College and University Attorneys (NACUA). NACUA offers continuing education and research to attorneys and their institutions on topics related to international programs.
www.nacua.org/

- National Association of College and University Business Officers (NACUBO). NACUBO produces resources on business operations affected by international activities.
www.nacubo.org/

- Overseas Security Advisory Council (OSAC). OSAC was established by the U.S. Department of State to promote dialogue with the private sector on security issues abroad. OSAC delivers safety and security-related information, public announcements, warden messages, travel advisories, significant anniversary dates, terrorist groups' profiles, country crime and safety reports, special topic reports, and foreign press reports. It also has staff who are international security research specialists who advise the private sector.
www.osac.gov/Pages/Home.aspx

- SAFETI Clearinghouse Program Audit Checklist. The Center for Global Education, based at California State University-Dominguez Hills, developed the checklist to help institutions evaluate health and safety policies and procedures. It includes sample resources from other study abroad programs.
globaled.us/safeti/program_audit_checklist.asp

- University Risk Management and Insurance Association (URMIA). URMIA is an international nonprofit association that promotes the advancement and application of risk management principles and practices for colleges and universities. URMIA offers resources for

developing an international risk management plan and for effectively
supporting programs abroad.
www.urmia.org/home

- U.S. Department of State (DOS). DOS launched a new system for
  issuing travel advisories in January 2018 that evaluates the relative risk
  of a country and region on a scale of 1 (exercise normal precaution)
  to 4 (do not travel) and based on the category of risky activity (e.g.,
  crime, terrorism, civil unrest, health notices, natural disaster, time-
  limited activity). The DOS website also includes the Smart Traveler
  Enrollment Program (STEP), which permits enrolled travelers to
  receive communications from the local consulate on emergencies
  affecting U.S. citizens abroad.
  step.state.gov/step/

Additional Resources

Albrecht, Teri J., ed. 2015. *Crisis Management in a Cross-Cultural Setting:
   International Students and Scholars.* Washington, DC: NAFSA: Association of
   International Educators.

Funaki, Julia, Brian Flahaven, Joanna Grama, Mark McConahay, Mary Chapin,
   Tracy Locklin, Caroline Donovan White, and Joann Ng Hartmann. 2018.
   *Implications of the General Data Protection Regulation: An Interassociation
   Guide.* American Association of Collegiate Registrars and Admissions Officers,
   Council for Advancement and Support of Education, EDUCAUSE, Indiana
   University-Bloomington, National Student Clearinghouse, and NAFSA:
   Association of International Educators. https://www.aacrao.org/signature-
   initiatives/trending-topics/gdpr/gdpr-interassociational-guide/.

Martin, Patricia C., ed. 2017. *Crisis Management for Education Abroad.*
   Washington, DC: NAFSA: Association of International Educators.

U.S. Department of Education. 2018. "Family Educational Rights and Privacy Act
   (FERPA)." Washington, DC: U.S. Department of Education. https://www2.
   ed.gov/policy/gen/guid/fpco/ferpa/index.html.

U.S. Department of Health & Human Services. n.d. "HIPAA FAQs for
   Individuals." Washington, DC: U.S. Department of Health & Human
   Services. https://www.hhs.gov/hipaa/for-individuals/faq/index.html.

References

Association of International Education Administrators (AIEA). 2016. "Standards of Professional Practice for International Education Leaders and Senior International Officers." Durham, NC: Association of International Education Administrators. http://www.aieaworld.org/assets/docs/Standards/b03.02. standardscolor.pdf.

Lehigh University. 2018. "Global Engagement Directory." Bethlehem, PA: Lehigh University. https://lehigh.moveonca.com/publisher/2/eng.

Lindeman, Barbara, Natalie Mello, Joseph L. Brockington, Margit Johnson, and Les McCabe. 2005. "Maximizing Safety and Security and Minimizing Risk in Education Abroad Programs." In *NAFSA's Guide to Education Abroad for Advisers and Administrators, Third Edition*, eds. Joseph L. Brockington, William Hoffa, and Patricia C. Martin. Washington, DC: NAFSA: Association of International Educators.

McQuaid, Meredith, and Sabine Klahr. 2018. "The Senior International Officer: Managing Risk and Liability." In *Leading Internationalization: A Handbook for International Education Leaders*, eds. Darla K. Deardorff and Harvey Charles. Sterling, VA: Stylus Publishing.

NAFSA: Association of International Educators. 2015. *NAFSA International Education Professional Competencies*. Washington, DC: NAFSA: Association of International Educators. http://www.nafsa.org/competencies/.

Rhodes, Gary, and Roger Ludeman. 2012. "Legal, Health, and Safety Issues: Crisis Management and Student Services in International Higher Education." In *The SAGE Handbook of International Higher Education*, eds. Darla K. Deardorff, Hans de Wit, John D. Heyl, and Tony Adams. Thousand Oaks, CA: Sage Publications.

Stoller, Eric. 2015. "Student Affairs Social Media Crisis Communication Thoughts." *Inside Higher Ed.* April 9, 2015. https://www.insidehighered. com/blogs/student-affairs-and-technology/student-affairs-social-media-crisis-communication-thoughts.

International Strategy Development: University of Calgary Case Study

Dru Marshall and Janaka Y. Ruwanpura

In this highly interconnected world, students, staff, and faculty are increasingly engaging in a wide range of international activities. Internationalization of a higher education institution focuses on the establishment and implementation of specific international relationships and activities that have definable educational, research, and community engagement goals (McCabe 2001). Given finite resources, internationalization strategies must clearly identify the goals, activities, and initiatives through which the international portfolio, led by the senior international officer (SIO), helps to drive the larger strategy of the institution.

This chapter highlights the development of an institutional international strategy at the University of Calgary, in Canada, and identifies how it has contributed to broader impacts and outcomes that support the university's vision and academic and research plans.

Institutional International Strategies

Institutional international strategies should not be stand-alone strategies. They must be driven by the vision of the university community and help to facilitate relationships and international activities in key priority areas. In order to be successful, international strategies require institutional-level investment of people, time, and funding.

An institutional international strategy should not inhibit the entrepreneurial efforts of individual faculty members in forging new relationships abroad. On the contrary, such activity by faculty members is crucial to the university achieving its internationalization goals. A great strategy supports the development of those relationships and ensures that they are productive and sustainable. While there are a number of approaches to developing institutional international strategies, this chapter examines the University of Calgary's approach as a case study.

Case Study: University of Calgary

The University of Calgary (UCalgary) formulated its "Eyes High" strategic vision in 2011 with the goal of serving as one of Canada's top five research universities and a global intellectual hub that is grounded in innovative teaching and learning and fully integrated with the community. UCalgary Academic and Research Plans were then developed and approved in 2012. Together, these plans contained 10 priorities that served as the road map to achieving the Eyes High vision. These same priorities guided human, capital, and financial resource allocations for the institution. These three guiding documents were developed with significant internal and external community consultation.

The process of developing the Academic and Research Plans was co-led by the provost and vice president (academic) and the vice president (research).

Figure 1. Academic Priorities

Source: UCalgary (2012b).

Following the data gathering phase for the Academic Plan, which included structured questionnaires and consultations, broad themes were identified from the input submitted by faculty, staff, and students. Seven academic priorities (see figure 1) emerged from the qualitative analyses of the data, one of which was internationalization.

The academic priority of internationalization was defined in the Academic Plan as follows:

> Our university will be a "global intellectual hub" where our students, staff, and faculty at the center of this hub will radiate new discoveries, ideas, and applications that have global impact. We will create a campus that also attracts scholars from around the world to this hub—one that promotes diversity of thought, culture, and respect for alternatives. We will leverage our expertise to share capacity with targeted institutions in the developing world. International partnerships will be equitable, respectful of differences in culture, and mutually beneficial. We will be a global source for objective information, expertise, and productive collaborations across all sectors of government, industries, and non-governmental organizations. Calgary is a global community—and we must prepare our graduates to work in a globalized world. (UCalgary 2012b)

The consultative processes involved in setting a university vision articulated by the Academic and Research Plans and gaining formal approval of these plans ensured the support for these key documents from critical university stakeholders (i.e., students, staff, faculty, and the Board of Governors). The specific priorities, strategies, and tactics established in the Academic and Research Plans allowed the university to progress in an intentional and systematic fashion. Since internationalization was identified as a key academic priority, an international strategy was developed, internationalization efforts were funded, more people were hired to support initiatives in this area, and facilities were developed to house activities and people.

Development of an International Strategy

Under the charge of developing an international strategy for UCalgary, the International Task Force—led by the provost and comprised of 24 individuals with broad representation from the university community—was established in April 2012. According to the *Terms of Reference for the Task Force*:

> It should identify ways to leverage our expertise, share capacity with targeted institutions in the developing world and it should encourage

faculty, staff and students to explore the world through linkages with partner institutions around the globe. (UCalgary 2012a)

The Task Force was formed to achieve two purposes. The first was to identify the specific goals, strategies, and tactics required to ensure that UCalgary became known as a global intellectual hub. The second purpose of the Task Force was to guide the allocation of resources for initiatives related to internationalization.

The Task Force proceeded through four steps: (1) orientation and data gathering; (2) identification of trends, principles, and goals; (3) consultations with internal and external stakeholders; and (4) approval of the strategy through the academic senate.

DATA GATHERING PHASE

To assess the status of UCalgary's current internationalization activities, a subcommittee of the International Task Force collected and analyzed data from across the institution, including data on international projects and research collaborations, international travel patterns by faculty members, and country of origin of all international students.

- International projects. The subcommittee requested current (2012) descriptions of all international projects from deans. "Projects" were defined as initiatives that involved more than one faculty member and were driven at the faculty level or higher. This delineation helped the subcommittee capture only the projects that were active and seen as priorities at either the decanal or provostial level (see figure 2).

- International research collaborations. Using the InCites database, the subcommittee obtained the countries and institutions of international authors who cowrote papers with UCalgary investigators. (For more on international research collaborations, see chapters 14 and 15).

- International travel. To map out the global reach of the university's international activities, the subcommittee analyzed the geographic patterns of travel by faculty members for research and presentations, as represented by purchases made through the university travel agency. While these data may not completely capture all faculty travel data (as not everyone books through the same service), they are unlikely to be systematically biased geographically.

- International students. The subcommittee obtained registration data, by country of origin, for the 2011–12 international student cohort.

Figure 2. International Projects by Type, Products, and Participants (N=115)

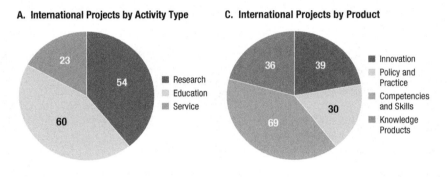

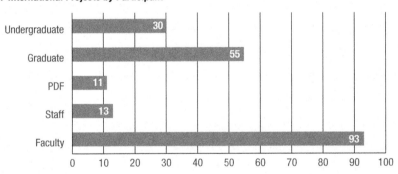

Source: UCalgary (2012a).

Note: The percentages in A and C exceed 100 because some projects involve more than one category. Similarly, the totals in B exceed 100 because most projects involve more than one participant type.

Given that every institution has finite resources, the types of data gathered help to identify the key areas of the world where the institution does and should focus its strategic activities.

IDENTIFICATION OF TRENDS

The next step in developing UCalgary's international strategy was understanding global and local trends relevant to internationalization. Macroeconomic, demographic, and technological trends can create both opportunities and challenges for a university. In the context of mounting pressure from a variety of sectors for globalized and internationally integrated academic and research systems, the International Task Force identified the following trends that were considered in planning the international strategy:

- Governments and employers are increasingly seeking graduates with a global perspective and cross-cultural competencies that contribute to successful performance in multicultural teams and international settings. To meet this demand, universities must offer curricular and cocurricular experiences that underpin the development of such competencies.

- Internationalization is a growing priority among postsecondary institutions worldwide. There are several drivers for this trend, both internal and external to the sector. The result is that universities are increasingly competing for international students and strategic international partnerships.

- More and more research is being conducted in large international teams. There is a trend toward expanding funding opportunities for teams at both the national and international levels.

- Massive open online courses (MOOCs) and other technology-enabled initiatives are gaining popularity as means used to enhance the international reputation of universities.

- Consortia among universities, government, and nongovernmental agencies are progressively recognized as key elements in developing solutions to large-scale global challenges (e.g., energy conservation, water pollution, and food hygiene). (For more on the role of consortia, see chapter 18.)

- Governmental research and development plans tend to favor partnerships with private sector organizations, many of which have international scope.

- Many governments see the recruitment of international students as an element of a broader strategy to address skilled labor shortages. Research has shown that many international students stay in the cities or regions in which they are trained (Alberta Minister of Enterprise and Advanced Education 2012).

Gaining an awareness of the trends relevant to higher education in general and internationalization in particular is crucial for developing an effective international strategy that can weather different paths. This assessment can also help SIOs to identify crucial opportunities and challenges for their institution in the years ahead.

Principles for International Strategy

Using the data gathered on the university's international activities and the global and local trends, and based on the goals of the Academic and Research Plans, the International Task Force established a set of principles to guide the development and implementation of the international strategy across the university:

1. International partnerships. Partnerships are essential tools for internationalization, but must be approached strategically:

    a. International partnerships must be focused, with clearly defined objectives that align with the broader strategic goals. Where possible, existing resources and strengths should be leveraged.

    b. International partnerships must be sustainable and multifaceted, where appropriate. This involves:

        i. Mutual benefits to both institutions;

        ii. Reinforced synergies among multiple points of contact, when appropriate; and

        iii. Projects and partnerships that are sufficiently limited in number so that they can be sustained given available resources.

    c. Whenever possible, the university must strategically work with universities and organizations that are highly ranked internationally, within their geographic area or specific fields of expertise or interest. Exceptions to this principle are made when the partnership accomplishes particular educational, research, or service objectives that relate to unique circumstances at the potential partner institution.

2. Entrepreneurism. Faculty members must maintain networks of international collaborations. The international strategy must encourage and facilitate international interactions at the faculty and student levels.

3. Structure. A university-level strategic plan for internationalization must include an effective organizational structure, agency at the institutional level to implement the plan, and visionary and effective senior leadership.

4. Incentives. Sustaining international activities must involve creating and maintaining incentive structures at the faculty level that will drive achievement of the goals of the international strategy.

5. Capacity building. As unique repositories of knowledge, universities must leverage their expertise to contribute to civil society and capacity development globally.

6. Risk management. The operation of all international activities must proceed within an enterprise-wide risk management framework that includes reputational and financial risk assessment. The safety and security of students, faculty, and staff is paramount.

7. Sustainability. The value of international initiatives and activities must be assessed relative to their overall impact. Once partnerships are established, technology-enabled solutions to maintain activities should be explored whenever possible.

These principles set the stage for discussions with internal and external stakeholders and helped secure support and approval of the international strategy from the leadership.

CONSULTATIONS WITH INTERNAL AND EXTERNAL STAKEHOLDERS

With an understanding of the major trends in international higher education in hand, along with the underlying principles of the strategy, the International Task Force engaged in consultations with multiple units across campus, including other vice presidential portfolios of the institution (research, finance, alumni engagement, development), faculties, and schools to test preliminary ideas generated by the Task Force and to ensure breadth in the international strategy. This consultation resulted in the drafting of the strategy.

Once a formal draft of the institutional international strategy was complete, the president and provost of UCalgary invited a select group of 25 external community members— comprising representatives and leaders from the business sector, nonprofit organizations, and local and provincial governments— to review and provide feedback on the strategy. This final consultation led to some changes to the strategy that made it more relevant to the local community. For example, areas where the institution's data matched up with critical geographical markets for local companies in the community were identified, considered, and included in the international strategy.

APPROVAL OF THE STRATEGY

The international strategy was unanimously approved by the academic senate and the Board of Governors of the university in 2013. An annual report on strategy progress is presented each year to the academic senate, the university Board of Governors, and the provincial government.

International Strategy

Based on the principles and analyses of all the data collected, the International Task Force developed four strategic goals, with three target metrics, to ensure that the university moved toward its vision of becoming a global intellectual hub:

1. Diversity: Increase the diversity of UCalgary's campus communities.

    a. Target: 10 percent of the undergraduate population will be international.

    b. Target: 25 percent of the graduate population will be international.

2. Cross-cultural competencies: Improve the global and cross-cultural competencies within the campus communities.

    a. Target: 50 percent of students will have an international experience before they graduate.

3. Partnerships: Enhance opportunities for international collaborations and partnerships in research and education.

4. International development: Leverage areas of expertise to engage in international development.

These goals are supported by specific strategies and tactics that drive the achievement of the international strategy. These, in turn, support the larger "Eyes High" vision and the university's Academic and Research Plans.

STRATEGIC REGIONAL FOCUS

In addition to the four key goals, the International Task Force developed a country/regional framework to bring more intentional focus to UCalgary's international activities around the world. Given the finite resources available, the Task Force analyzed the current (2012) location and focus of different international activities and, in conjunction with the academic and research priorities, pinpointed where the most appropriate partnership opportunities existed.

These countries and regions of emphasis represented areas where there were already ongoing institutional relationships, strong ties to the university's academic and research priority areas, and potential connections to industry in both Calgary and in the country or region of emphasis. In addition, the Task Force examined whether strong diasporic or immigrant populations from each of these countries and regions existed in Calgary.

The countries and regions of emphasis identified for the international strategy (2013) include:

- China. The sheer scale and speed at which its economy and higher education system are developing has made China a tremendous opportunity and challenge to any university. China is a nexus for many important collaborations.

- East Africa. UCalgary has a diverse and strong pattern of integrated education and research partnerships in East Africa, including in Kenya, Tanzania, and Uganda, particularly related to international development and health.

- Germany. Western Europe is a hub of research collaboration, and Germany has a strong postsecondary system.

- Mexico. The convergence of geographic proximity, trilateral agreements with Canada and the United States, and the strength of ongoing collaborations in Latin America has made Mexico an attractive partner. In particular, energy innovations are predicted to form the basis for strong collaborations in research and education.

- Middle East. UCalgary has a nursing campus located in Doha, Qatar, and broader research opportunities exist there. Qatar also provides a bridge to opportunities in other countries in the region, particularly around energy, engineering, and health research.

- United States. The highest density of the UCalgary's international research collaborations is in the United States. It is considered a center for international consortia that could tackle large-scale problems of importance to society.

In addition to these areas of emphasis, the International Task Force identified 13 other countries and regions of interest to explore and consider for internationalization activities. These include Australia, Brazil, France, India, Japan, Malaysia, Norway, Singapore, South Korea, Spain, Thailand, United Kingdom, and Vietnam.

Leadership and Governance

The efforts of university leadership have focused on these designated areas and on institutions within these geographic locations, with the appropriate funds allocated to support internationalization efforts. The selection of these countries and regions of emphasis is not intended to prevent activities from happening in countries that are not so designated, but certain institutional activities became very focused in these particular regions. Figure 3 shows the leadership and governance structure for implementing the international strategy across the various countries and regions of emphasis.

Figure 3. Governance Structure for International Strategy Implementation

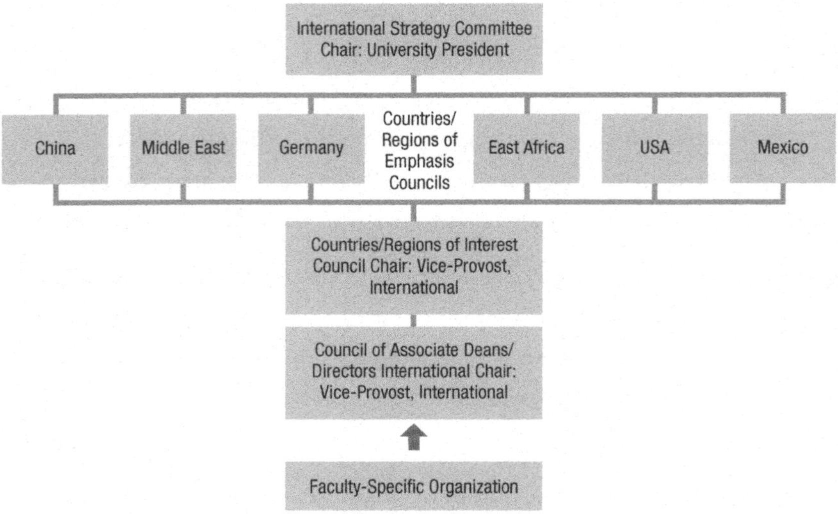

Source: UCalgary (2012a).

After an extensive international search, a vice-provost (international) (VPI), equivalent to the SIO, was hired to oversee and lead the implementation of UCalgary's international strategy. Aligning the university's international activities with the Academic and Research Plans, the VPI was responsible for advancing the institution's efforts in international research, academic programming, staff and student mobility, programmatic partnerships, service, and development. In this particular case, the selected VPI was also a member of the International Task Force that developed the international strategy.

After the academic senate and Board of Governors approved the international strategy, an overarching International Strategy Council (ISC) was formed. It is chaired by the president of the university and includes the chairs of the Countries/Regions of Emphasis Councils. The ISC is responsible for the implementation of the international strategy, including making decisions on country and regional designations.

The ISC makes its decisions based on data provided by the Countries/Regions of Emphasis Councils. Each of the six Countries/Regions of Emphasis Councils is led by a senior executive officer (e.g., president, provost, vice president research) and joined by invited members of the academy who have strong ties to the particular country or region, industry partners, and significant Calgary community leaders. Each member remains in effect for a period of 3 years and may be renewed pending satisfactory review by the ISC. The purpose of each of these councils is to develop a strategic direction for education and research activities related to the designated country or region of emphasis; to monitor trends and opportunities in the designated country or region; and to ensure that key performance indicators and other measures of impact are developed, measured, and reported for the designated country or region.

To further support the ISC's efforts, UCalgary established an Associate Deans/Directors Council (ADCI). The purpose of the ADCI is to engage with faculties in developing and maintaining international collaborations. This council, chaired by the VPI, has mitigated some of the bureaucratic and academic issues that previously stalled the development and implementation of projects initiated by faculties and international and external partners.

Although a single Countries/Regions of Interest Council was supposed to be established and chaired by the VPI to coordinate and monitor engagement activities within these countries and regions, it was later decided that the VPI would work with faculties through the ADCI.

Assessment of International Strategy

UCalgary has had years of successful internationalization efforts. UCalgary International (UCI), an office led by the VPI, includes staff members who work on executing elements of the international strategy. UCI staff members measure the progress of the international strategy goals regularly through the key performance indicator (KPI) dashboard. The dashboard includes exemplar metrics such as the proportion of international students at the undergraduate and graduate levels, proportion of students participating in international experiences, number of international partnerships, number of publications with international partners, and amount of research grants. Figures 4, 5, and 6 show a sample of the metrics of diversity, cross-cultural competencies, and partnerships, respectively, in the KPI dashboard for the 2016–17 academic year. An annual report on KPI metrics is presented to the academic senate and the Board of Governors of the university.

Figure 4. Diversity Key Performance Indicators

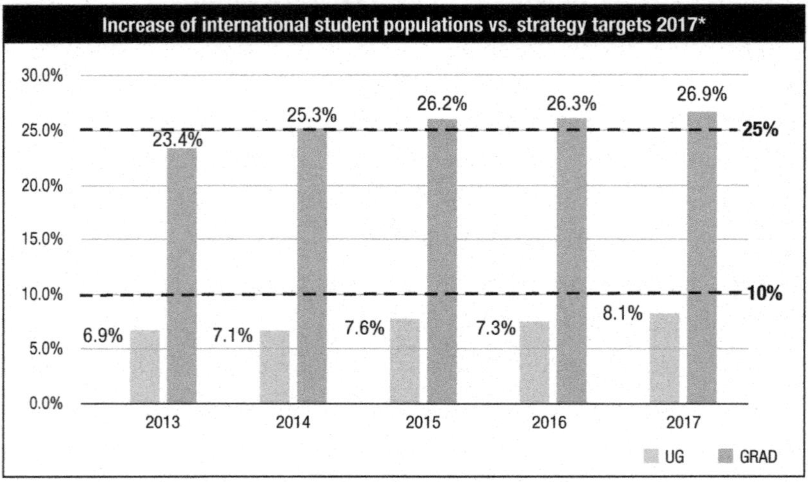

Increase of international student populations vs. strategy targets 2017*

*All international students weighted student headcount divided by total fall weighted student headcount.
Data Source: Registrar's Office (RO), as of 9/14/2018.

Top 10 countries of origin for international students 2017*					
Rank	**Country**	**UG**	**GRAD**	**Total**	**%**
1	China	514	303	817	21.3
2	India	149	157	306	8.0
3	Iran	19	264	283	7.4
4	USA	66	93	159	4.2
5	Nigeria	67	51	118	3.1
6	Pakistan	77	28	105	2.7
7	Bangladesh	37	54	91	2.4
8	Mexico	16	64	80	2.1
9	Brazil	26	42	68	1.8
10	Egypt	32	34	66	1.7

*All international students weighted student headcount divided by total fall weighted student headcount.
Data Source: Registrar's Office (RO), as of 9/14/2018.

Source: UCalgary (2018).

Figure 5. Cross-Cultural Competencies Key Performance Indicators

YOY share of students with an
international experience*

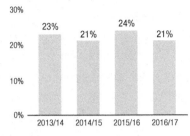

* UCalgary formula used: UG students with an international
experience (IE) divided by UG graduates for each year.

UCalgary students with an international
experience vs. national average*

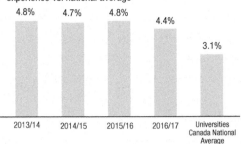

*Based on data reported by the Study Abroad Office, faculties and
other units as of end of Winter 2017. Formula is fulltime UG IE
students (UCI) divided by enrolled fulltime UG (RO).

% of students on intl. experience
programs receiving UC grants*

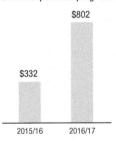

1135 students in 2016/17

UC grant dollars per student
on intl. experience programs*

*Number of grants (382 and 622
respectively), divided by students with
an intl. experience. Investment dollars
allocated by UCI for students divided by
students with an intl. experience. Individual
cases may differ. Data Source: VPI

Source: UCalgary (2018).

Rank	Country	Headcount	Percent of Total
1	United States	223	20.0%
2	United Kingdom	88	7.9%
3	China + HK + Taiwan	76	6.8%
4	Japan	71	6.4%
5	Spain	63	5.7%
6	Switzerland	55	5.0%
7	Germany	54	4.9%
8	Australia	46	4.2%
9	South Korea	39	3.5%
10	Italy	34	3.1%

Figure 6. Partnerships Key Performance Indicators

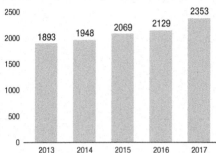

Top research output from international collaborations expressed via number of joint publications*

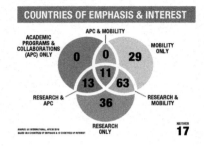

International Partnership Assessment Rating Index (IPARI)

*Joint publications related to countries/regions of emphasis and interest. All numbers have been amended from previous dashboard due to redefining search criteria for increased accuracy. Data source: Scopus database, UCI.

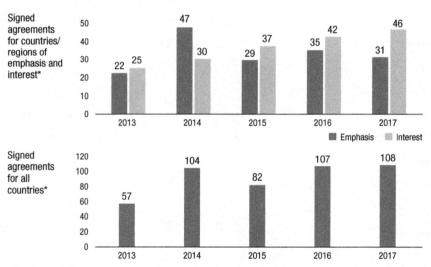

Signed agreements for countries/regions of emphasis and interest*

■ Emphasis   ▨ Interest

Signed agreements for all countries*

* Signed agreements for all countries and countries of emphasis/interest pulled by agreement start date from Jan 1 to Dec 31 that particular year. Figures follow the Calendar Year. Agreements may still be active or may be expired, depending on what it is stated in the individual agreements. Data assumed as accurate as possible. Numbers amended from previous years for accuracy. Data Source: MoveOn database, UCI.

Source: UCalgary (2018).

Some of the key outcomes of the international strategy include:

- International undergraduate enrollment grew from 5.1 to 9.2 percent between 2012 and 2018, representing an 80 percent increase, and international graduate enrollment increased to more than 27 percent, surpassing the target of 25 percent.

- UCalgary students have consistently participated in more international learning experiences compared with the national average (see figure 5).

- The number of joint research publications with international collaborators increased from 1,893 articles in 2013 to 2,353 articles in 2017, representing a 24 percent increase (see figure 6).

- Signed agreements with international entities increased from 57 agreements in 2013 to 108 in 2017, representing an 89 percent increase (see figure 6).

- Established global research initiatives and sites focused on energy in China and Mexico, leading to an increase of more than CAD$57 million in research funding.

- Raised more than CAD$20 million for international development projects in low- and middle-income countries.

Internationalization also contributed to enhancing the student experience. UCalgary has created or built up support programs to improve student success, satisfaction, and inclusiveness across all dimensions of diversity, including socioeconomic, race, ethnicity, gender, sexual orientation, faith, and age. The university has implemented a number of cocurricular and cross-cultural activities to help students maximize their academic and personal success. Examples of these initiatives and programs include:

- Established an international recruitment model that is founded on nine values: inclusivity, quality, student success, enhancement, customization, integration, sustainability, institutional autonomy, and agility;

- Developed and implemented an International Foundations Program to help academically qualified students gain English language proficiency;

- Delivered full-time, noncredit English training to approximately 5,000 students from 51 countries;

- Offered courses in languages, intercultural competency, and teaching English as a second language;

- Launched a welcome center for international students to help them successfully transition to life on campus;

- Expanded support services for international students across multiple units; and

- Trained an international student adviser as a registered Canadian immigration consultant.

UCalgary's community-based internationalization strategy advances multiple priority areas for the university. These efforts have resulted in multiple awards from national and international organizations, including the Association of Public and Land-grant Universities's Institutional Award for Global Learning, Research, and Engagement and the Canadian Bureau of International Education's Board of Directors's Award for Comprehensive Internationalization.

The SIO of the UCalgary International Strategy (2012) designed a seven-point model (see figure 7) called "Recipe for Success for Internationalization" (Ruwanpura 2018).

These seven points summarize the critical steps to establishing and implementing an international strategy that can be applied to various institutions around the world.

1. Identify internationalization as a campus-wide academic priority.

2. Craft a clear and focused international strategy with specific goals, objectives, and tactics focused on carefully selected geographical areas.

Figure 7. Seven-Point Model for Internationalization

Source: Ruwanpura (2018).

3. Establish a governance structure to oversee the implementation of the strategy and include leadership from the highest levels of the institution.

4. Create new programs and projects anchored within academic units.

5. Design international projects to support faculty teaching, research, and service.

6. Develop an empowering organizational structure for the central international office.

7. Allocate new and innovative funding models to sustain and grow internationalization.

This model can be customized to align with the vision and academic and research priorities of any institution to successfully design and employ an institutionally appropriate international strategy.

Conclusion

At a time when a rise in nationalism and protectionism is affecting many countries throughout the world, universities must play a key role in upholding and advancing internationalization efforts. These efforts should be strategic in nature, align with the institutional vision, and take into consideration data from across campus, global trends in the field, and input from internal and external stakeholders. SIOs, and the different leaders and councils with which they work, must identify and implement the international strategies that will add value to all academic and administrative units and serve the needs of the students, faculty, staff, and institution.

Additional Resources

Hudzik, John K. 2018. *Comprehensive and Strategic Internationalization: Lessons Learned and Future Prospects.* Washington, DC: NAFSA: Association of International Educators.

Hudzik, John K., and JoAnn S. McCarthy. 2012. *Leading Comprehensive Internationalization: Strategy and Tactics for Action.* Washington, DC: NAFSA: Association of International Educators.

Landorf, Hilary, and Stephanie Doscher. 2014. "Making Data Come Alive: Diverse Methods for Engaging Stakeholders in Meaningful Assessment." NAFSA e-Learning Seminar. Washington, DC: NAFSA: Association of International Educators. https://www.nafsa.org/Professional_Resources/ Learning_and_Training/e-Learning_Seminars/Making_Data_Come_Alive__ Diverse_Methods_for_Engaging_Stakeholders_in_Meaningful_Assessment/.

University of Calgary (UCalgary). 2013. *Becoming a Global Intellectual Hub: Highlights of the University of Calgary International Strategy.* Calgary, Canada: University of Calgary. https://www.ucalgary.ca/uci/files/uci/ucalgary- international-strategy.pdf.

References

Alberta Minister of Enterprise and Advanced Education. 2012. *Campus Alberta Planning Resource 2012: Profiling Alberta's Advanced Education System.* Alberta Minister of Enterprise and Advanced Education. https:// open.alberta.ca/dataset/0fe6d666-290e-422f-91a1-4690310f0b41/ resource/57d6dc0f-0745-4529-bd3e-212d85dce1af/download/5873415-2012- campus-alberta-planning-resource-2012.pdf.

McCabe, Lester T. 2001. "Globalization and Internationalization: The Impact on Education Abroad Programs." *Journal of Studies in International Education* 5, 2:138–145.

Ruwanpura, Janaka. 2018. *7 Steps to a Successful International Strategy Implementation.* Calgary, Canada: University of Calgary. https://go.ucalgary. ca/7stepsstrategy-ebook.html.

Universities Canada. 2016. "Student Mobility Is Essential to Canada's Global Future." Universities Canada. December 2, 2016. https://www.univcan.ca/ media-room/media-releases/opinion-student-mobility-essential-canadas-global- future/.

University of Calgary (UCalgary). 2012a. *International Strategy.* Calgary, Canada: University of Calgary.

University of Calgary (UCalgary). 2012b. *University of Calgary: 2012 Academic Plan.* Calgary, Canada: University of Calgary. http://www.ucalgary.ca/provost/ files/provost/academicplan2012.pdf.

University of Calgary (UCalgary). 2018. "International Strategy Key Performance Indicators (KPI) Dashboard 2016/17." Internal document. Calgary, Canada: University of Calgary.

PART 2
Administration

5 | Administration

Victoria Jones

The field of international higher education is still in a stage of rapid and relatively early development. As such, the criteria for measuring success for institutional leaders are still being articulated and defined. There is a wide range of job descriptions within the category of senior international officer (SIO) (see chapter 1). The SIO's responsibilities depend on the institution type, its mission, and the community it serves, as well as the institution's stage of, and commitment to, internationalization.

Career success is then determined by the fit between the individual SIO and the specific demands of the position he or she holds at a particular institution at a precise moment in time. Identification and obtainment of a generic set of characteristics or benchmarks are not predictive of success for SIOs. This chapter explores the administrative aspects of finding the right match between the institution and the SIO, which includes further consideration of the needs of the institution, its various stakeholders, the position search, and the campus leadership team.

Institutional Needs

Given the very wide range of internationalization stages at institutions, one particularly useful approach to the SIO hiring process is a contingency approach, which considers the institutional situation and identifies appropriate leadership styles to match. While situational approaches assume that leaders must be flexible and adapt their styles to match a variety of situations that change frequently, contingency approaches prioritize fit between the institutional situation at a moment in time and a leader's well-defined and practiced style and experience (Peretomode 2012). In the contingency approach, the ideal candidate not only possesses a specific set of skills and experiences for a generic job title, but also has experience working with institutions and projects that are in the same moment of development (Shao, Feng, and Hu 2015).

For example, in one scenario, a university that is hiring its first SIO in the newly created position might prefer to hire someone with director-level experience who has started several offices of education abroad and launched new programs at institutions just beginning to internationalize the campus. This individual will have the background, knowledge, and demonstrated skills to start internationalization efforts from the ground up, including working with stakeholders, vetting services, and securing funding. Conversely, hiring an experienced SIO who has held the position only at institutions where the role is already well established might not be as good a fit for this university because the individual may not have the experience or skill sets needed to build something new. In another scenario, a university with well-established programs and modest goals for growth may not be a good fit for an entrepreneurial SIO who is innovative and motivated by change. The school may instead prioritize candidates who have been solid contributors in established programs.

Another factor critical to SIO success is whether the SIO and the institution have similar expectations about what can be done in global engagement given the available resources and campus climate. A candidate accustomed to a well-staffed and generously funded program may not be a good fit for an institution with more modest resources. It is important that the SIO and the institution are a good fit in terms of institutional goals and mission, phase of internationalization, and size of staff.

Management and Leadership

At most institutions, the SIO is part of the senior leadership team, most often reporting directly to the provost (Kwai 2014). There is an extensive body of applied management literature that addresses differences between "management" and "leadership" (see Zaleznik 2004; Bennis 2003; Wall Street Journal 2009). Managers are generally described as people who effectively execute and coordinate the activities of their teams, while leaders are typically described as visionaries who inspire people. This is another area where fit should be considered. Is the institution in need of someone to provide vision, inspiration, and motivation, or is efficient management of operations and staff the priority? There are campus administrators who are often better suited to one or the other.

Additionally, although the SIO position may be next in the sequential hierarchy from a director position, it is an exponential jump in responsibility and scope, not an incremental one. Literature from the field of management describes a "T" shape of knowledge that is required for senior leaders, where the base of the T is a depth of knowledge in a single area, such as international student and scholar services, and the cross bar at the top of the T is a familiarity with many areas across the institution, such as education abroad, export control, finance and budgeting, human resources, English as a second language (ESL), etc. (Kelly 2018).

Those who aspire to be in an SIO position should strive to obtain significant, measurable levels of knowledge about functional areas beyond their own, which can be done by serving on cross-functional committees, developing strategic partnerships with other units, etc. Deep experience in one area is not sufficient for success or growth in a senior leadership role. As the position and the field of international education both continue to expand and mature, it is imperative that SIOs searching for positions equip themselves with the necessary skill sets and experiences to find the best-fit institution at which to advance their careers.

Position Search

Professional international education associations such as NAFSA: Association of International Educators and the Association of International Education Administrators (AIEA) offer a variety of publications and resources (e.g., *International Educator* magazine, NAFSA's International Education Leadership Knowledge Community, AIEA listserv, etc.) on news about SIO careers. Other common sources include general higher education associations, such as the American Council on Education (ACE) and the Association of Public and Land-grant Universities (APLU), and publications such as the *Chronicle of Higher Education*. (For more on professional associations, conferences, and career development resources, see Appendix B.)

It is common for universities to hire search firms that specialize in higher education to conduct searches for these positions that are increasingly integral to the leadership team. Compared with faculty and director positions, the search for an SIO usually involves a broader range of stakeholders from across the campus. Often there are many units invested in the hiring decision because the position is heavily matrixed.

The first response to a job posting is the written application, usually submitted through web-based software. It is not recommended to contact the supervisor of the position or search committee members at this stage. The human resources staff are usually responsible for the initial screening of candidates. Additionally, supervisors must uphold hiring requirements that ensure that all candidates are treated equally. Thus, supervisors cannot engage with candidates outside of normal, approved institutional procedures.

Application

When applying for the first time for a senior leadership position, general career guidance may be helpful, though it is important to note that procedures may vary from institution to institution and any specific instructions for the position must be followed precisely. As with other professional applications, a résumé should be limited to two pages and a cover letter to one page (University of California-Davis Internship and Career Center n.d.). If the candidate comes from a faculty background, using a curriculum vitae with unlimited pages is acceptable for listing the work history, but the one-page cover letter limit still applies. Candidates might consider creating their own professional websites to provide supplemental information and include photos and videos that exhibit their skills and experience.

Rather than merely listing previous professional responsibilities, candidates should tailor their application documents to focus on demonstrating their leadership readiness, establishing that position requirements are met, and making a case for fit to the specific position. For senior leadership roles, it is often more important to show significant impact and measurable contributions than it is to provide a comprehensive list of duties.

For example, if a candidate previously served as the director of an education abroad office, it is implicitly understood that the role included program promotion and risk management. Instead, the application documents should highlight what the candidate personally contributed. Under the individual's leadership, did program participation increase significantly? Did the candidate implement programs that broadened the demographics of participants or provided more diverse offerings? If the candidate overhauled policies to align with best practices or created a capacity development program that provided support to 10 percent of the faculty, those are the types of specific accomplishments that show readiness for leadership.

As much as possible, candidates should avoid using broad, generic statements and repeating qualifications that appear on the job posting such as "responsible for all risk management" or "provided oversight to peer advisers." These statements do not convey the unique skill sets and experiences that the candidate has and can bring to institutions. Alternatively, specific, personal contribution statements show leadership readiness and are presented in phrases like "increased faculty participation by 15 percent," "convened a cross-functional team that updated all risk management policies," and "proposed new programs that increased annual revenue." The more qualitative and quantitative outcomes validate the candidate's qualifications in a more tangible manner that often resonates with hiring committees and staff.

Interviews

Candidates should be prepared for the interview process to begin with technology-mediated conversations that may eventually lead to a series of in-person interviews with members of the search firm or committee and a final in-person interview held on campus with various faculty, administrators, and student leaders. The first interview is typically conducted using synchronous distance technology like Skype or Zoom or possibly by an audio-only conference call. The search firm representatives or search committee members generally convene in person so that they can ask follow-up questions of the candidate. Thus, the candidate may appear on a screen in front of several people at a time and answer questions from different members. It is important for candidates to be as natural as possible because committee members are getting their first sense of each candidate's personality during these interviews.

At this stage, the interview questions are usually identical for every candidate, and the number of candidates in the interview pool is usually between five and 10 people. The committee is looking for specific characteristics or experiences and may probe for this particular information. Candidates should try to understand the intent of each question and answer it clearly with brief and specific examples.

Campus Visit

Following the first round of interviews, the pool of candidates is usually narrowed down to three or four. These candidates are invited to campus for in-person interviews, which usually take a full day. Candidates take part in a series of meetings that generally kick off with the search committee and may also include groups and individuals such as deans, faculty, students, staff (usually in director roles of their various units), senior administrators, the provost, and the president. A campus tour and business lunch or dinner may provide opportunities for more informal interactions, but they are still a part of the active evaluation. Everyone that the candidates meet will likely have a voice in the final decision, so it is imperative that the candidate treat every person, regardless of rank, with professionalism and respect.

The on-campus interview usually has less structure to the questions than those from the earlier interviews. The many stakeholders involved in the interviewing process have their own priorities and concerns, and the search committee is now tasked with probing for individualized concerns, such as whether the candidate is truly willing to do the dull as well as the more interesting parts of the job, whether the individual is methodical and well organized, and whether the individual works well in a team. All participants of the interview process submit what is usually a combination of numeric scores and open-ended comments regarding their interactions with each candidate.

Throughout the process, it is important to keep in mind that candidates should be, in essence, interviewing the institution and future coworkers as much as they are being interviewed. Candidates should establish their own set of priorities and concerns that they wish to investigate during their interview before they come to campus. Some observations to make include:

- What is the supervisor's style and level of commitment to international activities?

- Is there an adequate number of support staff in place to implement initiatives?

- Is the campus generally in a period of abundance and growth or cutbacks and reductions?

- Are people forthcoming about challenges as well as opportunities? Candidates should also consider the day-to-day responsibilities.

- Where is the office located and is the space adequate?

- Are the institution's facilities in disrepair?

- Is the search committee fractious or equable in person?

- What is the social atmosphere like?

- What is the direction for global engagement?

There is usually only one visit to campus and it is important to use the opportunity to gather as much contextual information as possible. After the job offer has been made, the power balance shifts toward the candidate, who now has greater liberty to ask more sensitive questions about personality, culture, and fit.

Contract Negotiations

Contract negotiation is part of the hiring search and process. Both the candidates and institutions can withdraw from the process at any stage if they learn of anything unsettling about the fit or expectations. Among the things to be negotiated and put in writing either in an email or an employment contract include:

- Job title, including faculty appointment and tenure or payroll classifications;

- Salary and benefits, including how much travel is expected because it can be a significant factor in terms of job satisfaction;

- Budget, including the level of funding available for basic operations such as travel and programming and how many staff lines are funded and whether they can be reclassified or increased;

- Partner involvement, including whether the organization supports spousal hires and flexibility to work at a distance or allow for visits with family; and

- Participation and/or membership in professional associations, including whether this is encouraged and funded.

Campus Leadership

As part of the senior leadership team on a campus, the newly hired SIO must understand the fundamental overarching priorities of the institution and provide the international perspectives and strategies that will advance them. SIOs provide direct oversight to the units under their supervision, but they must also advocate and collaborate across other units at many levels. The international functions of a campus not only complement but also intersect and overlap with several basic functional areas.

Units that might report directly to an office of global engagement include partnerships, education abroad, intensive English programs, international admissions, international student and scholar services, etc. To provide the basic services of these units, SIOs must collaborate with other functional areas such as admissions, academic personnel and human resources, risk management, legal counsel, continuing education, office of research, and academic units like schools and colleges. Relationships and procedures with these units must be positive and well defined, or it can lead to confusion, conflict, or competition. The SIO position is heavily matrixed even when the international functions are centralized, and especially when they are decentralized.

Campus Partners

While SIOs may interact most frequently with their direct supervisor and with their direct reports, engagement with a wide range of internal stakeholders is critical. Deans are usually the main point of contact for SIOs when developing academic activities such as teaching and research. Some deans may delegate international activities to an associate dean or a designated faculty liaison. Since deans are the heads of their schools and act with considerable autonomy within their respective school, it is important for SIOs to meet individually and regularly with deans. Although working with senior leadership may be new to some first-time SIOs, the same leadership and people skills developed throughout their career also apply in the SIO role.

It can be advantageous to identify the colleagues who will be champions and allies. Sometimes these meetings between SIOs and deans serve to identify opportunities where there are "low-hanging fruit" for internationalization efforts, such as preparing guidelines for hosting visiting scholars, providing logistics support for delegations, opening a student exchange with a long-standing research partner, and securing funds for international programming. In large universities, there may be deans for graduate and undergraduate programs or for student services, in addition to the deans who oversee the academic colleges and schools. These administrative deans often have less autonomy but significantly more power to create policies that span the entire campus.

Another crucial group of on-campus partners for SIOs is the faculty. Faculty members are the beating heart and existential imperative of any college or university. Their critical role in teaching and research gives them both a collective and individual position of power and prestige. Faculty collaborators are indispensable; indeed, the SIO role is largely about setting up structures and processes that facilitate the work of faculty. SIOs who do not come from the faculty must cultivate a deep understanding of the faculty role and sincere respect for their perspectives. (For more on faculty engagement, see chapter 12.)

COLLABORATION

SIOs generally develop their strategies in collaboration with the most senior leaders on campus, and yet, execution often requires working with people at a more operational level. It is important for SIOs to determine when to begin with their peers who supervise the operational staff in other areas, and when to go directly to the operational staff for collaboration. Getting this wrong can be perceived as interfering in another leader's area or going over the head of a person unnecessarily. This is a judgment call that requires understanding about the individual leaders and staff involved.

Within the SIO team, it is possible to be more directive—though heads of individual units generally should be given as much independence as reasonable to direct their own units. This allows SIOs to focus on developing comprehensive strategies and policies, and it empowers directors to act where they are closest to the issues and concerns. Generally, SIOs may wish to ask their directors how they can be of support, rather than trying to take over the directors' operations. SIOs and directors can design strategies and develop priorities together or meet at regular intervals to set goals.

Career Progression

The career progression for SIOs has been evolving in response to student, institutional, and global needs. At one time, these roles were primarily held by faculty who were active in academic areas related to international education or who were active in international programming, such as faculty-led study abroad. Today, SIOs may also come from the ranks of experienced staff whose credentials are more administrative than academic. A doctorate is often still a job requirement; although at some institutions, a doctorate is only "preferred" and a master's degree is required. Increasingly, the doctoral degree may be either professional (as opposed to academic) or may be academic preparation for professional careers (as opposed to teaching and research).

Career progression after the SIO role has a unique trajectory as well. While it is possible to move from smaller to larger or lesser to more prestigious universities, generally, the SIO position is the terminal role in the international education leader career track. Although there is only anecdotal data at this time, few SIOs go on to become deans, provosts, or presidents. It is more likely that they transition to faculty roles, leave academia for the private sector, or establish consulting practices.

Conclusion

SIOs must work across a broad range of responsibilities, functional areas, and geographically expansive territories. A good fit between the individual SIO and the particular needs and resources of the institution at a given point of time is critical for success. Developing appropriate relationships across a broad spectrum of stakeholders is also essential. As part of the senior leadership team of a university with an expansive portfolio that usually includes a variety of distinct functions, the SIO must be able to prioritize and establish reasonable expectations. And it is essential that those practical expectations be combined with a clear vision that is shared by both the campus leadership and internationalization teams. When the fit is right, there are few positions as interesting and rewarding as that of an SIO.

Additional Resources

Lambert, Susan, Riall Nolan, Norman Peterson, and Deborah Pierce. 2007. *Critical Skills and Knowledge for Senior Campus International Leaders.* Washington, DC: NAFSA: Association of International Educators. https://www.nafsa.org/uploadedFiles/delphi.pdf.

NAFSA: Association of International Educators. 2015. *NAFSA International Education Professional Competencies.* Washington, DC: NAFSA: Association of International Educators. http://www.nafsa.org/competencies.

References

Bennis, Warren. 2003. *On Becoming a Leader.* New York, NY: Basic Books.

Kelly, Andy. 2018. *Model T Leadership: From Good Manager to Great Leader.* Independently published.

Kwai, C. K. 2014. "A Survey on Senior International Education Officers, Their Institutions and Offices." Durham, NC: Association of International Education Administrators. https://www.aieaworld.org/assets/docs/Surveys/sio%20survey%20summary.pdf.

Peretomode, Otaroghene. 2012. "Situational and Contingency Theories of Leadership: Are They the Same?" *IOSR Journal of Business and Management* 4, 3:13–17. http://iosrjournals.org/iosr-jbm/papers/Vol4-issue3/C0431317.pdf.

Shao, Zhen, Yuqiang Feng, and Qing Hu. 2015. "Effectiveness of Top Management Support in Enterprise Systems Success: A Contingency Perspective of Fit Between Leadership Style and System Life-Cycle." *European Journal of Information Systems* 25, 2:131–153. https://link.springer.com/article/10.1057/ejis.2015.6.

University of California-Davis Internship and Career Center. n.d. "Resume and Materials." Davis, CA: University of California-Davis. https://icc.ucdavis.edu/materials.

Wall Street Journal. 2009. "What Is the Difference Between Management and Leadership?" *Wall Street Journal.* Adapted from *Wall Street Journal Guidebook*, Alan Murray. Harper Business. April 7, 2009. http://guides.wsj.com/management/developing-a-leadership-style/what-is-the-difference-between-management-and-leadership/.

Zaleznik, Abraham. 2004. "Managers and Leaders: Are They Different?" *Harvard Business Review* 82, 1:74–81.

6 | Budgets and Finance

Jesse Lutabingwa

In recent years, many U.S. institutions of higher education, especially public ones, have experienced significant reductions to their budgets as legislatures continuously slash financial support. To make up for these cuts, institutional leaders often increase tuition, add fees, and eliminate certain academic programs and services. Global engagement programs and activities are often threatened and among the first to be chopped. This has weakened U.S. economic and national security (Committee for Economic Development 2006) and created a situation the Modern Language Association (2007) refers to as "the current language crisis." Not surprisingly, between 2013 and 2016, more than 650 foreign language programs at U.S. colleges and universities were eliminated (Johnson 2019).

One of the functions of senior international officers (SIOs) is to generate revenue in order to support their operations, develop budgets, and manage the finances of their office (Hudzik and Pynes 2014; Kwai and Deardorff 2012). Many SIOs, especially the relatively new ones, are not trained in identifying new, nontraditional, and sustainable revenue streams to support the mission of their office (Kwai and Deardorff 2012), despite NAFSA: Association of International Educators (2015) identifying financial stewardship as one of the cross-cutting competencies across all international education domains.

This chapter provides a broad discussion on revenue streams that support the operations of international offices. It discusses traditional sources that are increasingly becoming unstable and some creative streams that have the potential to be more sustainable over time. Additionally, the chapter discusses the important role that SIOs play in developing and managing budgets of their units.

There are many different types of institutions within the U.S. higher education landscape, and it is dangerous to overgeneralize. This chapter, therefore, is more relevant to SIOs at comprehensive and smaller public institutions than the large research institutions and private ones. However, this does not mean that SIOs at those institutions may not find information in this chapter to be useful. Additionally, information in this chapter is generally more relevant to SIOs at U.S. institutions than higher education institutions outside the United States.

Traditional Revenue Streams

With some variations, there are at least seven traditional or common revenue streams that most SIOs at public institutions rely on: state funds, tuition, university foundation streams, fundraising efforts, education abroad enrollment fees, intensive English programs, and fees for international student and scholar services. While not all of these revenue streams apply to private institutions, there is still significant overlap.

State Funds

Almost all public institutions rely on funds provided through legislative action. State funds provide base operating budgets for global engagement efforts on most campuses. These funds are used to support staff lines and other basic operations of international offices. At some institutions, state funds also support faculty and staff's travel abroad and international visiting scholars.

In recent years, however, this stream of revenue has been declining and has become very unstable. Overall, state funding for public two- and four-year colleges in the 2016–17 academic year was nearly $9 billion below its 2008 level, after adjusting for inflation (Mitchell, Leachman, and Masterson 2017). In some cases, revenue from state funds has remained stagnant even though the needs have increased and services have expanded. As such, SIOs cannot depend only on state-provided funds.

Tuition

As allocations from state funds have dwindled, many institutions have increased tuition rates to cover the difference. In 2017, for the first time in the history of the United States, public higher education institutions in most states received the majority of their revenue from tuition rather than government appropriations (Brownstein 2018). International offices often receive a substantial portion of their operating budgets from the tuition revenue stream. This is a particularly important revenue stream for private colleges and universities.

In the past few years, however, there has been a growing uproar about the amount of money students at public institutions have to pay for their education (Brownstein 2018; Seltzer 2018). As such, SIOs and international offices cannot expect that the share of their budgets from this revenue stream is going to increase significantly in the foreseeable future. In fact, the reverse might be true.

University Foundations

University foundations provide a reliable revenue stream for international offices. At many institutions, revenue from university foundations helps to cover various cost items that cannot be covered by state funds or student tuition, such as food and other operating costs. This type of funding is more flexible than state funds in terms of how the money may be spent. At some institutions, for example, funding from these sources is used to host meals for various purposes, rent apartments for international visiting faculty members, and purchase gifts for international visitors. It is also customary for scholarship monies raised from private individual donors to be placed in university foundation accounts (discussed in detail below). SIOs should engage with the foundation staff on their campus to see how they can help to grow this source of revenue for their operations.

Fundraising (Sponsorships and Donations)

At many U.S. institutions, fundraising efforts generate significant financial resources that support the operations of international offices. These include scholarships for students to study abroad and for international students to study at the U.S. institutions, as well as monies to support faculty and staff travel abroad for various purposes and international visiting scholars coming to U.S. institutions. Additionally, funds can be raised to support specific academic or nonacademic programs with a global focus.

Fundraising is an ongoing and very common effort at most U.S. colleges and universities. University presidents/chancellors and deans are expected to fundraise for their colleges and schools, yet few job descriptions for SIOs include fundraising as an expectation. Some SIOs at large U.S. research institutions are actively engaged in fundraising. However, many other SIOs expect their institution to provide them with the financial resources to support their operations, without having to contribute to efforts in generating those resources. This way of thinking is becoming, or may soon become, outdated.

SIOs can enhance these needed fundraising skills by developing close working relationships with university advancement colleagues on their campus, as well as by attending various fundraising professional development activities. NAFSA has offered preconference workshops on fundraising and international alumni since 2013 and will continue to do so during its annual conference. There are several other organizations that provide training in fundraising, including the Council for Advancement and Support of Education, Academic Impressions, and the Association of Fundraising Professionals. (For more on fundraising and alumni engagement, see chapter 20.)

Education Abroad Applications and/or Administrative Fees

Many colleges and universities in the United States charge a fee to students who apply for and enroll in various education abroad programs (Heisel and Kissler 2010). The education abroad fees vary widely across institutions and may even vary within an institution, based on the length and type of the education abroad program (e.g., year- or semester-long programs, short-term faculty-led programs, internships, student teaching abroad). Many education abroad offices are heavily dependent on this revenue stream to cover their operations, including staff salaries and programmatic activities.

The challenge with using education abroad enrollment fees as a primary revenue stream is that it can fluctuate depending on the number of students recruited and enrolled in the various programs (Stubbs and Carpenter 2014). As such, it is essential for SIOs and their teams to develop a minimum number of students who must be recruited annually in order to generate the necessary revenue to support the education abroad operations.

While not ideal, the self-support model is workable as long as financial pressures do not affect ethical judgments. In the current environment where students are complaining about the cost of education, SIOs must be sensitive to how high this cost can increase without triggering similar complaints heard about the rising tuition and fees.

Intensive English Programs

Intensive English language programs, also called intensive English programs (IEPs), have generally been a particularly strong revenue generator for international offices. At most colleges and universities in the United States, IEPs are stand-alone, self-supporting centers that are often, but not always, located within international offices. The revenue generated by IEPs can often support the operations of the programs themselves; some IEPs even generate excess revenue. A portion of the excess revenue is used to support other international programming activities on campus and abroad.

Recently, however, many international offices that once relied heavily on this revenue stream were forced to scale down their operations in order to meet basic financial needs. This shift has been a result of dwindling numbers of international students coming to study English in the United States (Eaton 2017). Consequently, this traditional revenue stream has become unstable over the past few years.

Some IEP leaders have voiced complaints that many SIOs have tended to see IEPs as cash cows to generate revenue for other international programs on campus. This sentiment is best reflected in a comment made by Mark Algren, executive director of the Center for English Language Learning at the University of Missouri. He states that: "institutions need to avoid the 'cash cow' syndrome of draining their IEP of its resources. Most IEPs are self-funded, but many of them are regularly drained of their resources to fund other programs; reinvestment in an IEP is essential to maintain a quality program with qualified instructors" (Algren 2016).

Many IEP programs are reinventing themselves to cope with the new reality of decreasing enrollment numbers. At the same time, there are other U.S. institutions that are establishing new IEPs as part of their efforts to recruit and retain international students on their campus.

Fees for International Student and Scholar Services

A national study commissioned by Vanderbilt University (2015) cites immigration as the fifth most costly area of regulatory compliance for colleges and universities in the United States. As the cost and complexity of immigration compliance grows, it is becoming increasingly common for institutions to charge an extra fee to international students as a means of funding immigration services (Redden 2015). These fees vary greatly in their amount and may be assessed on a one-time basis or for each term of enrollment. Some public institutions even charge differential tuition for international students over and above the standard rate for nonresidents. The fees provide support and programming services for international students and their dependents.

International offices responsible for serving visiting scholars or processing employment-based immigration sponsorship petitions may also charge fees for their services. Such fees may be required before the international office staff will issue a DS-2019 form for a visiting scholar or before they will begin work on an H-1B or other employment-based petition. Unlike the student fees, these costs are typically the responsibility of the sponsoring academic or administrative department rather than the visiting scholars or employees.

It is important for SIOs to understand the nature of these fees and to participate in the decisionmaking process on how much to charge the sponsoring departments in order to generate sufficient revenue to continue providing those services. This decisionmaking process may involve discussions with academic leaders who are unfamiliar with the importance of international students and scholars at institutions. SIOs should be prepared to make a case as to why these fees are important to the provision of the needed services for visiting international scholars.

Sustainable and Innovative Revenue Streams

There are some clear challenges with regard to the stability of the traditional revenue streams upon which international offices rely. In order to continue to support their operations, SIOs must become more creative in developing other innovative revenue streams. Some potential revenue streams are discussed below; there may be others not discussed here.

Considering that there are myriad ways that SIOs can approach revenue generation for their international office, it is important that they remain engaged with their various campus partners and take the time to evaluate what options might work for their institution. It is also vital for SIOs to take a gradualist approach to the suggestions made here. Some approaches may require a long-term perspective, while others may be low-hanging fruit that SIOs can implement within a short period of time.

Study Abroad Fees

In order to raise scholarship monies for students to study abroad, some U.S. colleges and universities charge every student a small fee per semester; it can range from $5 to $20, depending on the institution. This fee is similar to the athletics fee charged to all students at most U.S. institutions, whether or not students attend athletic events. At several colleges and universities, students have voted in favor of this fee in order to make study abroad more affordable for their peers (Heisel and Kissler 2010).

This fee has great potential in building a healthy scholarship fund to support students to study abroad. Most importantly, because this measure is often initiated and supported by the students, it may have an enduring effect. It is the responsibility of SIOs and their education abroad team to educate their campus communities on the importance of studying abroad and generating broad support from student bodies for such a fee. However, as with the education abroad application fee, SIOs must remain sensitive to broader complaints about the increased cost of higher education in the United States.

Tuition Reinvestment from International Students

In some U.S. states, there is a three-tier system for tuition rates: in-state, out-of-state, and out-of-the-country rates. International students are charged an out-of-the-country rate that is much higher than the other two (Redden 2015). Under a tuition reinvestment approach, portions of the higher tuition that international students pay are then reverted to international offices to support their various functions.

A relatively new approach is the "performance-based reinvestment model" used by the State University of New York (SUNY) and advocated by Mitch Leventhal (2011). According to Leventhal (2011), this approach is designed to create the financial resources needed to achieve sweeping internationalization goals of the university. At SUNY, 18 percent of the first year's international student tuition is reinvested to support the university's global engagement efforts (Leventhal 2011). Leventhal argues that this is an effective and sustainable revenue stream even as budgets are being cut.

Even though this approach has been applied in only a handful of institutions, it is an innovative way to generate revenue to support the operations of international offices. However, it does have limited application in many U.S. states and institutions, especially in some states such as North Carolina where legislatures are very restrictive on how tuition monies can be used. In those states, institutions do not have as much freedom in using tuition money as they wish. For such states, the argument for recruiting international students is not because of the tuition monies they bring with them, but the other non-financial contributions they make on campuses (Wainwright 2016).

For those interested in some comparative data in other countries, the Australian Universities International Directors' Forum conducts an annual *Benchmarking Australian University International Operations* study that may be of great value (Olsen 2013).

Cost-Sharing Approaches

There are various cost-sharing approaches that SIOs should also consider as part of a broader, sustainable revenue portfolio for international offices. These include, but are not limited to, partnering with other administrators on campus to support specific international activities, partnering with student government organizations or associations on campus events, and splitting the cost of international student recruitment with the offices of undergraduate and graduate admissions. These approaches do not necessarily generate revenue, but they may be considered as money saving methods for international offices. While these approaches may or may not work at all institutions, they are worth considering.

PARTNERING WITH OTHER ADMINISTRATORS

SIOs and the units they lead must recognize that the work of internationalizing the campus is a collective effort. There are several ways through which international offices can partner with other administrators on campus to support various international activities. For example, at several institutions, international offices provide financial support to faculty for their international travel on the condition that department chairs and college/school deans also contribute money to support their faculty. This approach holds faculty accountable to their chairs and deans, and it also helps to stretch the financial resources.

As another example, some international offices have been able to encourage the deans to contribute money to support education abroad scholarships for students from their colleges or schools. International offices are able to send more students abroad with the financial support. At the same time, colleges and schools can rely on the international offices to manage the logistics of administering the scholarships. With this approach, each unit wins.

PARTNERING WITH OFFICES OF STUDENT AFFAIRS AND STUDENT ORGANIZATIONS

At some U.S. institutions, international offices have partnered with the offices of student affairs to cover some costs, especially when it comes to student-related activities. At one university, the international office has developed a close working relationship with the Division of Student Affairs such that students' meals during international student orientation are completely paid for by Student Affairs.

On many U.S. campuses, student government associations (SGAs) are allocated funds, mainly from student fees, to support student activities.

International offices can partner with SGAs and other student organizations and associations to share the costs for activities that have a global focus.

SHARING COST OF INTERNATIONAL STUDENT RECRUITMENT

There are many institutions where the international student recruitment function is housed within international offices. One effective tactic is for international offices and admissions offices to share the cost of travel for the purpose of undergraduate and graduate student recruitment. This approach has been used successfully at a few small- and medium-sized institutions where, sometimes, resources for recruiting international students are scarce or not adequate.

Fees to Academic Departments for Immigration Services

It is a common practice on many U.S. campuses to charge a small fee to academic departments for immigration applications and petitions (e.g., J-1, H-1B, O-1, TN, E-3, green card, and others) filed by international offices on behalf of international faculty members and researchers from those departments. While a large portion of the costs are prescribed by the U.S. Department of Homeland Security or U.S. Department of State, international offices can add a small fee for the services rendered. At large institutions with a significant number of international faculty members and researchers, this can be a valuable and sustainable revenue stream. However, for smaller institutions with fewer international faculty and researchers, this may not be a worthwhile avenue.

Fees for Services

International offices can charge fees for several other services, such as taking passport photos, offering professional training for international groups, and delivering cross-cultural training for local businesses, to name a few. Some institutions provide services to their global partners and then charge a fee for those services (e.g., hosting faculty-led programs and conducting short-term training programs).

The relevant services that international offices are able to provide depend on the needs, creativity, and capacity of SIOs and their teams. Several U.S. institutions have set up an entire unit devoted to international training and development activities, and these units are completely self-supporting. Often, these units generate extra revenue, of which a small percentage is shared with the SIOs to support broader global engagement efforts.

Entrance or Participation Fees to Campus Events

International offices can generate additional revenue by charging entrance or participation fees for some of the events they organize at their institutions, such as cultural festivals and film viewings. These events may even be of interest to the community at large. This can become a sustainable revenue stream, especially if international offices organize the same event annually and it becomes popular.

Additionally, at some institutions, international offices charge a small fee to various exhibitors to participate in education abroad fairs on their campus. The fees generated by these events are reinvested in education abroad operations.

Revenue from University Merchandise Sales

In the United States, colleges and universities have licensing agreements for branded institutional merchandise such as T-shirts, cups, scarfs, ties, and other products. Some international offices have been able to negotiate a small percentage of the revenue from the sale of this merchandise to go toward supporting student scholarships. To bolster this effort, some international offices have helped with campaigns that encourage students and parents to purchase university branded products.

In a slightly different approach, some campus bookstores have partnered with international offices to provide scholarships to support international students in purchasing their school supplies from the university bookstores. At one university, the bookstore provides 20 international students with $300 each to use toward school supplies from the bookstore.

Rounding Down Approach

A lesser used revenue source for international offices is the "rounding down" approach. Even though this revenue stream is not frequently used on many campuses, it has shown some potential on campuses where it can work. With this approach, all campus personnel are asked to voluntarily have their salaries rounded down, and then all of the small cents from rounding down are deposited into accounts of international offices to support education abroad scholarships and other services. For example, if the actual payment is $10.49 per hour, then it is rounded down to $10.00 and the remaining $0.49 is deposited into the international office account. The administration of this approach can be very tricky and, oftentimes, it works best on smaller campuses. However, if there is broad campus support, it can be a good, sustainable revenue stream.

Contracts and Grants

Contracts and grants are other potential sources of revenue that many institutions of different types have used to fund their global engagement efforts. In order to use this revenue stream effectively, there must be interest in and capacity for writing grant proposals and implementing externally funded projects.

It is important to understand the differences between contracts and grants (see table 1). In a contract, there is an item (product and/or service) and the contractor is legally bound to deliver on that item. Failure to deliver can result in the contractor being found in default. In a grant, however, there is no legal consequence if the item is not delivered. A grant is an assistance mechanism, and a contract is a mechanism for acquiring services, supplies, or research for the direct benefit and use of the funding entity.

Table 1. Differences Between Contracts and Grants

Contracts	Grants
Legally binding agreements to deliver goods and/or services for the direct benefit or use by the funding entity in exchange for financial consideration.	Provide funding assistance to achieve some results, but have no legally binding requirement to achieve the results. Flexible funding to support public purpose.
Failure to perform can result in potential legal action or financial consequences.	Failure to perform not likely to result in legal action or financial consequences.
Relatively inflexible as to the scope of the work, budget, and other changes. Very specific in defining the scope of the work and outcomes.	Flexible in defining the scope of the work, budget, changes, and outcomes.
Governed by statutes, rules, and regulations (e.g., Federal Acquisition Regulation in the United States).	Governed by the terms of the grant agreement. More freedom to adapt the project and less responsibility to produce results.
Require frequent reporting and more fiscal requirements.	Usually involve only annual (or semiannual) reports and more flexibility in the use of funds.
Final payment based on deliverables.	Full payment usually awarded in lump sums or a "drawdown" system.

Source: Adapted from Grants.gov (2018) and includes information from other sources.

There are different types of contracts and grants:

- Solicited, whereby an institution responds to a specific announcement for grant proposals;

- Unsolicited, whereby an institution approaches a funder with a project idea; and

- Invited, whereby an institution is requested to submit a proposal to a funder for a specific purpose.

There are many grant opportunities that support or complement the work of international offices that SIOs should note. Some of the U.S. federal government entities that support globally focused grants include the Department of State, Department of Education, U.S. Agency for International Development, Department of Agriculture, National Science Foundation, and others. In addition, there are many organizations that work on large federal government grants that are always seeking to partner with colleges and universities to implement projects as subcontractors or sub-awardees.

There are numerous other organizations that solicit grants for various purposes, including United Nations agencies such as the World Health Organization; United Nations Children's Fund; International Labor Organization; United Nations Educational, Scientific and Cultural Organization; and others. Individual countries around the world, especially developing countries, also provide contract opportunities for U.S. colleges and universities. Additionally, there are private foundations that offer grants to support focused research in certain areas and different causes.

In order to take advantage of available grant opportunities, SIOs and their teams need to develop grant writing skills or engage the services of grant writers. Many institutions provide grant writing workshops or courses on campuses. Furthermore, SIOs and their teams must develop skills that will help them to understand what it takes to successfully implement and manage externally funded grants.

Budget Development and Financial Management

Most new SIOs receive little to no formal training on developing and managing budgets and office finances. Yet, on a daily basis, SIOs need to make decisions that affect their unit's financial performance. These decisions might include scheduling program activities for their operations, approving investment in a new program or activity, sending invoices for payment or approving payments, preparing a budget, and managing the human resource components of the office.

Budget Development

SIOs must know how to prepare their unit's budgets and their action plans for the next fiscal or academic year. SIOs should use the budget preparation process as a time to question how resources are being used and to determine if those resources could be used more efficiently (Shacklett 2016). The spending should be directly tied to the objectives, strategies, and action plans for the budget year and aligned with the unit and institutional strategic plans.

Financial Management

Managing a budget requires continuous monitoring, controlling, and reporting—all of which can be accomplished by hiring qualified budget or financial managers. Working closely alongside SIOs, the budget or financial managers may be based in international offices or assigned to international offices through a shared services system that can ensure proper checks and balances. It is important that disagreements and challenges are discussed in private, and that publicly, SIOs and budget or financial managers present a united front (McCray and Rosenbloom 2015; Shacklett 2016).

SIOs should monitor sources of revenue and expenditure, know how to minimize costs, be able to identify or investigate problematic areas and rectify them, and efficiently manage and authorize expenditures. SIOs must have access to accurate and management-oriented financial data, know how to interpret and use the data to inform decisions, and be able to incorporate financial data into a story about where their unit is headed (McCray and Rosenbloom 2015). Proper management of the international office's revenue and budget is the foundation for successful internationalization efforts on campus and abroad.

Conclusion

Increasingly, SIOs are expected to acquire certain financial skill sets that have not been as critical to the operations of international offices in the past. Relatively new SIOs must understand that some of the responsibilities and functions that they are expected to perform include generating revenue to support operations, developing budgets, and managing office finances. In order to support global engagement efforts, SIOs must increasingly develop new and sustainable revenue streams, many of which were discussed in this chapter. With this knowledge, along with the professional development resources available, SIOs can fulfill their fiscal responsibilities while advancing the internationalization agenda on their campus.

Additional Resources

Bethel, Krista Buda, and Margaret McCullers. 2017. "Creative and Innovative Solutions to Study Abroad Financing." e-Learning Seminar. March 15, 2017. Washington, DC: NAFSA: Association of International Educators. https://www.nafsa.org/Professional_Resources/Learning_and_Training/e-Learning_Seminars/Creative_and_Innovative_Solutions_to_Study_Abroad_Financing/.

References

Algren, Mark. 2016 "How Intensive English Programs Contribute to Campus Internationalization." *EvoLLLution*. October 26, 2016. https://evolllution.com/revenue-streams/global_learning/how-intensive-english-program-contribute-to-campus-internationalization/.

Brownstein, Ronald. 2018. "American Higher Education Hits a Dangerous Milestone." *The Atlantic*. May 3, 2018. https://www.theatlantic.com/politics/archive/2018/05/american-higher-education-hits-a-dangerous-milestone/559457/.

Committee for Economic Development. 2006. *Education for Global Leadership: The Importance of International Studies and Foreign Language Education for U.S. Economic and National Security*. Washington, DC: Committee for Economic Development. https://www.ced.org/pdf/Education-for-Global-Leadership.pdf.

Eaton, Sarah Elaine. 2017. "Perceptions of ESL Program Management in Canadian Higher Education: A Qualitative Case Study." *International Journal of Learning, Teaching and Educational Research* 16, 9:13–28.

Grants.gov. 2018. "What Is a Contract? 5 Differences Between Grants and Contracts." *Community Blog*. May 9, 2018. https://blog.grants.gov/2018/05/09/what-is-a-contract-5-differences-between-grants-and-contracts/.

Heisel, Margaret, and Gerald R. Kissler. 2010. *Financial Strategies for Expanding Study Abroad: Models, Mission, Management, and Means for Growth*. Washington, DC: NAFSA: Association of International Educators and Association of Public and Land-grant Universities. https://www.nafsa.org/uploadedFiles/NAFSA_Home/Resource_Library_Assets/Networks/CCB/StudyAbroadFinancing.pdf.

Hudzik, John K., and Penelope J. Pynes. 2014. *Developing Sustainable Resources for Internationalization*. Washington, DC: NAFSA: Association of International Educators.

Johnson, Steven. 2019. "Colleges Lose a 'Stunning' 651 Foreign-Language Programs in 3 Years." *Chronicle of Higher Education*. January 22, 2019. https://www.chronicle.com/article/Colleges-Lose-a-Stunning-/245526.

Kwai, C. K., and Darla K. Deardorff. 2012. "A Survey of Senior International Officers: Individual and Institutional Profiles." Durham, NC: Association of International Education Administrators. http://www.aieaworld.org/assets/docs/Surveys/2011siosurveyexecutivesummaryfinaldraft5b15djune2012.pdf.

Leventhal, Mitch. 2011. "US: New Funding Models for International Education." *University World News* 158. February 13, 2011. http://www.universityworldnews.com/article.php?story=20110211204106430.

McCray, Alex, and Philip Rosenbloom. 2015. "The Importance of Financial Leadership." *Nonprofit Finance Fund* (blog). November 24, 2015. https://nff.org/blog/importance-financial-leadership.

Mitchel, Michael, Michael Leachman, and Kathleen Masterson. 2017. "A Lost Decade in Higher Education Funding: State Cuts Have Driven Up Tuition and Reduced Quality." Washington, DC: Center on Budget and Policy Priorities. August 23, 2017. https://www.cbpp.org/research/state-budget-and-tax/a-lost-decade-in-higher-education-funding.

Modern Language Association. 2007. *Foreign Languages and Higher Education: New Structures for a Changed World*. New York, NY: Modern Language Association. https://www.mla.org/Resources/Research/Surveys-

Reports-and-Other-Documents/Teaching-Enrollments-and-Programs/
Foreign-Languages-and-Higher-Education-New-Structures-for-a-Changed-
World.

NAFSA: Association of International Educators. 2015. *NAFSA International
Education Professional Competencies*. Washington, DC: NAFSA: Association of
International Educators. http://www.nafsa.org/competencies.

Olsen, Alan. 2013. "2013 Research Agenda: Australian Universities International
Directors' Forum." Presentation to Australian International Education
Conference, October 9, 2013. http://www.spre.com.au/download/
AIEC2013AUIDFResearchPaper.pdf.

Redden, Elizabeth. 2015. "Fee for Being Foreign." *Inside Higher Ed*. May 8, 2015.
https://www.insidehighered.com/news/2015/05/08/some-public-universities-
are-charging-differentiated-tuition-rates-or-raising-fees.

Seltzer, Rick. 2018. "Tuition Grows in Importance." *Inside Higher Ed*. March
29, 2018. https://www.insidehighered.com/news/2018/03/29/state-support-
higher-ed-increased-2017-so-did-tuition-revenue.

Shacklett, Mary. 2016. "How to Manage a Departmental Budget: A Guide for
Beginners." *Tech Decision Maker*. July 20, 2016. https://www.techrepublic.
com/article/how-to-manage-a-departmental-budget-a-guide-for-beginners/.

Stubbs, Nancy and Ken Carpenter. 2014. "Financial Aid & Study Abroad:
Basic Facts for Administrators." Washington, DC: NAFSA: Association of
International Educators. https://www.nafsa.org/Professional_Resources/
Browse_by_Interest/Education_Abroad/Network_Resources/Education_
Abroad/Financial_Aid___Study_Abroad__Basic_Facts_for_Administrators/.

Vanderbilt University. 2015. *The Cost of Federal Regulatory Compliance in Higher
Education: A Multi-Institutional Study*. Nashville, TN: https://news.vanderbilt.
edu/files/Regulatory-Compliance-Report-Final.pdf.

Wainwright, Philip. 2016. "International Students Are Worth More Than
Their Tuition Fees." *Times Higher Education*. June 8, 2016. https://www.
timeshighereducation.com/blog/international-students-are-worth-more-their-
tuition-fees.

7 | Administration of Education Abroad Programs

Brett Berquist

Education abroad (EA), or international learning mobility, has long been the most visible component of internationalization in U.S. higher education institutions. The basic idea of a reciprocal semester exchange and students swapping seats at partner universities is understood by the general public. Most university people are also familiar with shorter faculty-led programs, where U.S. instructors take students overseas to deliver their teaching in-situ, far from the home campus.

Many senior international officers (SIOs) have had previous experience with study abroad, as faculty members perhaps or as student participants themselves. However, fewer have taken an in-depth look at the inner workings of the policies and systems that guide each institution's approach to learning abroad. This chapter covers some of the core concepts to help new SIOs engage with their institution's EA efforts, as well as current trends in the field.

History of Study Abroad

Education abroad has a long tradition in the United States, beginning between the two world wars in the twentieth century and replicating the European Grand Tour tradition for the elite (Gore 2005). William Hoffa produced a two-volume (Hoffa 2007; DePaul and Hoffa 2010) definitive history of education abroad for *Frontiers: The Interdisciplinary Journal of Study Abroad* that offers an excellent read on how the field has developed. EA has gradually shifted from academic term courses on foreign languages and intercultural skills to shorter programs carefully designed to maximize learning impact through an in-situ learning context far from the classrooms of the home campus.

The shorter format, intended to accentuate the home curriculum and often delivered by faculty from the home campus, has been the source of growth in enrollments for the past 2 decades as the traditional semester or year abroad model has plateaued. This shorter programming is also driving growth in other recent entrants to the study abroad landscape, e.g., Australia, Canada, the United Kingdom, etc. At the same time, this shorter approach has empowered a focus on access and inclusion, broadening the possibility of study abroad to students who previously could not envision reorganizing their lives for an entire semester or year abroad. Increasing access to underrepresented populations is becoming the mantra of the education abroad field (Barclay Hamir and Gozik 2018), displacing the previous push for growth in participation. The emphasis has increasingly become about who participates, rather than how many (Twombly et al. 2012).

The 'Business' of Education Abroad

Access and underrepresentation intersect with the cost of education abroad and the business of how campuses stage and promote such opportunities. Beyond the classic "swap seats" exchange model easily understood by laypersons, the financial and administrative arrangements of education abroad are often a mystery to faculty and senior administrators primarily because these systems have risen in the United States as optional curricular or cocurricular add-ons rather than core requirements. EA offices are often self-funded, generating revenue from the participants or student "clients" to sustain and develop activities. An understanding of EA financial and partnership models is important for the SIO's oversight role.

Finances

Private colleges frequently base their financial planning on the size of the overall student body. Many private colleges follow a "home tuition" model in which tuition for study abroad is the same price as tuition for the home institution. This is a common model because sending a significant portion of the cohort abroad in a given year would otherwise affect the institutional revenue model. The EA office must manage the variations in program costs, ranging from more or less expensive than the home campus, and, in some cases, must return an overhead contribution "profit" to the central administration. In this model, a student's budget is relatively steady and extra administration fees are usually not charged.

Other schools, usually public, operate their programs at cost, with program fees varying widely depending on the location and overhead required. In this spirit, the home school may run a "tuition waiver or remission" program that zeroes out the home tuition charge so that the EA office can post a program fee that encompasses the expenses the office needs to cover for the program, e.g., host institution tuition, accompanying faculty costs (if appropriate), lodging, travel included in the program, etc. For these types of programs, the funds to administer the EA office are prorated into the comprehensive program fee paid by the students. For universities running a large EA operation, the business model can become quite complex, requiring professional accountant support, forecasts for currency fluctuation, enrollment trends, etc. (For more on budgets and financial management, see chapter 6.)

Providers

Study abroad programs can be labor intensive. It is not always cost-effective to stage all aspects of the study abroad operations directly from the home university due to the nature of the arrangements, the need to reach a minimum enrollment to cover the expenses for group programs, etc. Commercial organizations, commonly called "third-party providers," partner with institutions to help them administer their program portfolios. Many of these organizations are nonprofit, but a growing number work with private equity. This relationship can offer a range of benefits for both the school and the provider.

For example, the EA office can promote several group program sites run by a specific provider, thus enabling the home institution to send small numbers of students abroad by joining forces with a cohort drawn from multiple institutions. On the other side, the provider can help organize various labor-intensive components of a faculty-led program, e.g., local housing, excursions, guest lecturers, etc. Whether for-profit or nonprofit, there are a number of long-standing providers that share some of the educational goals of the institutions they serve. Professional associations such as NAFSA: Association of International Educators and The Forum on Education Abroad offer guidelines on the strategies and ethics of working with providers.

Regulations

In addition to the sometimes complex finances of programs, SIOs should pay close attention to and undertake training for the regulatory environment for education abroad. Most SIOs at U.S. institutions will already be familiar with the Family Educational Rights and Privacy Act (FERPA), the Americans with Disabilities Act (ADA), and the Health Insurance Portability and Accountability Act (HIPPA). Additional regulations designed for the U.S. higher education context also regulate educational activities overseas, such as:

- The use of federal financial aid (Title IV) for study abroad;

- Civil rights and nondiscrimination (Title IX) regulations; and

- The reporting of crimes (Clery Act/Title IX/WAVA).

SIOs should ensure that their EA administrators have access to training not only from their campus, but also through their professional associations. Furthermore, a strong alliance with the institution's general counsel is a necessary component for all EA offices.

Risk Management

The regulatory environment informs the institution's risk management policies and procedures as well. According to Julie Friend, director of the Office of Global Safety and Security at Northwestern University, there are currently more than 100 professionals dedicated full time to health and safety matters in U.S. international offices (personal communication, October 28, 2016). Sending students overseas into the care of a trusted partner university or with a quality provider usually includes a vetting process to ensure that adequate support and protocols are in place. When the program is staged by the home institution and delivered by home campus faculty, the duty of care is somewhat greater and a clear process for approving and monitoring destinations and program design choices is required.

Crisis management plans that connect an overseas situation back to appropriate campus resources have become the norm for EA operations. This plan should outline processes for various scenarios, such as deciding whether to resume programming after a crisis situation or approving a program to operate in a country with a raised government travel advisory. SIOs benefit from a close, proactive, and mutually beneficial relationship with their risk management office. (For more on risk management and crisis communications, see chapter 3.)

The Balance of Academics and Business

At the interface between academics and the business operations of education abroad is the need to ensure that the programming offered by the home institution is integrated into the curriculum. Gone are the days where education abroad was an option for the lucky few who could afford to add time to their degrees. Now, there is strong evidence that EA participants are often more engaged and enjoy higher retention rates and faster degree completion times (Barclay Hamir 2011). However, true to the complexity of research on education, it is difficult to demonstrate causality in the age-old chicken or egg question: Do EA participants show these characteristics as a result of the experience, or are those characteristics what drove them to study abroad?

In any case, the concept of curriculum integration has become a core expectation for U.S. study abroad programming. The core idea of this integration is to ensure that academic programs have identified curricular options for their students abroad that enhance the home curriculum and keep the students on schedule to degree completion.

The EA field offers a wealth of resources on curriculum integration. Professional associations such as NAFSA and The Forum have developed best practice guidelines by inviting input from those in the field. The Forum's *Standards of Good Practice for Education Abroad* is not intended to be prescriptive, but instead includes open-ended questions intended to enrich campus thinking on program design (Anthony and Whalen 2017). The field provides such guidance to help institutions and administrators make choices in various situations that are aligned with their institution's distinct goals, priorities, and values.

Strong alignment with the home institution's curriculum is also beneficial when education abroad programs are reviewed by regional or professional accrediting bodies, which have had an increasing impact on education abroad and have established rubrics that encourage international learning. The approach of the review varies among the regional accrediting bodies in the United States but are frequently a feature in the accreditation cycle. A new SIO may wish to ascertain the next scheduled visit of the university's regional accrediting body and anticipate a review of education abroad strategies and the possible visit of a small sample of programs. Harnessing the university-wide energy devoted to accreditation review, particularly at the self-study phase, can be a useful opportunity to review and strengthen the direction of the institution's education abroad portfolio.

SIOs who have risen to the role from an academic faculty background will have a deep knowledge of the research in their academic field. Likewise, there is a valuable body of literature that looks at the philosophy of EA and examines the effectiveness of pedagogical and program design choices.

Education Abroad Research

Research conducted to inform EA programming choices, outcomes, and impact has accelerated as the role of scholar-practitioners' work has become more established (Streitwieser and Ogden 2016). Multiple resources highlighting the landmark studies of the field are available (Potts and Berquist 2014; Vande Berg, Paige, and Lou 2012; Twombly et al. 2012). The literature notes a shifting paradigm—away from a previous belief that learning abroad will inevitably happen through students' exposure to different cultures—toward an emerging school of thought that advocates for intervention and cultural mentoring to ensure learning outcomes (Vande Berg, Paige, and Lou 2012).

It may be challenging for a new SIO to navigate all of the literature, given the range of academic fields that inform the research approach. Therefore, it can be useful to categorize the literature through the stages of the student participant's higher education experience (Potts 2016). Each stage brings a different focus and may utilize different research approaches, from predeparture to program evaluation (see figure 1). Many studies over the past 20 years have addressed the development and facilitation of learning outcomes. Participants' preuniversity choice factors and the long-term impacts of education abroad are the current leading edge of the work in the field.

Figure 1. Learning Abroad Research Schematic

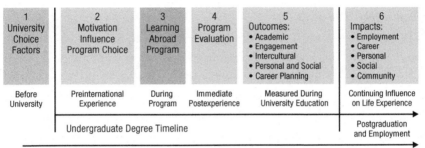

Note: Used with permission from Potts (2016).

The institutional SIO is responsible for the overall direction of EA programming, which often involves a broad and deep network of dedicated faculty members bringing their own perspectives to the institutional strategy. A research focus can be a useful approach to effect institutional change, and several primers are available to help an SIO facilitate an evidence-based campus discussion on the state of the field and strategic directions.

For example, at Michigan State University, the education abroad staff ordered a new print run of an issue in the American Society of Higher Education (ASHE) series (Twombly et al. 2012), held a series of book club lunch discussions, and hosted coauthors Susan B. Twombly and Mark H. Salisbury in a lecture series. These efforts helped bring together around 300 faculty program leaders and their wide range of academic and personal perspectives for a discussion on the state of the field.

Trends in Education Abroad

As political, environmental, economic, and educational movements emerge on the global stage, colleges and universities have become more intentional in the scope and outcomes of their EA programming. To prepare students for the increasingly interconnected workforce, institutions are prioritizing strategies aimed at expanding the demographics of the EA participant pool and strengthening the personal and professional development that students receive while abroad.

Participation Rate Goals

The most closely watched trends in education abroad focus on participation rates, and the SIO is ultimately responsible for the institution's goals in this area. Generation Study Abroad, the Lincoln Commission, the Senator Paul Simon Study Abroad Program, the New Colombo Plan, and 100,000 Strong in the Americas are examples of the numerous initiatives implemented in many countries seeking to increase the number of students participating in international learning experiences during their university studies.

Participation rates and goals can be confusing, as evidenced by Canada's recent conflicting national goals for its emerging outbound strategy (Berquist and Goddard 2018). Often, media or senior administrators new to the field will cite low participation rates such as, "only 2 percent of U.S. students study abroad." However, this calculation divides the number of institutionally reported study abroad students by the entire higher education enrollment in that country, which is inaccurate. The goal of many institutions is not to send students abroad each year, but that students have at least one international learning experience before graduating. Canada's recent reporting on outbound participation used these two different calculations, causing some confusion within the international education field as to the country's goals and current state (Berquist and Goddard 2018). Consequently, institutions should use the following formula for tracking institutional participation rates:

{Number of students abroad in a given cycle / Number of undergraduate degrees awarded = participation rate.}

This is not the same as tracking the actual behavior of individual students. While that might be possible at small four-year colleges, it is simply not feasible at large institutions; therefore, participation rates are reported in the aggregate, both in the United States and in other countries (Berquist, Blahnik, and Ramirez 2018). This explains why some small four-year colleges occasionally spike above 100 percent participation rates in the Institute of International Education (IIE)'s *Open Doors* report when the graduating senior class is followed by a much larger junior class. The graduate-level participation rate is another matter and a subject of research (Dirkx et al. 2014), but most institutional goals are based on undergraduate-level participation.

Some relative newcomers to the education abroad field, such as New Zealand, have adopted a broader definition than the one used in IIE's *Open Doors* in that they include nonresidents as well as noncredit activities. *Open Doors* began counting education abroad in 1985 and excludes international student participants (IIE 2018). IIE has run an additional survey on noncredit education abroad for several years (still not including non-U.S. resident participants).

Some newer institutional entrants have implemented a larger scope of recording all learning activities undertaken by students through their affiliation with the institution (Huckel and Ramirez 2017). This distinction is salient given the rising presence of international students on many campuses as well as the growing demand for experiential learning, which may not always be credit bearing. SIOs may find themselves responding to a learning activity overseas that has been undertaken through the relationship with the home institution but for which administrative systems do not provide the same level of management oversight as for credit-bearing activities. It is important for SIOs to understand the institutional participation metric in the context of a range of practices used in different reporting systems.

Education Abroad and Employability

Today's generation of students is more pragmatically oriented than many institutions may recognize. While intercultural competence is firmly embedded in the learning goals of most U.S. institutions—and understood in the larger concept of global citizenship that is present in the mission statements or strategic plans of many U.S. colleges and universities—modern students are increasingly driven by a desire to stand out in the job market.

IIE's *The World Is the New Classroom: Non-Credit Education Abroad* report points out that most noncredit learning abroad participants chose their programs through their home institutions' portfolio of offerings (Mahmoud and Ferrugia 2016). Essentially, they went "shopping" inside their home campus store. The outlier was internships abroad, for which students were far more likely to shop outside their home university. There is a gap between this generation's motivation to pursue learning abroad for potential employability gains and what institutions are actually offering, with nearly half of U.S. universities failing to offer international internships to their students (Helms and Brajkovic 2017).

Students and their families sometimes see study abroad as a market distinguisher, a way to stand out from the crowd in the search for the first career job after university. Employability is an important driving factor for study abroad engagement, often more than intercultural competence as a goal in itself.

For example, New Zealand's young people are highly mobile, with 31 percent of domestic bachelor's degree graduates and 41 percent of domestic doctoral degree graduates living overseas 7 years after graduation (Park 2014). Traditionally, this overseas experience (OE) has been undertaken outside of university, either as a gap year or after graduation. This has changed significantly with today's generation of students who are seeking to start their OE during their university studies. Australia took a similar historical approach to international experience as New Zealand (i.e., OE not during university), however, Australian OE participation rates are now at 20 percent (International Education Association of Australia n.d.) and have surpassed U.S. rates at 15.5 percent (IIE 2017) in a little over a decade.

The International Education Association of Australia (IEAA) recently published a critique of nine major studies since 2014, examining the link between education abroad and employability (Potts 2018). This critical review is representative of the state of the field because it calls for more robust statistical analysis and recognition of the challenge inherent in educational research to control variables sufficiently to confirm causality. The fact that there were nine significant studies in 4 years illustrates the importance of employability as a driver for education abroad, students, their families, and their institutions.

While other national strategies to increase international learning as part of higher education emerge, the discourse in the United States has begun to shift from a focus on quantity to one on learning outcomes and access. To sum up, the literature asserts that not all study abroad is created equal and not all programs share the core intercultural competence goals that for so long formed the foundation of the field (Twombly et al. 2012). The conversation is increasingly less centered on how many students studied abroad and more about who studied abroad and what they learned from the experience.

Conclusion

This chapter introduced some of the key concepts and resources to advance the new SIO's thinking on what is often considered the most visible part of the institution's internationalization work: education abroad. But the field has a long history, deep body of literature, standards for best practice, and numerous professional development opportunities upon which the SIO can build. A new SIO usually comes to the role with a strong related disciplinary background, some experience of university administration, and insightful personal international experience. As the SIO connects with the role and professional associations, it is important to take a broad view of the institution's education abroad activity to determine strategies for moving forward given the current trends of the field.

Additional Resources

Chieffo, Lisa, and Catherine Spaeth, eds. 2017. *The Guide to Successful Short-Term Programs Abroad, Third Edition*. Washington, DC: NAFSA: Association of International Educators.

Hernandez, Magnolia, Margaret Wiedenhoeft, and David Wick, eds. 2014. *NAFSA's Guide to Education Abroad for Advisers and Administrators, Fourth Edition*. Washington, DC: NAFSA: Association of International Educators.

Martin, Patricia C., ed. 2017. *Crisis Management for Education Abroad*. Washington, DC: NAFSA: Association of International Educators.

References

Anthony, Bill, and Annmarie Whalen. 2017. "A Conversation with Bill Anthony," April 6, 2016, in Forum Storytellers, produced by The Forum on Education Abroad, podcast, 39:56. https://forumea.org/podcast/s2-episode-5-a-conversation-with-bill-anthony/.

Barclay Hamir, Heather. 2011. "Go Abroad and Graduate On-Time: Study Abroad Participation, Degree Completion, and Time-to-Degree." Doctoral dissertation. UMI No. 3450065.

Barclay Hamir, Heather, and Nick Gozik. 2018. *Promoting Inclusion in Education Abroad: A Handbook of Research and Practice.* Sterling, VA: Stylus Publishing and NAFSA: Association of International Educators.

Berquist, Brett, Brook Blahnik, and Keri Ramirez. 2018. "Using Comparative Data to Enhance Learning Abroad Strategies." Presented at the NAFSA 2018 Annual Conference & Expo, Philadelphia, PA.

Berquist, Brett, and Trevor Goddard. 2018. "Why Should Canada Get Serious on Outbound?" Presented at the British Columbia Committee on International Education 2018.

DePaul, Stephen C., and William W. Hoffa, eds. 2010. *A History of US Study Abroad: 1965—Present.* Carlisle, PA: Frontiers: The Interdisciplinary Journal of Study Abroad and The Forum on Education Abroad.

Dirkx, John, Kristen Janka Millar, Brett Berquist, and Gina Vizvary. 2014. "Graduate Student Learning Abroad: Emerging Trend?" *International Higher Education* 77, Fall 2014. https://ejournals.bc.edu/ojs/index.php/ihe/article/view/5677.

Gore, Joan Elias. 2005. *Dominant Beliefs and Alternative Voices: Discourses, Belief, and Gender in American Study Abroad.* New York, NY: Routledge.

Helms, Robin Matross, and Lucia Brajkovic. 2017. *Mapping Internationalization on U.S. Campuses: 2017 Edition.* Washington, DC: American Council on Education.

Hoffa, William. 2007. *A History of US Study Abroad: Beginnings to 1965.* Carlisle, PA: Frontiers: The Interdisciplinary Journal of Study Abroad and the Forum on Education Abroad.

Huckel, Dimity, and Keri Ramirez. 2017. *New Zealand International Education Benchmark, 2017.* Sydney, Australia: Studymove.

Institute of International Education (IIE). 2017. "Open Doors Executive Summary." Institute of International Education.

Institute of International Education (IIE). 2018. "About Open Doors." Institute of International Education. https://www.iie.org/Research-and-Insights/Open-Doors/About-Open-Doors.

International Education Association of Australia. n.d. "Sector Stats." Melbourne, Australia: International Education Association of Australia. Accessed July 15, 2018. https://www.ieaa.org.au/about-us/sector-stats.

Mahmoud, Ola, and Christine Ferrugia. 2016. *The World Is the New Classroom Non-Credit Education Abroad: A Study of Student Participation in Non-Credit Education Abroad and U.S. Institutions' Data Collection Processes.* New York, NY: Institute of International Education. https://www.iie.org/Research-and-Insights/Publications/The-World-is-the-New-Classroom-Non-Credit-Education-Abroad.

Park, Zeneta. 2014. *What Young Graduates Do When They Leave Study: New Data on the Destination of Young Graduates.* Wellington, New Zealand: New Zealand Ministry of Education.

Potts, Davina. 2016. *Outcomes of Learning Abroad Programs.* Canberra, Australia: Universities Australia and International Education Association of Australia.

Potts, Davina. 2018. *Learning Abroad and Employability: Researching the Connections. IEAA Research Digest 13.* Melbourne, Australia: International Education Association of Australia. https://www.ieaa.org.au/documents/item/1267.

Potts, Davina, and Brett Berquist. 2014. "Researching the Outcomes of International Learning Mobility: Taking the Next Steps." *IEAA Research Digest 1.* Melbourne, Australia: International Education Association of Australia. https://www.ieaa.org.au/documents/item/256.

Streitwieser, Bernhard, and Anthony C. Ogden, eds. 2016. *International Higher Education's Scholar-Practitioners: Bridging Research and Practice.* Oxford, United Kingdom: Symposium Books.

Twombly, Susan B., Mark H. Salisbury, Shannon D. Tumanut, and Paul Klute. 2012. *Study Abroad in a New Global Century: Renewing the Promise, Refining the Purpose.* ASHE Higher Education Report: 38:4. San Francisco, CA: Wiley.

Vande Berg, Michael, R. Michael Paige, and Kris Hemming Lou, eds. 2012. *Student Learning Abroad: What Our Students Are Learning, What They're Not, and What We Can Do About It.* Sterling, VA: Stylus Publishing.

8 | Administration of Intensive English Programs

Jun Liu

Intensive English programs (IEPs) are multifaceted entities. Both the development of the field of foreign language teaching and the emergence of the field of applied linguistics were responsible for the establishment of IEPs in the mid-twentieth century. As international students began to study at universities in the United States after World War II, these students' specific and unique needs surfaced and, in response, English as a second language (ESL) programs were created, of which the IEP is a subset.

The first IEP in the United States was established in 1941 at the English Language Institute at the University of Michigan (Clifford 2013). IEPs have existed in many other English-speaking countries in the form of English language centers since the 1950s (Hamrick 2015). According to Hamrick (2015, 321), the purpose of IEPs is to "serve full-time English language students who seek to develop their English skills rapidly in an immersion setting by offering a comprehensive program of study that emphasizes accelerated learning." For many international students whose first language is not English, IEPs enhance the pathway to success in their academic studies and professional careers.

This chapter provides an overview of IEPs, IEP administration, and the benefits that IEPs have brought to the field of language education and to U.S. higher education. However, there are also emerging operational and curricular issues that must be addressed, with the help of senior international officers (SIOs), to meet the needs of the new generation of non-native English-speaking international students. A concrete model of IEPs is proposed that may offer SIOs and their institutions an effective approach to making IEPs more relevant to international student success in the increasingly globalized environment.

Benefits of Intensive English Programs

IEPs have numerous positive effects on non-native English-speaking international students and their universities. Some of the most obvious benefits include:

- IEPs help non-native English-speaking students enhance their language skills, such as listening, speaking, reading, and writing, as well as strengthen their knowledge of pronunciation, vocabulary, and grammar for academic success.

- IEPs serve as a gateway for conditionally admitted students whose academic performance has met the admissions criteria, but their English language skills need further improvement. As such, IEPs serve as a pipeline for degree-seeking students to universities.

- IEPs give non-native English-speaking students an opportunity to acculturate and feel comfortable and competent in communication before they matriculate into a heavy courseload in their respective disciplines.

- IEPs generate tuition revenue and program fees that benefit both the programs and the universities.

- IEPs provide programs (e.g., workshops, activities, events) that allow for socializing between students, scholars, and their peers.

In sum, IEPs play an important role for recruitment, for language enhancement and acculturation, and for the retention and success of international students who need additional help before they officially start their English-medium degree programs.

Complexities of Intensive English Programs

Despite the benefits discussed above, there are a number of issues related to IEPs that make them complex to manage. These issues include, but are not limited to, institutional placement, changes in admissions requirements for English proficiency, faculty status, and the ever-expanding responsibilities of IEP directors.

Organizational Placement

Due to their unique mission and scope, IEPs are often difficult to accurately place within the institutional structure. Some IEPs are affiliated with academic departments, such as English or linguistics. In such cases, the IEP may operate on the periphery of the department's core academic mission. This can lead to a variety of challenges in terms of institutional identity because (a) the mission of IEPs tends to be both unique and specialized when compared with the home academic unit; (b) IEPs are tangential to curricula that have been in place for decades; and (c) IEP faculty, who are often hired part time without the prospect of tenure, may not have the same status as other faculty in the department (Kaplan 1997).

Some IEPs may be housed within foreign language departments, with the understanding that ESL is viewed as another foreign language program, such as Chinese, Japanese, Italian, and French. However, many IEP instructors find it odd to be treated as foreign language teachers when their missions are so uniquely different. Therefore, some IEP instructors may consider it peculiar that they are considered as a subset in foreign languages departments.

At other universities, IEPs are situated in the division of continuing professional education or in other general academic structures, such as undergraduate education and graduate schools, with the assumption that the greater administrative and budgetary flexibility offered in those tangential sites would permit IEPs to earn more revenue for the university. The courses in IEPs are often structured in such a way that the units provided are not tied to academic credits. (For more on the relationship between IEPs and continuing professional education units, see chapter 13.)

Other IEPs are placed in the college of education because part of the mission of the college is to prepare students for teaching ESL. Thus, graduate students in teacher training programs can act as ESL teachers or interns for IEPs. This arrangement allows for both a readily available practicum and a steady supply of teachers.

Finally, some IEPs are partially or wholly administered by outside entities through a services-for-hire or revenue-sharing agreement with the institution. In these instances, IEP faculty may not be considered as employees of the college or university, and they may lack access to core benefits and services such as employee parking passes, student information systems, and advocacy through shared governance.

Many of these placement options for IEPs are based on historical factors and may not be ideal for serving increasing numbers of non-native English-speaking students whose backgrounds, needs, and demands are drastically different at preadmission, undergraduate, and graduate levels.

English Language Proficiency Requirements

It is common for universities to publish cut scores—the lowest possible score that a student must earn to either "pass" or be considered "proficient"—for internationally accepted high-stakes tests, such as the Internet-Based Test of English as a Foreign Language (iBT/TOEFL), the International English Language Testing System (IELTS), the Cambridge English Exams, and the Michigan English Language Assessment Battery. Some universities also have differential cut score requirements for different majors. For instance, some universities choose low cut scores for less popular programs in order to increase their applicant pool and enrollment, while raising English proficiency requirements for their most popular programs, such as computer science or business, to moderate the surplus in applications to those in-demand programs. Some programs, such as journalism and comparative literature, may require higher proficiency scores simply to ensure that students can succeed in meeting the academic expectations. This variance in score requirements can be challenging for IEPs to manage and coordinate in terms of their policy, course placement, evaluation, and content design. The more diverse the student profiles, the more complex the placement and course design.

Faculty Status

Because the coursework may be noncredit, or even considered remedial, IEPs may not be considered as regular academic units. Consequently, the lecturers and instructors are often not tenured and may be the same level as the support staff. These differences in status can lead to IEP faculty feeling sidelined or marginalized at some institutions (Eskey 1997).

It is therefore important for SIOs who are in charge of global affairs and international activities to serve as key allies of IEPs and advocate for this important group of stakeholders. This is particularly essential on campuses where the IEP director reports to a department chair or associate dean or is otherwise placed lower within the institutional hierarchy than the directors of other international education units.

Expanded Roles and Responsibilities of Program Directors

Despite the possible lack of support provided at some institutions for IEPs, the scope of responsibilities of IEP directors is often expanding and evolving to meet student and institutional needs. While the required and expected tasks vary across institutions, some of the major areas of responsibilities are listed in table 1.

Table 1. Major Responsibilities of International Education Program Directors

Responsibility Areas	May Include...
Academics	Accreditation; curriculum design; syllabus development; testing; student placement; articulation and placement among levels; test development and curriculum trialing; special program training; teacher training; and teacher evaluation
Administration	Operations; infrastructure planning; organizational planning; policy development; staff development; regulatory compliance; and record-keeping
Finances	Long- and short-term budget development; day-to-day control of expenses, purchasing, and equipment maintenance; planned acquisition of office and instructional equipment; and grants and contracts
Institutional Priorities	Liaisons with higher-level administrators; liaisons with committees such as admissions, faculty, governance, language education, and student and faculty advocacy
Management	Meetings; structuring committees; staffing; hiring and firing procedures; grievances; counseling; personnel issues; and legal action
Recruitment	Program promotions; marketing materials; interactive websites; and virtual and in-person recruitment
Relationship Building	Institutional policy development; external professional organization development; liaisons with clients; and liaisons with accrediting agencies, funding agencies, international agencies, and sponsors

As evident in table 1, IEP administrators have a wide range of responsibilities, from recruitment to placement, curriculum to instruction, and enrollment management to faculty evaluation. The list might be overwhelming to some; however, according to Panferov (2015, 11), it is "representative of the range of responsibilities that language program directors typically face, although the time frame in which these responsibilities occur varies depending on the context." Given increased competition and global economics, it is always challenging for IEP administrators to prioritize their responsibilities in order to ensure not only the recruitment and enrollment but also the management and coordination of their programs.

Challenges Facing Intensive English Programs

In part due to the complex issues described above, IEPs face unique challenges in today's higher education landscape. Some of the major challenges confronting IEPs include decreased enrollment, lack of funding or institutional commitment, conventional curriculum, and differences in cultural customs. SIOs can take the time to meet with IEP directors to better understand these challenges and find opportunities for collaboration and shared support.

Decreased Enrollment

In recent years, IEPs across the United States have experienced sharp decreases in enrollment. According to the Institute of International Education, enrollment in IEPs at U.S. institutions dropped 20 percent from 2016 to 2017 (Redden 2018). The decreased enrollment is due to several factors. First, many schools that prepare students for tests and examinations (nicknamed "cram schools"), international schools, and college preparatory programs in foreign countries are aggressively recruiting students and opening classes for those who want to study abroad but do not meet the English proficiency admissions criteria. These programs specifically offer test prep courses, and some are very effective in teaching test taking skills.

Second, in their competition for students, many universities have lowered their English proficiency admissions requirements so that those students who should go to IEPs end up enrolling in the universities directly. This places an undue burden on content faculty and staff at tutoring centers who are often unequipped to handle ESL-related issues.

Third, due to recent tightening of visa policies, some IEP hopefuls have not been granted visas for unspecified reasons, making them unable to attend schools in the United States. Finally, many IEPs do not have the personnel or resources to develop and implement targeted marketing plans and recruitment strategies.

Lack of Funding or Institutional Commitment

Since many IEPs operate on a self-sufficient model, the funding needed to proceed largely depends on the enrollment numbers. Decreased enrollment directly results in a lack of funding to retain instructors and sustain programs. Given such budgetary constraints, many IEPs around the country have had to let instructors go, which affects the productivity and sustainability of programs.

However, at both the undergraduate and graduate levels, many majors, especially engineering and business, have relied heavily on international student enrollment. (For more on international enrollment management, see chapter 9.) Therefore, IEP staff can coordinate recruitment and marketing efforts with these colleges and schools for the benefit of both. It is important for universities to allocate substantial funds to support international student success across campus.

Pedagogical Challenges

A phenomenon worth noting is that, in recent years, the majority of international students at U.S. universities have come from a few countries. In the 2016–17 academic year, China was the top origin country for international students, representing 33 percent of the total, followed by India at 17 percent (Zong and Batalova 2018). Since English is already an official language in India, the majority of students learning English in IEPs are naturally Chinese. This influx can require some adjustment on the instructor's part to navigate cultural and classroom customs.

For example, many Chinese students are quiet in class, but their silence cannot be simply attributed to any single factor. Chinese international students are often working through various transitional experiences, including culture adjustment, language barriers, and the lack of social connection. Many international students identify their English proficiency as the biggest shield blocking them from classroom participation. This lack of language competence can have a negative impact on students' self-esteem, influence their decisionmaking, and, ultimately, restrict their levels of participation and contribution. IEP instructors who are cognizant of diverse cultural norms can adopt a variety of teaching methods to engage learners from different parts of the world.

Under the right circumstances, the benefits of the intensive English training last long after the completion of the programs. Many factors can contribute to a positive experience for IEP students, including an immersive environment, the dedication of professional trainers and instructors, cultural activities coupled with language learning, and the learning of academic English related to learners' respective disciplines. SIOs can work with IEP directors and staff to develop optimal learning environments for these students. In order to make IEPs more cost-effective, motivating, and relevant to the academic success of non-native English-speaking students, a centralized model is proposed here that incorporates best practices and is reflective of the changing needs of students.

Center for ESL Programs

One proposed model to help improve the efficacy of IEPs is to establish a university-wide center for ESL (CESL) that is directly administered by the SIO and housed within the central global affairs division. Within the CESL, there are at least three interrelated programs: IEPs, English for academic purposes (EAP), and English for specific purposes (ESP). A set of sample course offerings in each of the three programs is provided in table 2.

CESL Programs

IEPs provide skills-focused courses to students who want to improve their overall communication competence with regard to listening, speaking, reading, writing, and critical thinking. The curriculum has multiple levels of skills that prepare students to handle academic tasks in both oral and written communications. IEPs are most suited for prematriculated students and conditionally admitted students.

EAPs deal with the use of English in study settings, particularly in higher education where the main purpose of language learning is to prepare undergraduate students to be familiar and comfortable with university settings and academic discourse. The curriculum is intended to help learners hone the skills that are necessary in academic settings. EAPs are most suited for admitted international undergraduate students.

ESPs are designed for non-native English-speaking international graduate students who are learning with an identified purpose and clearly specified needs. The curriculum is designed in such a way that it accounts for each student's chosen academic discipline, such as humanities, social and behavioral sciences, natural sciences, engineering, or medicine. A subset of courses is offered for international teaching assistants who teach general education courses to university students.

Table 2. Sample Course Offerings at a Center for English as a Second Language

Intensive English Program (IEP)	English for Academic Purposes (EAP)	English for Specific Purposes (ESP)
Level 1 Communication Skills I	Academic English I	English for Specific Purposes I
Level 2 Communication Skills II	Academic English II	English for Specific Purposes II
Level 3 Communication Skills III	Academic English III	English for International Teaching Assistants

Implementation Considerations

The success of a CESL relies on a number of factors and conditions. The primary factor is funding. It is recommended that universities allocate certain percentages of the revenue to support the CESL operations, for example, 3 to 5 percent of international student tuition and fees. Such an investment is appropriate because the success of the CESL will lead to a large positive impact on future international student applications and enrollment.

Second, the CESL has multiple curricular streams, so targeted curriculum development is central to success. Making courses relevant to each group—prematriculated students, undergraduate students, graduate students, and international teaching assistants—is of utmost importance to address these individuals' diverse needs and goals.

Another factor to consider is the CESL teachers. In order to teach ESP courses, teachers and instructors have to go through a series of professional development activities, or self-study certain disciplines, to be able to speak on the subjects with authority. Their teaching materials need to be developed accordingly, and their teaching methodologies must be reviewed with the support of content instructors.

Mini-committees of ESL instructors may need to do some research, conduct needs analyses of students, and interview content instructors to know what to teach, how to teach it, and when to teach it. Moreover, content professors in each major discipline, such as engineering, natural sciences, social sciences, and business, should be part of the curriculum innovation team and engage in the course development and articulation between their courses and ESP courses, especially at the graduate levels.

To maximize the effectiveness of the CESL, instructors can offer independent learning materials, such as digital materials, online platforms, DVDs, books, magazines, board games, and adaptive software, together with a flexible setting for hosting activities ranging from workshops and events to performances and competitions. The center can also offer elective courses as needed, such as public speaking, proposal writing, and thesis writing.

Conclusion

IEPs are an indispensable component of the ESL sequence and play a vital role in the academic success of prematriculated non-native English-speaking international students. While IEPs have served students for decades with language enhancement, cultural exposure, and academic training, they are now facing new challenges on different levels. SIOs are responsible for looking into these operations and providing needed support to integrate IEPs into global strategies. SIOs, in partnership with IEP directors, must come up with new curricular designs that will motivate students to learn, develop new courses to cater to students' academic needs, recruit and retain faculty with innovative methodologies facilitated by modern technology, and prepare international non-native English-speaking students for the global marketplace. This work calls for the collaborative support and effort from university administration, faculty in academic disciplines, IEP administrators, and professional associations in the field of language education and language program administration.

Additional Resources

Coombe, Christine, Mary Lou McCloskey, Lauren Stephenson, and Neil J. Anderson, eds. 2008. *Leadership in English Language Teaching and Learning.* Ann Arbor, MI: University of Michigan.

Di Maria, David L., ed. 2017. *Managing a Successful International Admissions Office: NAFSA's Guide to International Admissions.* Washington, DC: NAFSA: Association of International Educators.

Farrelly, Raichle, Shawna Shapiro, and Zuzana Tomaš. 2018. *Fostering International Student Success in Higher Education.* Alexandria, VA: TESOL Press and NAFSA: Association of International Educators.

Sandberg, Jessica Black, ed. 2017. *NAFSA's Guide to International Student Recruitment, Third Edition.* Washington, DC: NAFSA: Association of International Educators.

References

Clifford, Katy T. C. 2013. "History: 75 Years of the International Center at the University of Michigan." Ann Arbor, MI: University of Michigan. https://internationalcenter.umich.edu/about/history.

Eskey, David. 1997. "The IEP as a Non-traditional Entity." In *A Handbook for Language Program Administrators*, eds. MaryAnn Christison and Fredricka L. Stoller. Burlingame, CA: Alta Book Center.

Hamrick, Jim. 2015. "Intensive English Programs." In *A Handbook for Language Program Administrators, Second Edition*, eds. MaryAnn Christison and Fredricka L. Stoller. Burlingame, CA: Alta Book Center.

Kaplan, R. Bob. 1997. "An IEP Is a Many-Splendored Thing." In *A Handbook for Language Program Administrators*, eds. MaryAnn Christison and Fredricka L. Stoller. Burlingame, CA: Alta Book Center.

Panferov, Suzanne K. 2015. "Transitioning from Teacher to Language Program Administrator." In *A Handbook for Language Program Administrators, Second Edition*, eds. MaryAnn Christison and Fredricka L. Stoller. Burlingame, CA: Alta Book Center.

Redden, Elizabeth. 2018. "Intensive English Enrollments in U.S. Drop
    20%." *Insider Higher Ed.* May 31, 2018. https://www.insidehighered.com/
    quicktakes/2018/05/31/intensive-english-enrollments-us-drop-20.
Zong, Jie, and Jeanne Batalova. 2018. "International Students in the United
    States." Washington, DC: Migration Policy Institute. May 9, 2018. https://
    www.migrationpolicy.org/article/international-students-united-states.

9 | International Enrollment Management

George F. Kacenga

At many institutions of higher education, senior international officers (SIOs) oversee global engagement and international affairs, which involves international enrollment management (IEM). As international students have become increasingly integral to campus economies, many SIOs are accountable for managing the revenue-generating aspect of international students. Some of the related tasks include being cognizant of school, college, and program objectives; establishing intensive English program roles on campus or across campuses; maintaining service continuity across units internal and external to the SIO's purview; creating budget models; developing funding sources for recruitment; allocating sources for marketing; proposing partnerships; and providing evidence of return on investment (ROI). Yet, even above all these significant aspects of the SIO's job, one role towers highest of all: leader. No individual can successfully accomplish all that is expected on today's campuses regarding IEM and international affairs without cultivating a knowledgeable, competent, and confident team.

This chapter examines SIOs' complex, nuanced roles in IEM, which comprise recognizing trends, forecasting changes, formulating plans, and establishing communication channels so that campus leadership can react effectively and proactively to IEM conditions on the ground. To perform all of these operations, SIOs must be agile and laser focused on shifts in both societal conditions and institutional objectives to lead the IEM and international admissions team to success.

The Strategic International Enrollment Management Plan

The strategic international enrollment management plan (SIEMP) represents a synopsis of the SIO's macro- and micro-level IEM goals. IEM staff members may be tasked with autonomous oversight of the international students' experiences, from prospect through alumni, or given varying levels of responsibility requiring complex partnerships across divisions throughout campus. The SIEMP acknowledges this and includes strategies for recruiting and retaining international students; short-term and long-term student goals by academic level, admit type, and target market; strategies for achieving those student goals; fiduciary requirements for achieving objectives; and assessment measurers, key performance indicators, and ROI. The SIEMP lives at both the 30,000-foot level and the baseline; it articulates the SIO's statement of overarching themes and it empowers the IEM team to take on a list of necessary action items.

Development of the SIEMP

A good IEM team can aggregate eclectic and disparate data, process that data, and distribute the processed data as user-friendly, actionable information—this is how the SIEMP originates. Ongoing communication between the SIO, deans, and other internal and external stakeholders at a particular institution provides valuable input about both institutional idiosyncrasies and desired IEM outcomes. The SIO must also solicit input from the budget and finance office to (a) align enrollment goals and forecasts with recruitment budgets, and (b) draft accurate figures to reflect the impact of tuition from international enrollment. Furthermore, the SIO must gather data even more broadly to be cognizant of geopolitical forces that affect international enrollments. The SIO carries this information back to the IEM team members, who work collectively to draft and execute targeted strategies.

Maintenance of the SIEMP

The SIEMP is not a one-off project; it is a living document that needs to be adapted over time in response to changes made at the institutional, state, national, and international levels. In short, if the SIEMP outlines strategies for a three- to five-year period, it must be acknowledged that a lot can change during that time frame. Therefore, the SIO and IEM team must be sensitive to subtle on- and off-campus changes in the conditions surrounding international education.

Primarily, this involves forecasting future enrollment trends and identifying viable markets for recruiting new students, often for intensive English, undergraduate, and graduate programs. One effective strategy is gaining an understanding of the current international student body and demographics and then researching target markets. Learning who the current international students are and why they selected the institution is vital to modifying recruitment strategies and keeping the SIEMP fresh.

By inviting the leadership of the institution's schools and colleges to align their objectives with the evolving SIEMP, the SIO can maintain stakeholder buy-in. The SIO can prompt the IEM team to pursue stakeholder participation in SIEMP maintenance through routine solicitation of input (for more on stakeholder engagement, see chapter 2). Providing a list of compelling questions to help campus leadership and other stakeholders evaluate their realities and opportunities is often the best way to achieve that input.

Specific Areas of Focus

Effective SIOs are concerned with a long list of issues, some of which are discussed here. These areas of focus are dynamic because different times and circumstances necessitate different points of emphasis. Maintaining this kind of vigilance may seem like a lofty and unapproachable goal, but it is often as simple as meeting two or three times a year with the IEM team to discuss current realities in key areas of focus. The SIEMP can then be updated and shared with any oversight committees or advisory boards.

Campus Internationalization

If an SIO is in place at an institution, by title or responsibilities, there is either a strategic effort at campus internationalization or an opportunity to initiate one. Unfortunately, at many institutions, the IEM team or functional lead can often feel cast out from the broader enrollment management effort.

Intentional or not, it is common for international admissions to be viewed as an afterthought, or even as a nuisance, by the staff focused on domestic admissions given (a) how difficult it is for institutional systems to accommodate specialized data collection, and (b) how much effort it takes to assure the clarity of written communications for non-native speakers of English.

To combat this exclusionary practice, the SIO needs to champion the IEM team across different departments. The parlance of the day is for departments "to avoid being silos." The international division itself may often be viewed as self-isolating because of the high level of expertise required and the complicated nature of its work. However, many times, it is the apprehensive nature of campus colleagues to engage with international affairs that builds a silo from without.

The SIO can help tear down these walls and instead build bridges toward understanding and cooperation. At institutions where an overarching enrollment management strategy is not in place, the IEM team can serve as an excellent incubator for new practices on campus, thus setting a new standard. The SIO can help to develop and nurture relationships with the registrar, institutional research, budget and finance, and domestic admissions units to generate and analyze data that add value to the broader campus conversation. Demonstrated success in IEM can lead to the systematic deployment of a comprehensive enrollment management plan.

Campus Support

As the campus community comes to understand the complex, yet rewarding nature of IEM, it will more readily buy into the process. IEM needs and priorities can be financially supported in many ways. Often there is a dedicated line of resources from the central administrative body, but the costs for staff salaries with benefits, student workers, operating expenses, office supplies, furniture, software, marketing, recruitment, professional development, and special projects add up fast. In response, many IEM offices have begun to cost-share international recruitment activities with different schools and colleges, undergraduate or graduate, in accordance with their goals.

The IEM team may offer to cover the cost of event registration and shipping materials for a recruitment trip, for example, while the school or college covers travel and per diem costs. This strategy also applies to armchair recruitment done at the office, virtual activity and social media engagement online, and active recruitment abroad. The SIO should insist that anyone who travels for the purpose of recruitment must have the capacity and training to recruit for the entire institution, rather than just an individual school, college, or program. The recruiters should be able to answer basic questions about the institution as a whole. It is a lost opportunity when prospective international students are speaking with an institutional representative in their home country just to be told that the staff member can speak about only a small percentage of the programs available.

Budgets

Over the past half-century, while the competition for domestic enrollment has increased and public funding for higher education has diminished, many colleges and universities have come to rely on the income generated by international student enrollment. The SIO can involve the IEM team in campus discussions designed to understand the impact of international tuition on the institution budget and the ways those funds are managed and allocated. This involvement can further motivate the IEM team to excel, and it can highlight the value of the team's efforts among colleagues.

At some institutions, international tuition is not incorporated into the overall budget, so the occasional turbulence of international enrollment (that which is beyond the control of professional staff) does not impact critical expenditures like salaries or operating budgets. In these cases, international tuition is allocated toward one-time projects or temporary activities.

At other institutions where international tuition is pooled with other revenue sources in a centralized account, the role of the IEM team in anticipating increases and decreases in enrollment becomes all the more essential. A recruitment cycle can last well past a year or 18 months, and ROI data often reveal that activity from 3 or more years previous may still yield enrollment today.

The SIO can insist upon achieving clarity by setting enrollment goals and allocating the resources to achieve them. This model commonly begins with a budget meeting for the coming fiscal year. Members of the IEM team may be asked to share what they believe can be achieved, or a goal may be given to them. The IEM team can then outline the necessary activities to achieve the desired outcomes and the associated costs. If funding is not adequate, discussions are initiated until the outcomes and means to achieve them align.

Programs, Initiatives, and Markets

It is not yet clear if the online delivery of programs is (a) stimulating demand from international students who would not have otherwise considered attending a U.S. institution, or (b) cutting into in-country degree program enrollment. In other words, do online programs expand the pie or simply cut it into smaller slices? Similar questions surround the off-shore delivery of popular degree programs. In either event, technology continues to prompt a wider range of institutions to offer more and more platforms for program delivery.

Collaboration with overseas partners for the off-shore delivery of programs can take a variety of forms, including sharing curricula, designing boutique summer programs, sending faculty abroad, and even building an entire campus across borders. These details of the relationship should be carefully articulated in a memorandum of understanding (MOU) or other institutional partnership agreement, as prescribed by the institution's legal counsel. Sometimes, the MOU is a brief document of introduction indicating little more than professional camaraderie. The MOU can also take the form of a lengthy legal document describing a wide variety of protocols (e.g., fiduciary accountability, renewal and termination policies). (For more on MOUs and partnerships, see chapter 16.) Managing MOUs is a routine part of the SIO's role, and the IEM team members are often at the front end of the process. Providing guidance to help the team members recognize potential opportunities and filter prospects will save the SIO a great deal of time and involve the IEM team in an essential, professionally rewarding function.

The SIO must also assess market trends when deploying a finite budget. New markets need to be researched (exploring), markets that have received an initial investment must be nurtured (developing), and productive existing markets must be supported (sustaining). Articulating where and how the IEM team will invest and divest funds demonstrates fiduciary accountability, which is an attribute respected by would-be partners. The SIO's process of evaluating budgets, learning about market trends, and understanding the relationships among programs available to international students can help in shaping the strategies. To stay on top of trends, the SIO must read from the wealth of information available online and provided through professional organizations, third-party providers, and international recruitment agents. The IEM team members appreciate and are strengthened by an SIO who shares in the responsibility of "environmental scanning."

Student Recruitment and Enrollment

Most international students who are looking at U.S.-based higher education options were born in the twenty-first century. This means that they expect fast, digital, and customized experiences wherever they go. Enrollment managers have begun using customer relationship management (CRM) software to meet the demands. CRMs allow for savvy messaging and marketing campaigns that accommodate transactional and relational messaging in both static and dynamic formats. Static messages are issued at a scheduled time to fit a particular audience, such as applicants who need to be reminded of an upcoming deadline. Dynamic messaging is the reverse and is issued to a defined audience at whatever time a particular status is achieved, such as issuing a congratulatory message a few days after admitting a student. An engaged SIO can help the IEM team members get creative with the messaging.

If admissions teams are not using a CRM yet, they will likely be doing so soon. Some advancement and alumni offices have had one in place for years. CRMs are powerful tools, but they do not replace the impact of a print brochure about the campus with beautiful pictures or targeted information on academic programs that can be shared with friends and family, thus extending the reach of the message. CRMs can supplement more traditional marketing and promotional communications to help boost student enrollment.

The SIO and IEM team may be asked to answer questions about overall enrollment numbers on a regular basis, so the SIO must stay familiar with up-to-date institutional data. Retention and graduation rates fall outside the sphere of influence controlled by the IEM team alone, but if the team members are recruiting students who do not persist, that feedback must get back to the SIO so that strategies can be altered and the SIEMP can be updated.

The SIO may have the opportunity to get campus buy-in on initiatives that may lower or level-off enrollment for a defined period of time, with the promise of recruiting students with improved English language proficiency scores, higher math abilities, and/or increased overall GPAs. These student success indicators can and should work in tandem with any existing scholarships, or they may be part of a proposal to launch an international student scholarship program. Many institutions in the United States are leveraging the #YouAreWelcomeHere scholarship initiative to this very end.

Aside from enrollment analytics, the SIO might also be concerned with English language proficiency scores, GPAs, AP courses, IB courses, A-Levels, etc. The exercise of applied comparative international education, or foreign credential evaluation, is a profession unto itself, with dedicated professional organizations and resources. The SIO needs to sort out the best approach for the campus because there are pros and cons to in-house versus external credential evaluation strategies. Faculty senates or policy committees may be involved in that decision. If the decision is to use in-house credential evaluation services, the SIO needs to support the professional staff members who conduct the internal evaluations. On the other hand, the use of third-party credential evaluators is also a proven strategy—but take caution and employ mechanisms that ensure consistent interpretations of credentials if there is a compelling case to use a mixed-methods approach.

Student Yield

One of the most important roles of the SIO is to mitigate the complications that can arise from the effort to ensure continuity among related service areas in international affairs. A complication in the enrollment process could result in a student enrolling elsewhere due to a lack of confidence in the institution.

Students may first be recruited by an intensive English program or IEM team member, work with the institution's international student advising staff to obtain a visa document to apply for a visa to enter the country, work with IEM again to gain admission to a degree program, and then again work with either the institution's international student advising staff or admissions staff to prepare or update visa documents. There are lots of people and steps involved in the enrollment process, and SIOs can help facilitate by documenting and clarifying the process for students.

Program Effectiveness and Accountability

All of the efforts and initiatives carried out by the IEM team should include an instrument for assessment. Knowing the ROI for the myriad activities of the IEM team allows the team members to focus on the most productive activities in future cycles. In addition to measuring the number of prospects or applications yielded from a recruitment activity, or knowing how much it costs to recruit an international student, it is valuable to speak with new students and reverse engineer the exercise to determine what they think were the factors that brought them to the institution. For example, IEM data may indicate that a recruitment trip to a specific high school was worthwhile, but the students themselves may say that it was a webinar that made all the difference in their decisionmaking process.

Often, the most effective recruitment approach is the use of multipronged activities to reach different students and their unique needs. The SIO can support the IEM team by using data to make a case to the IEM or international affairs advisory board, budget and finance team, or provost that multiple contact points across modalities in the recruitment cycle can lead to higher student enrollment, not lone investments in discrete activities. This is an important point to raise during budget talks.

Conclusion

Teams rise and fall on the strength of their leadership. The members of the IEM team need an effective SIO who can accurately communicate both their needs and the institution's needs to the right audiences. In addition, leading the IEM team means that the SIO must cultivate and manage stakeholder relations, provide resources for professional development (e.g., conferences, credential evaluation workshops, professional organizations, online databases), and empower the IEM professionals to craft a strategy and execute it.

The SIO's purview extends to every corner of the globe, and the SIO's fundamental duty is to develop and maintain an evolving, living global strategy. By building a capable team, the SIO can enlist help in shouldering the work of international enrollment management and make invaluable contributions to any institution of higher education.

Additional Resources

Di Maria, David L., ed. 2017. *Managing a Successful International Admissions Office: NAFSA's Guide to International Admissions*. Washington, DC: NAFSA: Association of International Educators.

NAFSA: Association of International Educators. n.d. *IEM Spotlight Newsletter*. Washington, DC: NAFSA: Association of International Educators. https://www.nafsa.org/iemspotlight.

NAFSA: Association of International Educators. 2019. "International Enrollment Management Knowledge Community." Washington, DC: NAFSA: Association of International Educators. http://www.nafsa.org/Connect_and_Network/Networking_with_NAFSA/Professional_Networks/IEM_KC/International_Enrollment_Management_Knowledge_Community/.

Sandberg, Jessica Black, ed. 2017. *NAFSA's Guide to International Student Recruitment, Third Edition*. Washington, DC: NAFSA: Association of International Educators.

Sinclair, Julie, ed. 2014. *International Enrollment Management Strategic Planning: An Integrated Approach*. Washington, DC: NAFSA: Association of International Educators.

Temple University International Affairs. n.d. "Fall 2019 #YouAreWelcomeHere Scholarship." Philadelphia, PA: Temple University International Affairs. https://www.youarewelcomehereusa.org/scholarship/.

10 | Administration of International Student and Scholar Services

Heather Housley

Since as early as 1784 (Bevis and Lucas 2007), international students have traveled to the United States to pursue higher education. As the population of international students and scholars increased over time, the support services offered to them grew to not only include the cultural programming described in chapter 8, but also immigration services to help manage federally mandated regulatory compliance responsibilities.

Following the events of September 11, 2001, federal immigration regulations became much more complex and demanding with the government's creation of the Student and Exchange Visitor Information System (SEVIS). The immigration landscape is constantly changing, whether from a new federal policy, procedure, or interpretation. If immigration compliance is neglected, it can lead to the loss of legal status by international students or scholars, as well as federal fines for the institution and withdrawal of the institution's authorization to host international students, scholars, and others. As a result, compliance is a critical institutional responsibility that demands vigilance and the investment of human, fiscal, and technological resources.

While not all senior international officers (SIOs) need to have detailed knowledge of specific immigration regulations, they are expected to be aware of critical university compliance and reporting obligations, resources for important subject matter expertise and guidance, and tools to support institutional compliance and student success. This chapter provides an overview of some of the key issues related to immigration advising and support services, also commonly known as "international student and scholar services" (ISSS), that SIOs need to address as they develop and lead campus internationalization efforts. This information is supplemented by Appendix A, a checklist that SIOs can use to increase their knowledge of how immigration services are administered at their institution.

International Constituents

The size and demographics of the international population vary from institution to institution, but the groups discussed below are among the most commonly represented on any given campus. Each constituent group has its own specific characteristics within the code of federal regulations that can impact, support, and complicate internationalization efforts. Thus, it is important that SIOs know the individuals and offices at their institution that are responsible for their institutional compliance, even if the SIOs are not directly responsible for immigration advising and support services.

International Students

Students from all over the world choose to attend U.S. colleges and universities to pursue their undergraduate and graduate degree programs, but they can also study in nondegree exchange programs and intensive English programs (IEPs). All academic programs that wish to enroll international students on F, J, or M visas need prior approval from the appropriate U.S. government agency (see Appendix A). The SIO, therefore, needs to know the individuals in the immigration services unit who serve the campus as the "principal designated school official" (PDSO), the role designated by the U.S. Department of Homeland Security to assist F and M visa students, as well as the campus "responsible officer" (RO), the role designated by the U.S. Department of State to assist J visa students. These key positions are responsible for the institution's regulatory compliance, including regular government reporting.

The PDSO and RO are critical partners that the SIO should consult regarding any new program or initiative that includes international students in the United States. When there is a change in the campus PDSO or RO position, the SIO should ensure that the role is appropriately delegated to trained employees who can maintain university responsibilities in the interim.

International Scholars

Faculty, researchers, and graduate students from foreign universities can be sponsored to come to the United States as visiting professors, lecturers, and researchers for the purpose of cultural exchange. The U.S. Department of State oversees the regulations that govern visiting scholar eligibility and activities, and the RO is responsible for monitoring institutional compliance. Due to their role in establishing exchange agreements with foreign universities, SIOs often play a diplomatic role in welcoming international scholars from those institutions to campus.

International Employees

U.S. colleges and universities frequently hire foreign nationals for various faculty and staff positions. Multiple visa types are available for this purpose, but complex and, often, fast-changing requirements from the various government agencies involved, along with the lengthy timelines needed for processing applications, can make the hiring process quite challenging. Institutions need to establish clear policies on when and how they will sponsor foreign nationals for employment and determine whether to use in-house experts or outside counsel for preparing immigration petitions.

Sponsoring international employees may require extensive collaboration and communication between many university units, including human resources, international student and scholar services, legal counsel, and various hiring units, as well as the U.S. Departments of Homeland Security, Labor, and State. Institutions that do not meet compliance requirements can be subject to hefty fines and even barred from hiring foreign nationals. SIOs need to ensure that staff who are responsible for compliance receive the training and ongoing professional development needed to stay abreast of regulatory changes. SIOs who oversee units responsible for filing employment-based immigration petitions must commit to providing sufficient funds and opportunities to support this endeavor.

International Visitors

Universities frequently invite international visitors to campus to present a lecture, participate in short-term cultural programs, or attend workshops, seminars, or conferences organized by the institution. While international visitors do not require formal visa sponsorship, federal regulations impact if and how they can be paid by the institution, as well as their access to university resources and information.

While the other groups discussed here are easily monitored due to the legal relationship that exists between the foreign national and the institution, international visitors are more difficult to track, especially if they are eligible to participate in the visa waiver program. The program "enables most citizens or nationals of participating countries to travel to the United States for tourism or business for stays of 90 days or less without obtaining a visa" (U.S. Department of State n.d.). Nonetheless, institutions should establish clear policies related to reimbursements, honoraria, benefits (e.g., library access), and restrictions (e.g., export control) that are applicable to international visitors. SIOs should be involved in creating these policies and helping ensure they are communicated effectively across campus.

SIOs should meet with international immigration staff on a regular basis to make sure that they have the resources they need to meet compliance requirements and have data on internationalization outcomes. As part of their role on the senior leadership team, SIOs may often be called upon to promote enrollment numbers and the contributions of the different constituent groups to the larger campus and community as part of the institutional strategy.

Administrative Considerations

At some institutions, the size of the international population plays a factor in the prominence, scope, functions, and even the more administrative elements of immigration services on campus. The location of immigration advising and support services within the university organizational structure varies by institution. SIOs should think strategically about the model that is most appropriate for their institutional culture and structure. The most common model positions the offices and units responsible for international students and scholars under the SIO's authority due to their central role in supporting comprehensive internationalization efforts. Typically, these offices include ISSS, study abroad programs, international partnerships and agreements, and the IEPs, if applicable. The close proximity of these related units can often help to spark collaboration in terms of policies, initiatives, and the sharing of resources, as well as a degree of unity under the SIO.

Advising Services

Just as there are different approaches to the location of immigration services, the advising models also vary from one institution to another. Some universities combine services for international students, scholars, and employees in the same office, while others locate them separately within different units. While it is quite common for different staff members to specialize in immigration support for particular constituent groups—students, scholars, or employees—an emerging model features advisers who are cross-trained in multiple areas. This more comprehensive role provides welcomed professional development opportunities as well as critical backup during peak seasons and when there is employee turnover. SIOs at institutions with resource constraints would be well served to consider this model because it enables a small staff to reach a larger number of international constituents.

For international employees, however, depending on the number of foreign national faculty and staff hired by the university each year, the institution may need to consider outsourcing immigration support to external legal counsel. Immigration attorneys selected for this purpose should be thoroughly vetted and approved by university legal counsel, and they should be informed of applicable institutional policies. Public institutions may be restricted to working with immigration lawyers previously approved or contracted by the state's attorney general.

Staff

Due to the critical compliance responsibilities involved, the U.S. Department of State requires program sponsors to ensure adequate staffing and sufficient support services (see U.S. Citizenship and Immigration Services n.d.) on campus. This is something to which the president, chancellor, or chief executive officer of the college or university attests each time he or she signs the institution's Exchange Visitor Program Application (Form DS-3036).

While there is no nationally accepted caseload for immigration advising, a 2011 national survey conducted by NACADA: The Global Community for Academic Advising found the median caseload to be 296 immigration advisees to one full-time adviser (Robbins 2013). According to Herlien et al. (2017), the determination of an adequate adviser caseload must include several key considerations, including:

- Types of clients based on immigration status and objective;

- Adviser duties in addition to immigration advising;

- Staff expertise, experience, and cross-training;

- Access to tools and support services, such as online scheduling, chat software, and immigration case management systems with SEVIS batch functionality;

- Management priorities in terms of cost, quality, and time; and

- Administrative support to assist advisers with clerical and front-end services.

Finances

At many institutions, the staffing structures are dependent on funding and space allocations. Care must be taken to establish adequate and diversified funding sources in support of immigration advising and support services. In situations where funding these immigration services is a challenge, consideration may be given to charging fees to students and scholars or partnering with other departments to help cover costs. Additionally, many institutions charge fees to international scholars and hiring departments for preparing immigration petitions. The SIO can work with immigration services staff to determine the best approaches for the institution. (For more revenue-generating and cost-sharing strategies, see chapter 6.)

Use of Technology

One of the major expenses related to immigration services is ensuring that advisers have access to the technology needed to help with their federal compliance and reporting requirements and data management. The myriad data points to be reported for each international student and scholar, per term, may be entered directly into SEVIS if the total international population is relatively small. However, with a larger international population, reporting compliance is usually best facilitated by the purchase of an immigration batching and case management system.

Multiple software options are available from third-party vendors that include not only batch management of immigration compliance and reporting responsibilities, but also customer relationship management (CRM) capabilities that allow the institution to proactively communicate with students and scholars regarding impending document expiration dates and other important deadlines. Depending on the capabilities of the institution's existing enterprise system, ISSS units may also choose to use the third-party software for data mining, case tracking, front desk management, event registration, and other helpful features. Many external systems can also support international payroll, taxation, and other administrative concerns.

The data collected through these software and CRM systems may help to support and advance internationalization efforts across campus. The SIO can promote enrollment and retention numbers to boost the institution's reputation on the global stage, which can, in turn, lead to more international students, scholars, employees, and visitors joining the campus community and contributing to other units.

Partners

Immigration support and advising services are, by nature, collaborative and require active partnership with other offices and units on campus. SIOs should endeavor to cultivate quality relationships in the following areas:

- University general counsel. General counsel should be consulted regarding the creation of and changes to institutional immigration policies; policies and processes for export control compliance; responses to federal policy updates and programs; questions regarding compliance of specific university or departmental programs, actions, or cases; and appropriate responses to staff errors.

- Outside counsel. SIOs may need to reach out to outside counsel when immigration expertise is required beyond what the PDSO, RO, or university general counsel can provide.

- Human resources. The office of human resources is involved in international employee hiring, institutional tax compliance, international employee/scholar data maintenance and reporting, and payments to international visitors.

- Institutional technology (IT). SIOs may be required to call on the support of IT staff regarding the configuration and maintenance of immigration compliance software and its connection to the institutional enterprise system. IT staff may also provide expertise on the latest data sharing and protection protocol.

- Government relations officers. These individuals can be strategically helpful when the institution needs state senators or representatives to advocate for international students, scholars, or employees who are facing extreme delays or challenges with the processing of immigration applications. SIOs can work closely with their government relations officers to coordinate accurate, impactful messages.

- Internal auditors. Auditors can provide insights and suggestions for streamlining operations and processes for increased data quality and compliance.

SIOs, along with ISSS advisers, can actively foster partnerships with different units to maximize resources, mitigate large-scale issues, serve the entire campus, and drive internationalization strategies.

Escalation of Issues

Inevitably, some cases will arise that require the SIO to alert the provost, president, or other senior-level administrators. Any situation involving international students, scholars, or employees that could end up in the media, is the result of an error on the part of the institution, or that otherwise puts the institution at risk should be escalated accordingly. In rare cases, it may be necessary to enlist the assistance of congressional representatives to help address particularly intractable scenarios and advocate on the beneficiary's behalf. In these cases, the relationships and communications channels that the SIO has built across campus units will come in handy.

Conclusion

International students and scholars enrich their host institutions and communities. They are a key part of any internationalization plan, enhancing the overall academic, cultural, and social experiences of their peers. The complex immigration laws and regulations attendant to inbound academic mobility require that key units stay informed, be adequately staffed, and have access to the resources and tools needed to maintain institutional compliance. SIOs play a critical role in the overall support of these areas, and thus must know who to contact and where to turn for related information and resources.

Additional Resources

SIOs and ISSS staff cannot operate in isolation and should seek information and resources from colleagues, peer institutions, and related professional associations whenever needed.

The Association of International Education Administrators (www.aiea-world.org) supports senior international education leaders by providing opportunities to share institutional strategies, create networks, and a serve as a voice on international education policy issues. Its programs and annual conference are targeted for campus SIOs.

NAFSA: Association of International Educators (www.nafsa.org) is the largest professional association working within international education and exchange. It provides many beneficial resources, including:

- Core Education Program (CEP) Workshops. CEP Workshops offer in-depth information and skill development regarding specific areas of international education, including F-1 and J-1 advising, the filing of H-1B petitions, and employment-based permanent residency. CEP Workshops are typically offered prior to NAFSA national and regional conferences and are ideal professional training opportunities, especially for new employees.

- NAFSA Adviser's Manual 360. This is a critically important online resource to immigration advising services professionals that provides regulatory guidance, best practices, and up-to-date information regarding all areas of immigration advising for international students and scholars.

- NAFSA's Immigration Classifications and Legal Employment of Foreign Nationals in the United States poster and quick reference guide. This handy tool provides a succinct summary of visa types relevant for college and university personnel.

The Society for Human Resource Management's Council for Global Immigration (www.shrm.org) brings together professionals involved in employment-based immigration from both corporate and educational institutions. Its annual conference, publications, and advocacy channels are useful resources for university staff involved in hiring foreign faculty and staff.

Subscribing to and maintaining memberships in associations such as these are critical for staff who address the operational, management, advising, and compliance functions of the ISSS unit. In addition, newsletters from reputable immigration legal firms, federal publications, and the U.S. Department of Homeland Security's "Study in the States" website (studyinthestates.dhs.gov) all provide useful and timely information pertaining to immigration regulations and policies.

References

Bevis, Teresa Brawner, and Christopher J. Lucas. 2007. *International Students in American Colleges and Universities*. New York, NY: Palgrave Macmillan.

Herlien, Charmagne, Tricia Schueler, Tami Renner, and Amber Tetreau-Segura. 2017. "Advising Caseloads: Finding the Right Fit." Presented at the NAFSA 2017 Annual Conference & Expo, Los Angeles, CA. https://www.nafsa.org/uploadedFiles/NAFSA_Dojo/Professional_Resources/Browse_by_Interest/International_Students_and_Scholars/advising_caseloads.pdf.

Robbins, Rich. 2013. *Advisor Load*. Manhattan, KS: NACADA: The Global Community for Academic Advising. https://www.nacada.ksu.edu/Resources/Clearinghouse/View-Articles/Advisor-Load.aspx.

U.S. Citizenship and Immigration Services. n.d. "Sec. 62. 9 General Obligations of Sponsors." Washington, DC: U.S. Citizenship and Immigration Services.

U.S. Department of State. n.d. "Visa Waiver Program." Washington, DC: U.S. Department of State. https://travel.state.gov/content/travel/en/us-visas/tourism-visit/visa-waiver-program.html.

PART 3

Faculty and Academics

11 | **Academic Programs Integration**

Lance R. Askildson

Oversight for curricula and academic degree programs is typically the domain of academic college and school deans, department chairs, and degree program directors. The role of senior international officers (SIOs) within academic programs should, therefore, be focused on advocating for and facilitating international education, campus internationalization, and global engagement in ways that align with and directly support the priorities of academic deans, chairs, and directors, as well as the pedagogical goals of faculty and the educational needs of students.

This chapter examines how SIOs can build and rely on their partnerships with academic deans, department chairs, and faculty governance bodies to help them integrate internationalization activities into academic curricula and degree programs, making that impact more sustainable within the academic mission of the university.

Internationalization Stakeholders

While SIOs typically report directly to provosts or related institutional officers, SIOs are ultimately accountable to the primary stakeholders within academic affairs, namely, relevant academic administrators (deans, chairs, etc.), the faculty, and the students. Thus, it is essential that these stakeholders also be central figures in the development, implementation, and reporting of SIO activities. Gathering their input and feedback at each stage of new international initiations is essential.

Internationalization of Academic Affairs

On an institutional scale, SIOs have a mandate to align and integrate their internationalization efforts with academic affairs as a means of directly supporting the teaching and research goals of the university. This begins with the development of a strategic plan for internationalization that draws upon input from academic affairs stakeholders and explicitly codifies how internationalization efforts will support and advance the university-wide strategic plan and academic mission.

The internationalization strategic plan can then be used to guide everything from institutional agreements to study abroad program development to internal funding opportunities for international education and global engagement. This plan should focus the efforts of international education offices by framing their work as not simply a vehicle for global and intercultural learning specifically, but also as a powerful instantiation of so-called "high-impact practices" and the associated impact of such academically engaging experiences on student retention, progression, and graduation (Kuh 2008). On the academic college and department side of the equation, the internationalization strategic plan can also help to clarify what types of institutional agreements (e.g., memoranda of understanding for exchange or articulation, dual and joint degrees, etc.) should be pursued and prioritized in service to the mission of academic affairs at large.

At Kennesaw State, for example, staff members in the SIO's office engage stakeholders across academic affairs to emphasize the impact of study abroad, international internships, international service-learning, and undergraduate research abroad as part of a broader phenomenon. The *Strategic Plan for Internationalization,* which was coauthored by faculty, is used to align internationalization activities with the university's institutional strategic plan and mission statement, while also developing programs explicitly intended to advance these points. One major outcome was the creation of an internal grants program, the Strategic Internationalization Grants (SIGs), which provides funding to faculty to advance one of the five major academic goals of the internationalization strategic plan. SIG funding has been provided for faculty members' international research, global course development, student learning outcomes assessment efforts, and new internationally themed degree programs. These efforts have significantly advanced the university's international goals, those of academic affairs, and the aims of constituent academic deans and department chairs.

In a similar manner, Kennesaw State recently refined its 35-year-old flagship internationalization program, the Annual Country Study Program (ACSP), to ensure that it is more closely integrated with the strategic goals of academic affairs and the university. The ACSP annually selects a foreign country or region and spends an initial year studying that country or region as a university learning community, followed by another yearlong public educational program with weekly academic events on campus. Recent changes made to the ACSP to better align its activities and outcomes have included the addition of a faculty advisory board, the creation of academic college "spotlights" for more focused disciplinary speakers and events, and new mandates to include additional interdisciplinary coursework for faculty and students from diverse colleges and majors. These changes have improved faculty and student engagement with the flagship program and enabled the SIO to better articulate and document the program's contributions and impact.

Faculty Academic Engagement

SIOs have a particular priority to engage faculty in the internationalization efforts of the institution. As educators who often draw upon global perspectives within their academic disciplines, faculty are natural allies for SIOs. However, faculty are also increasingly being asked to do more with less across their teaching, research, and service domains. Accordingly, it is important for SIOs to present themselves and their teams as resources that are available to help faculty accomplish their existing teaching and research goals. (For more on collaborating with academic faculty on internationalization, see chapter 12.) Offering financial support for professional development, opportunities for research and publication, and teaching resources and materials can help to incentivize faculty to partner with SIOs in ways that support shared institutional roles and objectives (Childress 2010).

For example, SIOs can invite national and international scholars of intercultural competence to the campus for collaborative faculty workshops and feedback sessions that produce new international courses, course modules, and faculty publications, thus advancing internationalization goals for the university at large. Staff members of the SIO's office can work to help faculty and departments bring in visiting scholars to address gaps in research and teaching specialties. These visiting faculty also provide students with alternative pedagogical approaches to their disciplinary coursework and the chance to engage with educators from other countries and cultures.

Of course, to achieve these faculty engagement outcomes, SIOs need formal structures through which they can consult and collaborate with faculty. Kennesaw State, for example, created formal shared governance bodies and numerous advisory boards and committees dedicated to internationalization, generally in conjunction with a diverse array of specific programs, initiatives, and events. And, importantly, the university continues to recognize the important role that faculty play in these activities through annual awards and events and letters of appreciation addressed to their chairs and deans.

Student Academic Engagement

Although SIOs have many stakeholders to consider in their role, the most important stakeholders should always be the students themselves. Here again, students are natural allies for SIOs. Many students understand, implicitly, that global engagement and perspectives have become requisite for personal and professional success after college. Students generally value diverse and intercultural perspectives within their academic experiences, alongside experiential learning opportunities (Bandyopadhyay and Bandyopadhyay 2015).

Like faculty, students are increasingly pressed upon to do more with their academic careers despite increased academic and financial demands. Offering additional cocurricular learning programs is oftentimes neither compelling nor productive to students who are already overwhelmed with their academic goals and have limited time, energy, and funding to complete their degrees on time. SIOs should, therefore, prioritize academically relevant international education opportunities that help students advance toward their degrees, while infusing that academic progression with global perspectives and experiences. Where direct academic integration is not feasible, SIOs should work with faculty and academic departments to create cocurricular experiences that are as integrated as possible within the established coursework and curricula.

For instance, staff members in the SIO office at Kennesaw State work closely with faculty to develop integrated and upper-division international education course requirement offerings, domestically and abroad, so that students can complete required coursework within their majors. The university offers study abroad coursework that meets general education requirements, as well as first-semester freshmen study abroad programs to improve freshmen engagement and retention. The SIO and staff also work closely with departments to offer cocurricular programming that is relevant to students' curricular goals and integrated wherever possible with their academic degree requirements. Additionally, students can earn a Global Engagement Certification that is noted on their academic transcripts. Identical strategies are implemented for international students, while also recognizing the increasingly high stakes regarding time restraints and progress to degree completion.

Internationalization Outcomes

The reporting of internationalization outcomes should include compelling data points that demonstrate the outcomes of the SIOs and their activities. For example, at Kennesaw State University, the Division of Global Affairs publishes highly accessible annual reports that are designed to showcase the university's international accomplishments. These reports include specific statistics regarding student, faculty, and academic impacts, alongside analyses of their relationships to student achievement and retention, progression, and graduation rates. Such reporting helps to situate the impacts of internationalization activity in service to the educational mission of the university and the advancement of academic degree program outcomes.

Conclusion

SIOs must carefully balance the diverse priorities of multiple institutional stakeholders, but the primacy of the academic mission of the university should be a guiding principal for these efforts. In addition to serving as diplomatic advocates for global engagement on campus, SIOs must understand how to implement international education initiatives within the structures of the university generally and the domain of academic affairs specifically. SIOs have to develop and sustain both administrative structures and collegial relationships, which involves an appreciation for the consultation of faculty, academic administrators, and students, as well as an ability to operationalize such stakeholder input within university governance structures and incentive models. Above all, SIOs should aim to inspire these stakeholders with the relevance, significance, and shared value of global learning for all involved.

Additional Resources

Hudzik, John K. 2011. *Comprehensive Internationalization: From Concept to Action*. Washington, DC: NAFSA: Association of International Educators.

Hudzik, John K. 2018. *Comprehensive and Strategic Internationalization: Lessons Learned and Future Prospects*. Washington, DC: NAFSA: Association of International Educators.

Hudzik, John K., and JoAnn S. McCarthy. 2012. *Leading Comprehensive Internationalization: Strategy and Tactics for Action*. Washington, DC: NAFSA: Association of International Educators.

References

Bandyopadhyay, Soumava, and Kakoli Bandyopadhyay. 2015. "Factors Influencing Student Participation in College Study Abroad Programs." *Journal of International Education Research* 11, 2:87–94.

Childress, Lisa K. 2010. *The Twenty-First Century University: Developing Faculty Engagement in Internationalization*. New York, NY: Peter Lang Publishing.

Kuh, George D. 2008. *High-Impact Educational Practices: What They Are, Who Has Access to Them, and Why They Matter*. Washington, DC: Association of American Colleges and Universities.

12 | Curriculum Internationalization

Anthony L. Pinder

In 1992, members of the Association of International Education Administrators (AIEA) espoused that no degree program could be considered adequate, then or at any time in the future, if it did not require minimal curricular exposure to international and global content (Klasek 1992). Interestingly, nearly 3 decades later, the majority of higher education institutions struggle to determine the appropriate levels and scopes of internationalization to implement on their campus (Leask 2015; Helms and Brajkovic 2017; Johnson 2019). Yet, the curriculum is one of the most obvious indicators of whether an institution is fulfilling its mission and the needs of its students, both domestic and international. This chapter considers the different perspectives, strategies, and responsibilities of senior international officers (SIOs) involved in internationalizing the curriculum. It also examines some of the challenges of the globalized society through a case study on Emerson College.

Curriculum Internationalization

Among the many elements of internationalizing a college campus, the curriculum stands out as the essential component of any effort rooted in global learning. However, internationalizing the curriculum is not a simple adjustment; it is a transformational and, sometimes, colossal effort. At the root, internationalization of the curriculum involves reforming of the curriculum to include a pervasive infusion of international dimensions. Such reform must be broad based and approached with the learning objectives and outcomes as the basis for the reform. It requires an ongoing, collaborative, and interdisciplinary approach that combines the support, knowledge, efforts, and skills of cross-culturally sensitive and globally oriented faculty, students, SIOs, and other academic leaders (i.e., provost, deans, and departmental chairs).

Institutional Perspective

The complexity of internationalization, the diversity of institutions, and the strength of disciplinary traditions present enormous challenges to comprehensive internationalization of higher education. At each institution that looks strategically at global learning, its leadership must develop a response and set of strategies that complement the institution's unique profile, mission, and goals. Additionally, faculty buy-in is essential to an institution's successful progression to an internationalized curriculum. SIOs can help advocate for such an important change by encouraging other stakeholders to conceive of the curriculum not as a collection of disconnected courses, but rather as an integrated and learner-centered system that fosters global learning.

Internationalizing the curriculum is the central mechanism that academic leaders and faculty can use to shape student learning. Although it is a complex task that requires attention to general education, the major, and pedagogy, the ability of faculty members to lead this important work requires constant attention to their own global learning. Internationalization affects all faculty, not just those who teach internationally focused courses in the general education curriculum or in a few majors. It provides a unique world perspective that affects how academics view their disciplines, scholarship, curricula, and campus life.

Significant Learning Experiences

While the goal of any educator is to support learning, there are different degrees and levels of learning that resonate with the learner. According to L. Dee Fink (2013, 7):

> significant learning is learning that makes a difference in how people live—and the kind of life they are capable of living. We want that which students learn to become part of how they think, what they can and want

to do, what they believe is true about life, and what they value—and we want it to increase their capability for living life fully and meaningfully.

Fink (2013) further makes the point that significant learning requires helping students connect what they learn in courses with their "life file" rather than just with their "course file." With this in mind, curriculum internationalization offers educators the opportunity to not only be intentional in creating significant learning experiences for students, but also expand each student's global mindset and "life file." Internationalization requires new pedagogies and ways of learning that enable students to fully experience how other cultures and belief systems work.

In order to support students' significant learning experiences, it is critical that faculty members be exposed to effective procedures for designing courses, whether for curriculum internationalization specifically or for their own professional development in general. Faculty must become adept with new approaches of pedagogy to be able to create more culturally inclusive teaching and significant learning practices. To do so, faculty must begin with an awareness of the barriers and gaps in the curriculum and in current teaching practices. However, faculty members are generally less likely to diversify their teaching techniques without an investment by their institutions.

There has never been a more appropriate time for faculty to receive the institutional support they need to create significant learning experiences. One strategy for ensuring that advocacy and support for curriculum internationalization is pervasive across academic departments is articulating global student learning outcomes. The establishment of outcomes makes it easier to estimate the potential effectiveness of academic programs and courses and their alignment with stated educational objectives, rather than simply hoping that they contribute to global learning (Shoenberg and Green 2006).

Strategies for Curriculum Internationalization

How the curricular reform looks (and is financed) is different from institution to institution. However, the research literature offers three common approaches to internationalizing the curriculum in higher education (Bond 2003a, 2003b):

- Add-on approach. This is the earliest used approach to internationalizing the curriculum and is characterized by adding international or intercultural content or themes to existing curricula and courses without modifying the original structure or pedagogical approaches (Banks 2004).

- Infusion approach. This approach infuses the curriculum (Bond 2003b) with content that enriches students' cross-cultural understanding and knowledge of diverse cultures (Whalley, Langley, and Villarreal 1997). The infusion approach focuses on the interdisciplinary nature of curriculum internationalization and exposes students in all fields of study to international and multicultural perspectives.

- Transformation approach. This approach is more difficult to adopt and is the least utilized approach to modifying the curriculum (Bond 2003a, 5). This approach, which is based on the tenets of critical pedagogy, "encourages new ways of thinking, incorporates new methodologies, so that different epistemological questions are raised, old assumptions are quested, subjective data sources are considered, and prior theories either revised or invalidated" (Marchesani and Adams 1992, pp. 15–16).

All three approaches have their merits, and there is opportunity to view them as progressive levels or steps. For some educators, the transformation approach is the most desirable because this type of curriculum aims to assist students with developing the required critical consciousness, values, awareness, skills, and knowledge of cross-cultural differences to thrive as global citizens. Furthermore, students are encouraged to explore and critically analyze their reality through the lenses of diverse cultural and ethnic groups (Banks 2002, 2004). Kitano (1997) also finds that the transformation approach to curriculum development provides the opportunity for students and teachers to share the power within the classroom and to learn from each other.

Regardless of the approach used, what will continue to sustain faculty interest in any institution's process of internationalization will be the additional institutional resources devoted to keeping this initiative alive and relevant in the minds and livelihood of faculty. At many institutions, one of the biggest issues is determining how to deliver resources to faculty members that not only underscore their collective hard work but also fuel their facilitated innovation. This is particularly critical in a resource-constrained environment. If institutions fail to provide resources to support their faculty's efforts to internationalize the curriculum, the institutions risk losing the pulse of the internationalization process. Thus, the task for the academic leadership at any institution is identifying the gaps between where the institution currently is regarding internationalizing the curriculum and where it wants and needs to be following the reform.

Role of the SIO

Ideally, the SIO will work closely with the academic leadership, along with diverse tenured faculty, in developing desired competencies related to new or reimagined global student learning outcomes. An initial charge of the SIO should be to help faculty members specifically frame their responses to the following three questions:

- What are the characteristics of an internationalized curriculum?

- What factors contribute to the effective implementation of an internationalized curriculum?

- What are the outcomes and effects of an internationalized curriculum?

The challenge may be in navigating diverse faculty opinions regarding (a) the definition of internationalization; (b) the scope of work to achieve internationalization; and (c) the extent to which faculty believe the current curriculum is already internationalized. The latter may present the greatest hurdle because faculty members can sometimes be parochial and somewhat less transparent in admitting that their own courses (thus, their scholarship) may not be contemporary or offer students a "global" lens.

An additional charge of the SIO is discerning the best way to keep faculty members away from defensive posturing when determining the international dimensions of existing curriculum in general and their courses in particular. The SIO must continue to move the reform initiative toward a congenial process of welcoming and generating ideas about how to broaden and deepen the level of internationalization across the curriculum. To that end, the SIO can support faculty as they determine the desired learning outcomes of internationalization, which then elicits a closer review of how the current curriculum helps students achieve those outcomes.

Faculty Engagement in Curriculum Integration

Research on the administration and supervision of instructional programs contends that all instruction is about initiating, expanding, and reinforcing. At the heart of any internationalization process and strategy should be the question, "What do we want our students to know?" Yet, how the SIO is able to convince faculty members that this particular priority merits high visibility and resources (both human and capital) is a challenge, considering that some among the faculty may have limited global exposure themselves. Nevertheless, a successful internationalization process incorporates faculty input on the different modes of study, curricular interests, and learning styles of diverse students.

To begin, the SIO can first validate the contributions of faculty members, recognizing their expertise and asking them to present examples of internationalization currently happening within their own disciplines. SIOs should be rather deliberate, albeit diplomatic, about keeping faculty members honest regarding producing demonstrated evidence that their courses have international dimensions. Many course syllabi make extravagant claims about the competencies and skills students gain, but the only evidence of such learning are the seat time and the grades (Mestenhauser and Ellingboe 1998).

Next, the SIO can empower faculty members to imagine what an infusion of international dimensions would look like in their division, department, and courses. Such validation and empowerment can often result in faculty from diverse disciplines joining together to construct more holistic approaches to understanding how to make their area specialties more culture bound and international in nature for the advancement of student learning. The facilitation of this key group of specialists is a delicate undertaking, which, if done correctly, can lead to revolutionary positive change resulting in the production of globally competent and conscious graduates. The collaborative relationship between SIOs and faculty is crucial at institutions across the globe, regardless of their size, mission, or specific internationalization goals.

FACULTY INCENTIVES

Faculty members are the pivotal agents in driving curriculum internationalization. Creating incentives for faculty to engage in internationalizing the curriculum may require new practices and resources, or a redirection of existing resources (Shoenberg and Green 2006). For example, some institutions offer internal faculty development funds as competitive incentive grants to create intentionality and greater visibility for the institution's focus on curriculum internationalization. (For more on faculty engagement, see chapters 11 and 15.) The case study of Emerson College illustrates how faculty engagement in curriculum internationalization initiatives can have far-reaching effects on the institution and the students.

Case Study: Emerson College

Emerson College, like many other institutions of higher education, continues to respond to the challenges presented by globalization in a myriad of ways. One response has been the pursuit of comprehensive internationalization of the Emerson campus. Another is the ongoing discussion regarding how the college can educate students as effectively as possible in an increasingly global twenty-first century. To underscore the college's mission to educate the world's future generations of artists and storytellers, the Office of Internationalization & Global Engagement (IGE) was established in March 2014, with the appointment of its charter SIO/associate vice president for internationalization and global engagement.

American Council on Education Internationalization Laboratory

Leadership at Emerson College recognized the importance of pursuing an intentional, institution-wide approach for achieving comprehensive internationalization, as well as securing an appropriate overarching infrastructure and additional financial resources to support the full achievement of the articulated internationalization goals. With this goal, Emerson seized the opportunity to pursue membership into the American Council on Education (ACE)'s Internationalization Laboratory as a vehicle to focus specifically on the comprehensive internationalization of the college.

The decision to internationalize the curriculum was made very early in the ACE Lab strategic planning process. As with most institutions that work to increase the number of students who graduate with an international experience, the 2014–15 academic year began a period of intense examination of the limitations of traditional models for international education. As a result, three key ACE Lab subcommittees were established to specifically examine student learning outcomes and efforts at internationalizing the curriculum and cocurriculum at Emerson. The subcommittees' work was grounded in and driven by the curriculum.

Curriculum Internationalization Studio

Once the newly articulated student learning outcomes, including a global outcome, received full consensus from the faculty assembly, the SIO successfully made the case to the president and provost to use the Presidential Fund for Curricular Innovation as the funding vehicle to support the creation of a new Curriculum Internationalization Studio. Under the auspices of the SIO, the goals of the Curriculum Internationalization Studio are to (a) encourage collaboration among faculty; (b) build the college's collective capacity to internationalize the curriculum; and (c) develop specific courses, course modules, and pedagogical and advising methods that contribute to these aims.

Teams of two to three faculty—led by a full-time faculty member and composed of tenured, tenure-line, term, and part-time faculty—are invited to apply to the Curriculum Internationalization Studio for support in the development of actionable projects that will contribute significantly to the internationalization of the Emerson curriculum. Projects might focus on, but are not be limited, to:

- Course content and course design (either a full course or course modules);

- Teaching strategies for enhancing the development of students' global knowledge and intercultural competencies;

- Instructional materials and equipment; and

- Academic advising.

Ultimately, the aim is to offer a curriculum that assists Emerson students in developing the required critical consciousness, values, awareness, skills, and knowledge of cross-cultural differences to thrive as global citizens.

Each awarded team member receives a monetary stipend, and the teams have the opportunity to apply for further funding for project-related expenses (e.g., travel, funds to hire student assistants, materials, etc.). Accepted teams participate in a series of professional development workshops (e.g., backward course design, aligning student learning outcomes, internationalizing the curriculum, etc.), during which they develop their projects, remain in dialogue with the other teams, and enhance their capacity to serve as a resource for colleagues interested in internationalizing the curriculum.

The intention of the Curriculum Internationalization Studio is to support projects that will become vibrant and enduring parts of the Emerson curriculum. All new curricula coming out of the Curriculum Internationalization Studio need to be approved through regular college and departmental processes. In total, since the studio's establishment, more than 45 faculty members have participated in producing 25 new, highly internationalized courses and initiatives across disciplines.

Conclusion

Institutions that seek to impact comprehensive internationalization on their campus cannot successfully do so without an intentional strategy. SIOs must effectively collaborate with administrators and faculty to engage their support, time, and effort in purposely designing curricular and cocurricular opportunities that serve the learning goals of students in this globalized world. Internationalizing the curriculum enhances faculty acumen, facilitates the research agenda of faculty and students, and strengthens overall engagement that promotes the application of knowledge.

Additional Resources

Helms, Robin Matross, and Malika Tukibayeva. 2013. "Internationalization in Action: Internationalizing the Curriculum, Part 1 - Individual Courses." Washington, DC: American Council on Education Center for Internationalization and Global Engagement. https://www.acenet.edu/news-room/Pages/Intlz-in-Action-2013-December.aspx.

Helms, Robin Matross, and Malika Tukibayeva. 2014. "Internationalization in Action: Internationalizing the Curriculum, Part 2 - Academic Program Components." Washington, DC: American Council on Education Center for Internationalization and Global Engagement. https://www.acenet.edu/news-room/Pages/Intlz-in-Action-2014-January.aspx.

Helms, Robin Matross, and Malika Tukibayeva. 2014. "Internationalization in Action: Internationalizing the Curriculum, Part 3 - Degree Programs." Washington, DC: American Council on Education Center for Internationalization and Global Engagement. https://www.acenet.edu/news-room/Pages/Intlz-in-Action-2014-March.aspx.

Helms, Robin Matross, and Heather H. Ward. 2014. "Internationalization in Action: Internationalizing the Curriculum, Part 4 - Disciplines." Washington, DC: American Council on Education Center for Internationalization and Global Engagement. https://www.acenet.edu/news-room/Pages/Intlz-in-Action-June-2014.aspx.

NAFSA: Association of International Educators. 2019. "Internationalizing the Curriculum." Washington, DC: NAFSA: Association of International Educators. https://www.nafsa.org/Professional_Resources/Browse_by_Interest/Internationalizing_Higher_Education/Internationalizing_the_Curriculum/.

References

Banks, James A. 2002. *An Introduction to Multicultural Education, Third Edition.* Boston, MA: Allyn and Bacon.

Banks, James A. 2004. "Approaches to Multicultural Curriculum Reform." In *Multicultural Education: Issues and Perspectives, Fifth Edition*, eds. James A. Banks and Cherry A. McGee Banks. Hoboken, NJ: John Wiley & Sons, Inc.

Bond, Sheryl. 2003a. *Engaging Educators: Bringing the World into the Classroom: Guidelines for Practice*. Ottawa, Ontario, Canada: Canadian Bureau for International Education.

Bond, Sheryl. 2003b. *Untapped Resources: Internationalization of the Curriculum and Classroom Experience: A Selected Literature Review*. CBIE Research Millennium Series No. 7. Ottawa, Ontario, Canada: Canadian Bureau for International Education.

Fink, L. Dee. 2013. *Creating Significant Learning Experiences: An Integrated Approach to Designing College Courses*. San Francisco, CA: Jossey-Bass.

Helms, Robin Matross, and Lucia Brajkovic. 2017. *Mapping Internationalization on U.S. Campuses: 2017 Edition*. Washington, DC: American Council on Education.

Johnson, Steven. 2019. "Colleges Lost a 'Stunning' 651 Foreign-Language Programs in 3 Years." *Chronicle of Higher Education*. January 22, 2019. https://www.chronicle.com/article/Colleges-Lose-a-Stunning-/245526.

Kitano, Margie K. 1997. "What a Course Will Look Like After Multicultural Change." In *Multicultural Course Transformation in Higher Education: A Broader Truth*, eds. Ann Intili Morey and Margie K. Kitano. Toronto, Canada: Allyn and Bacon.

Klasek, Charles B. 1992. *Bridges to the Future: Strategies for Internationalizing Higher Education*. Carbondale, IL: Association of International Education Administrators. https://files.eric.ed.gov/fulltext/ED362112.pdf.

Leask, Betty. 2015. *Internationalizing the Curriculum*. New York, NY: Routledge

Marchesani, Linda S., and Maurianne Adams. 1992. "Dynamics of Diversity in the Teaching-Learning Process: A Faculty Development Model for Analysis and Action." In *New Directions for Teaching and Learning: Vol. 52*, ed. Maurianne Adams. San Francisco, CA: Jossey-Bass.

Mestenhauser, Josef A., and Brenda J. Ellingboe, eds. 1998. *Reforming the Higher Education Curriculum: Internationalizing the Campus*. Washington, DC: American Council on Education.

Shoenberg, Robert, and Madeleine F. Green. 2006. *Where Faculty Live: Internationalizing the Disciplines*. Washington, DC: American Council on Education.

Whalley, Thomas Randall, Lin Langley, Linda Villarreal. 1997. *Best Practice Guidelines for Internationalizing the Curriculum.* Victoria, British Columbia, Canada: Ministry of Education, Skills and Training and the Centre for Curriculum, Transfer and Technology.

13 | Synergy Between International Education and Continuing Professional Education

Jeet Joshee and Geraldine de Berly

International education (IE) offices largely assist inbound and outbound undergraduate and graduate students at institutions. Continuing professional education (CPE) units, on the other hand, typically serve people in specific professions, adult learners, and business and industry partners locally and globally. While the participant demographics do deviate, the two units both function in expanding and supporting additional educational opportunities. As a result, some universities in the United States have combined their IE and CPE units into one. Though the merged model varies depending on the institutional context, some of the main reasons for choosing this arrangement are programmatic priorities, revenue expectations, growth potential, and sustainable funding. At universities where IE and CPE are viewed as enterprising in nature, increasing entrepreneurship within the institution serves as an additional motivation for joining the units.

The various administrative models of institutions impact how the senior international officer (SIO) and the senior continuing and professional education administrator (often referred to as the "CPE dean") function in relation to one another. The structures of the two units are best explored by looking at examples of how different institutions manage international programs within the CPE domain. This chapter provides perspectives on this emerging model and how the SIO and CPE dean can work together to support campus internationalization.

Leadership Roles and Responsibilities

Research into the range of responsibilities of SIOs and CPE deans who are engaged in international work indicates some overlap (de Berly 2015, 242). At some institutions, the CPE dean, with the necessary administrative infrastructure in place, also acts as the SIO. At other institutions, there is collaboration between the two, where the SIO's office provides the administrative support for global projects. At some other institutions, the CPE unit is a stand-alone operation with minimal interaction with the SIO, who may not have international program administration as a direct report (e.g., Student and Exchange Visitor Information System). Moreover, in some decentralized institutions, there are multiple individuals, including the CPE dean, who serve in SIO-like roles for particular units.

According to a 2017 Association of International Education Administrators survey on the SIO profile, the top three responsibilities of SIOs are reported to be international institutional relations and partnerships and linkages, strategic planning for internationalization, and representing the institution in institutional dealings (Kwai 2017, pp. 3–4). Other primary responsibilities include study abroad, risk management, faculty-led programs, and international student and scholar services (Kwai 2017, 4). Secondary responsibilities consist of language study, research, branch campuses, grants and fundraising, and service learning and internships (Kwai 2017, 4).

The University Professional and Continuing Education Association's *UPCEA Hallmarks of Excellence in Professional and Continuing Education* recognizes international education as a new frontier for continuing and professional education (UPCEA n.d.). The publication indicates that CPE units and their senior administrators are increasingly engaged in recruiting international students to U.S. campuses for English as a second language (ESL) as well as degree programs. Many CPE units also offer shorter professional development and training programs for global audiences, in partnership with institutions abroad either in-country or through their own satellite campuses and centers. At some institutions, CPE staff units deliver customized in-country and online professional development programs to public and private employees through partnerships with international governmental and corporate entities, licensing course materials to international partners and providing consultative or evaluative services and guidance in development work abroad.

To accomplish these and other tasks, SIOs and CPE deans often demonstrate strong entrepreneurial leadership. They must be innovators, calculated risk takers, and savvy fiscal managers, while aligning their work with the institutional mission. These individuals must be current with global political, economic, and social trends, and they must cultivate programs that attract sufficient enrollments. Given increasing competition among institutions, both SIOs and CPE deans must consider students' educational needs and the various arenas for internationalization activity, including (a) study abroad for outbound U.S. students; (b) programs for international students in the United States; (c) programs for international students on satellite campuses abroad; and (d) programs for niche market participants at home and in distant venues. However, CPEs that are stand-alone entities tend to have more autonomy than SIO offices regarding budgetary decisions and, thus, a merger between CPE deans and SIOs can boost creativity and entrepreneurship for both areas.

Institutional Expectations for New Revenue Resources

With the ever-growing need to support diverse student bodies and pursue creative programming directions, many institutions in the United States have struggled to find sufficient traditional revenue streams. Some of the reasons for the decline in revenue are decreasing domestic enrollment numbers, diminishing government support for public education, rising cost of personnel, and legal compliance. Consequently, alternative sources of funding are critical to fulfill the mission of the institution, and the areas of IE and CPE are increasingly seen as major sources of new revenue generation.

Education abroad is a prime example of the complex dynamic between institutional priorities and funding. The majority of U.S. education abroad participants are white, female undergraduates in their third or fourth year of college (Institute of International Education 2018). However, many institutions that are committed to expanding access to education abroad experiences to underserved populations find it challenging to do so. This is often due to a lack of financial resources needed to subsidize the opportunity costs of studying abroad. Such costs include passport and visa fees, airfare and other incidentals beyond the standard tuition fees, and room and board, which are compounded by the students' lack of employment during the time abroad. If the international program structure does not generate sufficient revenue to provide need-based subsidies or scholarships, then access to education abroad programs remains limited to certain segments of the student population. (For more on the administration of education abroad programs, see chapter 7.)

Other sources of funding can comprise central administrative funds, philanthropy efforts, corporate or nonprofit support, and third-party vendors, but these funds and sources can fluctuate and may not be sustainable in the long run. International students, however, provide a growing stream in revenue, and CPE-run education abroad programs, especially during the summer and winter terms, can generate substantial revenue to support major institutional priorities. This has led many institutions to take the strategic step of combining IE and CPE units to strengthen their capacities and funding sources.

The Integrated Model

In the integrated model, one administrative unit covering both the IE and CPE functions serves to increase operational efficiencies and entrepreneurial capacity. The model can vary greatly from one institution to another, depending on size and scope, from a fully integrated system (e.g., a college or division of continuing and international education) to merging only certain aspects of the operations (e.g., international training programs) to a revenue-sharing agreement between two or more administratively distinct units.

Traditionally, a CPE unit has a well-established structure in place with its own curriculum, marketing, recruitment, advising and support services, finance, and human resources departments. This centralized and autonomous structure allows the unit to quickly develop innovative programs and core services in response to market demands and opportunities, such as transnational education. Likewise, an IE department depends on operations such as marketing, recruitment, student services, and advising. While the target clientele might comprise different demographics, the support services are often closely aligned. For example, the strategy and approach for marketing and recruitment might be different for IE and CPE programs, but the skills and expertise needed for this functional area to be effective in international markets are similar.

There are both advantages and challenges to merging the IE and CPE units. One obvious advantage is lower operational costs due to the elimination of redundancies. Nevertheless, objective analysis and strategic principles must inform the decision to pursue an integrated model in order to address the inevitable challenges that will arise due to this significant organizational change. Table 1 includes some of the most common advantages and challenges.

Table 1. Advantages and Challenges of Combining the International Education and Continuing Education Units into One Model

Advantages of the Merged Model	Challenges of the Merged Model
All international programs are under one administrative unit	Each international program has distinct needs and priorities
Shared vision set by a single leader	Coordinating different priorities into one vision takes time, effort, and patience
Operational synergy	Separate way of doing things
Flexibility and cohesion	Programs have different cultural contexts and schedules
Comprehensive service to students	Different types of students need different services
Cost-effective programs	Two distinct programs that often require different types of resources
Joint marketing and recruitment efforts	Domestic versus international audiences are quite different
Cross-training	Difficult to find a leader who is knowledgeable in both areas
Greater autonomy	Distinct professional values

With buy-in and collective effort from the key stakeholders, an integrated IE and CPE unit can work to serve the university more efficiently and advance its global mission. Faculty, staff, and students can look to one unit for their needs and services, thereby streamlining efforts, capabilities, and outcomes.

Programmatic and Administrative Synergies

At many universities, it is common for CPE units to serve the students of intensive English programs and ESL programs, while the IE units assist degree-seeking international students. However, international student recruitment, whether it is for ESL programs or degree programs, requires similar strategies, resources, and personnel. A coordinated international recruitment strategy from a merged IE-CPE unit enables the institution to reach its target audiences in a more effective manner, with longer-term outcomes.

Case in point, ESL students often come to the United States to learn English first, but for many, their ultimate goal is to matriculate and get a college degree at a U.S. institution. Thus, by actively recruiting and supporting ESL students, the institution can develop a pipeline for prospective full-time students in the degree programs. A strategic recruitment approach could lead to long-term benefits for all international students and the institution.

Similarly, at some institutions, nondegree, fee-paying international students, sometimes referred to as "free-movers," may be served by the CPE unit, while the students enrolled through reciprocal exchange agreements may be supported by the IE unit. Thus, similar types of students may be categorized separately and have differing levels of access, support, and resources at an institution due to the fact that they are served by two distinct units.

As an example, in the California State University system, the traditional exchange students may pre-register for the courses they need, whereas the free-movers cannot register in advance, or they may have access to only limited courses until space becomes available. However, in a merged IE-CPE environment, some of these barriers can be lifted by having the same level of advising, student services, and visa processing services, as well as equal access to many of the same cocurricular activities. This unity provides better service and experiences to the students. Additionally, the management of the programs can be cohesively organized regardless of the status of the international student, thus reducing the amount of overlapping or duplicate work that must be performed by the staff.

Furthermore, at many institutions, CPE units manage the programs during the summer and winter terms, which is when many of the students have the time to partake in short-term education abroad programs. Thus, a merged IE-CPE unit that operates year-round could provide seamless service and constant resources to faculty and students participating in international programs.

A unified approach takes the university's strengths beyond the walls of the campus. As market needs are changing constantly, and globalization is blurring the borders between countries, the need for CPE programs designed for IE audiences is on the rise. The integrated IE-CPE model creates a partnership that can move internationalization efforts forward while ensuring the institution is capable of capitalizing on entrepreneurial opportunities.

Examples from the Field

More than half of the 23 campuses in the California State University (CSU) system have IE programs that are administratively and operationally combined with CPE units. In this model, the CPE dean is also the SIO, with a title of assistant/associate/vice president for global or international education. Although the organizational models vary from institution to institution, functional areas such as recruitment, education abroad, and institutional partnerships are managed similarly.

California State University-Long Beach (CSULB) merged its IE and CPE units in 2010. Prior to that, CSULB did not have clear strategies in place for international enrollment management. Other than case-by-case, one-time, and ad hoc funding, there was no regular source of funding to support the recruitment and retention of international students. The reorganization created much needed synergies that have resulted in growth of the international student presence and the establishment of several new and revenue-generating departments, such as the International Training Programs and the Study at the Beach Program. The newly merged unit allowed CSULB, for the first time, to view and serve all international students—matriculated students, English language students, and exchange students—collectively as part of the institution's vision of globalizing the campus.

Elsewhere in California, institutions within the University of California system have demonstrated great success in marketing certificate programs to international students. UCLA Extension, which is part of the University of California-Los Angeles's Division of Continuing Education, offers more than 40 F-1 visa approved programs lasting in duration from 9 to 12 months. These programs are attractive to international students seeking to advance or change their careers and include opportunities for practical training (University of California-Los Angeles UCLA Extension 2016).

Funding Model

As discussed earlier, many institutions in the United States and around the world are struggling to find new sources of revenue to fulfill their internationalization goals. A sustainable funding model is key to the success of such initiatives (Joshee, Leventhal, and Weller 2013, 1). A partnership between IE and CPE units that includes associated finances can ensure the long-term sustainability of programs and services, while also providing the fiscal flexibility to engage in new entrepreneurial activities.

Most CPE programs, especially at state institutions, are self-funded, and their only revenue source is from the tuition and fees charged to their students. No appropriations are made for these programs from the central or general fund. For IE programs, public universities often charge international students out-of-state tuition and additional international student fees, which means they usually pay a higher rate than any other population. In this regard, IE is also a self-funded program. The difference is that, unlike the CPE revenue, the IE revenue, in most cases, goes to the central pool and the IE unit eventually reaches a plateau in terms of program growth. However, with a merged IE-CPE unit, the pooled funding would be used for services and activities for all international students and, for those institutions that use the performance-based funding model (PBF), reinvested back into the unit.

The PBF is a sustainable funding model based on meeting clear performance metrics. In the PBF model, a portion of all new revenue from the first year's tuition, generated by increased international student enrollment, is set aside to directly support IE programs. While at many institutions, CPE's existing infrastructure will help cover certain aspects of IE operations, the PBF allocation allows for necessary staffing, coordinated recruitment efforts, and scalable support services. The funds are also used to advance other comprehensive internationalization initiatives, including scholarships for education abroad, seed funding for international research, and faculty incentives for incorporating global learning outcomes into the curriculum. Because the model is based on performance and the funds come from a portion of the tuition paid by new international students, the model costs nothing to the institution. Rather, it promotes a nimble and entrepreneurial business environment that actually grows revenue in ways otherwise not possible.

What portion of the new revenue is to be set aside is determined by the institution, depending on the circumstances, commitment, and priorities involved. While the concept is simple, it can be difficult to implement due to institutional policies, practices, and politics. Although a growing number of institutions already employ similar business models to support their partnerships with external entities, such as recruitment agencies and pathway providers, fewer seem willing to reinvest into their own IE programs. (For more examples of innovative budgeting and financial models, see chapter 6.)

Conclusion

Senior leadership must be in agreement regarding any major organizational change, such as partial or total integration of IE and CPE units. Furthermore, the leadership must clearly communicate the rationale for this change to all stakeholders, including faculty, staff, students, and external partners. The individual or team charged with leading this integrated unit must possess a range of skills, including fiscal accountability, entrepreneurship, knowledge of global issues and socioeconomic implications, programmatic vision, and strategic leadership. Under effective leadership, the IE-CPE model is more likely to succeed because goals, objectives, priorities, and roles are clearly delineated and understood. The basis of such a structural change cannot be solely about expanding the revenue stream, but instead should center on how the integrated model best supports the institutional mission and its priorities for external engagement.

Additional Resources

Alfred, Mary V., and Shibao Guo. 2007. "Globalization and the Internationalization of Adult and Higher Education: Challenges and Opportunities for Canada and the United States." 2017 Adult Education

Research Conference, Halifax, Nova Scotia, Canada. https://newprairiepress. org/aerc/2007/papers/1.

Di Maria, David L. 2018. "How to Make International Learning Opportunities More Accessible to Non-Traditional Learners." *The EvoLLLution.* May 3, 2018. https://evolllution.com/revenue-streams/global_learning/ how-to-make-international-learning-opportunities-more-accessible-to-non-traditional-learners/.

Grants.gov. 2019. "Grants.gov." https://www.grants.gov/.

Horn, Michael B. 2016. "Why Continuing Education Programs Are Poised to Become Hubs of Innovation." *EdSurge.* August 20, 2016. https://www.edsurge. com/news/2016-08-30-why-continuing-education-programs-are-poised-to-become-hubs-of-innovation.

Leventhal, Mitch. 2011. "US: New Funding Models for International Education." *University World News.* February 13, 2011. https://www.universityworldnews. com/post.php?story=20110211204106430.

U.S. Department of Commerce. 2019. "Trade Leads." Washington, DC: U.S. Department of Commerce. https://www.export.gov/Trade-Leads.

References

de Berly, Geraldine. 2015. "Continuing, Professional, and International Education: Converging Skill Sets." In *Centennial Conversations: Essential Essays in Professional, Continuing, and Online Education,* eds. Daniel W. Shannon and Robert Wiltenburg. Washington, DC: University Professional and Continuing Education Association. https://upcea.edu/wp-content/uploads/2017/09/ Centennial-Conversations-Essential-Essays-in-Professional-Continuing-and-Online-Education.pdf.

Institute of International Education. 2018. "Profile of U.S. Study Abroad Students, 2005/06-2016/17." *Open Doors Report on International Educational Exchange.* New York, NY: Institute of International Education. https://www. iie.org/en/Research-and-Insights/Open-Doors/Data/US-Study-Abroad/ Student-Profile.

Joshee, Jeet, Mitch Leventhal, and Jonathan Weller. 2013. "Closing the Loop: Funding Comprehensive Internationalization Through Inbound Recruitment – A Performance-Based Reinvestment Model." Presented at the American International Recruitment Council Annual Conference, Miami, FL.

Kwai, C. K. 2017. "The SIO Profile: A Preliminary Analysis of the Survey on Senior International Officers, Their Institutions and Offices." Durham, NC:

Association of International Education Administrators. https://www.aieaworld.org/assets/docs/Surveys/final-2017%20executive%20summary_sio%20profile%20survey.pdf.

University of California-Los Angeles UCLA Extension. 2016. "Certificate Programs for International Students." Los Angeles, CA: University of California-Los Angeles UCLA Extension. http://international.uclaextension.edu/certs/.

University Professional and Continuing Education Association (UPCEA). n.d. *UPCEA Hallmarks of Excellence in Professional and Continuing Education.* Washington, DC: University Professional and Continuing Education Association. https://upcea.edu/resources/hallmarks/.

14 | International Research: A Community of Practice and a Culture of Success

Kiki Caruson and Roger Brindley

Today's grand societal challenges will not be solved by one discipline or one single researcher. Complex issues such as mitigating the effects of climate change, managing dwindling natural resources, establishing healthier communities, ending poverty, and reducing geopolitical tensions all require diverse perspectives and approaches through the collaboration of researchers and practitioners from across the globe. Solutions to society's most vexing concerns require a vibrant international research ecosystem—and the role of universities in this ecosystem is critical.

> Universities are hubs for discovery, building new knowledge, and changing our understanding of the world. The public values the role universities play in education; yet as a sector, universities are less effective at highlighting their roles as the catalysts of new industries, homes for the fundamental science that leads to new treatments and products, or sources of the evidence on which policy decisions should be made. (Popowitz and Dorgelo 2018, iii)

This chapter examines the crucial role that senior international officers (SIOs) must play in articulating the importance of global engagement and the impact of higher education in globalized knowledge discovery, innovation, dissemination, and implementation. Scholarly inquiry is not only central to the mission of research universities, it should also be at the core of the institution's internationalization strategy.

Institutional Support

Ideally, international research engagement should be clearly articulated in an institution's mission and vision statements. The strategic plan should identify methods for achieving campus-wide goals associated with enhancing the international profile. Just as the goals of internationalization should pervade the campus organization, globalized research priorities should be embedded and cross-promoted at all levels of the university. This is significant not only for building a robust and productive global research portfolio, but also for increasing the public's awareness of the vital role that institutions of higher education play in the stimulation of scientific innovation.

The attention and support of the president or chancellor is imperative and sends a message to the entire university community about the importance and centrality of global research to the mission of the institution. The Association of Public and Land-grant Universities (APLU)'s Commission on International Initiatives asserts that "Presidents are positioned to ensure that the global dimension be 'intimately woven' into every aspect of the university's mission" and that if U.S. "universities aspire to ensure the continued primacy of their institutions on the world stage, presidents and chancellors must now double down on their global commitment" (APLU 2017, 29). But, to attract the attention of senior leaders and stakeholders, SIOs must be able to clearly demonstrate how internationally funded projects and globally engaged research contributes to the institution's larger research enterprise, to its reputation and prestige, and to student success.

Other key stakeholders that SIOs must engage include college/university trustees, governing boards, provosts, vice presidents, and deans. Their commitment empowers constituent organizations on campus that are represented by faculty, staff, and students, as well as the broader university community, including industry, government, and nongovernmental organization partners. It is essential that SIOs have the skill sets to work on behalf of and across this complex landscape.

Campus Connections

SIOs have a unique role to play as advocates for international research endeavors. While research operations are often housed beyond the international office,

SIOs and vice presidents for research (VPRs), or their equivalents, must possess a shared awareness and appreciation for the mission of the research enterprise and the centrality of international collaborations in order for fruitful cooperation between campus units to occur. To set the stage, it is important to create opportunities for administrators and staff in the research office and international office to interact, form personal relationships, and identify ways for fostering connections between the two units. For example, staff in the research and international offices might develop a set of common strategic and planning goals around issues relevant to both units, such as enhancing researcher success; engaging students; identifying corporate sponsors; leveraging partnerships; and supporting innovation, creativity, and discovery more generally. There are several ways to bridge the divide between the research office and international office:

- Educate administrators and staff about the roles and responsibilities of both offices (host an annual retreat, if possible) and share a "points of contact" list.

- Create a position or unit dedicated to advancing international research engagement and share the costs and benefits of this unit.

- Situate a research administrator in the international office, or vice versa.

- Agree to shared responsibilities and jointly funded positions (e.g., export control or international risk and security management personnel).

- Establish a committee or workgroup dedicated to identifying ways to improve support services for international research.

- Cultivate an environment where communication between the two offices is routine by creating different opportunities for interaction (e.g., cross-representation on internal workgroups or committees) and developing a common working vocabulary.

- Identify opportunities for international partnerships that center on faculty and student research and work collaboratively to document outputs.

Promoting and sustaining international research projects and collaborations requires support from all corners of the campus—not just the research and international offices. Other entities such as colleges, departments, graduate studies, undergraduate research, advancement, and student affairs, among others, are critical to the success of institution-wide efforts. Figure 1 illustrates a number of units that play a part in fostering and sustaining global research efforts.

Figure 1. Possible Internal Stakeholders of a Global Research Ecosystem

Source: Holbrook and Caruson (2017). Reprinted with permission from USF World and the University of South Florida.

It is vital at any institution aspiring to achieve pervasive internationalization that these different offices and myriad stakeholders work together to engage in the global research ecosystem.

Case Study: University of South Florida

The University of South Florida (USF) is one such institution that strives to build strong connectivity between offices for the larger international research objective. USF World, the university's international unit, worked in partnership with USF Research & Innovation, the university's central research office, and the Office for Strategic Planning, Performance & Accountability to establish the USF Global Research Operations Workgroup (GROW). GROW is comprised of a diverse group of stakeholders (depicted in figure 1), whose mission it is to create a university-wide forum for the exchange of ideas and knowledge that serves to promote international research endeavors and improve the university's ability to support and sustain global projects. Units across the university have proven willing to invest in the training and recognition of staff members who expand their capacity regarding the development and management of international research projects.

A key project of GROW involves populating an online toolkit with materials, templates, and information dedicated specifically to the development and management of global research projects. Components of the toolkit address topics such as how to get started (e.g., information about proposal development specifically for international projects), where to find funding, how to manage the project start-up process, how to negotiate contracts and sub-awards, and advice on how to work across cultures and time zones. Another section of the toolkit is devoted to legal and compliance matters and includes information regarding export controls, legal and tax issues, risk management associated with intellectual property and the commercialization of ideas from international partnerships, and laws and reporting requirements associated with clinical trials and the use of human or animal subjects abroad. (For information on export controls and research ethics and compliance abroad, see chapter 17.) The development of a digital resource can be used as a vehicle for cooperation across units and as a service to researchers themselves.

> There are many digital toolkits that offer information, best practices, and approaches for managing the tasks associated with global research projects. Here are a few examples:
>
> - Heidelberg University (Germany): www.uni-heidelberg.de/research/international/heidelberg/
> - North Carolina State University's Office of Global Engagement Research Resources: global.ncsu.edu/research/resources/
> - University of California System's Global Operations: www.ucgo.org/
> - University of Pennsylvania's Global Support Services: global.upenn.edu/gss
> - University of Queensland (Australia): global-engagement.uq.edu.au/about/our-global-network
> - University of South Florida's Global Research Toolkit: www.lib.usf.edu/globalresearchtoolkit/

Value of International Research

For faculty members who are successfully involved in international collaboration, their contributions must be valued by the institution. International engagement must matter at the time when researchers are hired, annually evaluated, promoted and tenured, and rewarded as senior scholars. It is crucial to include language that values international engagement (including research) in promotion guidelines across the institution.

Opportunities for faculty to become engaged in global work must be communicated and encouraged. The work should be facilitated and strategically resourced for time, funding, and support services. The outcomes must then be evaluated and recognized in clear and tangible ways. There are a number of services, ranging in size and cost, that SIOs and VPRs can collaboratively offer to promote and support international research activities.

- Distribute a newsletter or digital resource identifying global funding opportunities by region or discipline, with deadlines and other relevant information. Disseminate materials about international research opportunities via merged (international and research) email lists and listservs. Cross-promote relevant faculty, staff, and student accomplishments through web content and social media.

- Hold proposal writing workshops led by a research development administrator or a faculty member. The research and international offices can jointly offer a series of workshops for faculty or students that target different international opportunities. For example, the European Union's Horizon 2020 Marie Skłodowska-Curie actions provide grants for researchers at all stages of their career and are an excellent avenue for promoting international mobility among researchers of all disciplines.

- Provide access to international country and city guides and cultural advice, international travel and security risk mitigation services, and information on emergency and evacuation insurance for international business travelers.

- Establish internal funding opportunities supported by both the research and international offices that promote global research mobility, outbound and inbound. Seed-grant programs allow faculty and students to conduct pilot studies that affirm international partnerships and set the stage for larger external awards. Staff from the research and international units can work collaboratively to review proposals and promote project success. The two offices can share the responsibility of assisting scholars with applications for prestigious international awards (e.g., Fulbright, Humboldt Research Award, Rome Prize, Kyoto Prize, Killam Prize, Gottfried Wilhelm Leibniz Prize, etc.). The pooling of resources can also be used to offer international sabbaticals for current researchers and as an added incentive for hiring new faculty whose work is globally focused.

- Launch an academy or institute dedicated to supporting a cohort of faculty members who are engaged in international research. Support these researchers by developing a global network and identifying and securing resources for their work, including guidance about how to "pitch" their scholarship to funding agencies and how to articulate their research endeavors through a global lens. An excellent success story is Michigan State University's Academy for Global Engagement (www.globalacademy.msu.edu/). (For more on the Academy for Global Engagement, see chapter 15.)

- Invite international funding agencies and organizations to speak at events open to faculty and students, or establish a Fulbright program adviser on campus or Scholar-in-Residence.

- Encourage faculty and students to participate in activities (e.g., meetings, lunches, site visits) with international delegations and institutional partners during their visits to campus. Urge faculty members who are considering inviting international visitors to campus to engage with the SIO and the international office.

- Cohost an annual research awards celebration that recognizes the achievements of faculty, students, departments, and colleges. These events can range from smaller, more frequent gatherings (e.g., networking opportunities for J-1 scholars or poster sessions for Fulbright recipients) to an annual special ceremony hosted by the president or chancellor.

All of these approaches serve to acknowledge and support the research efforts of faculty, students, staff, administrators, and university organizations. These contributions work toward the betterment of the globalized society.

Assessment of the Global Research Footprint

A common challenge that institutions of higher education face is how to strategically manage, document, and report international research engagement. Historically, universities often have not looked far beyond familiar ground, simply turning to the well-known or high-profile international researchers among their faculties, or cobbling together ad hoc information concerning global activities and engagement. Most colleges and universities lack a system for aggregating internal data and information from different campus units including human resources, travel, research, international, faculty reporting, and corporate relations. Valuable data can also be found in subscription abstract and citation indexing services regarding publications and other research outputs with international coauthors.

SIOs will want to choose data and metrics that make sense in the context of their mission and institution. Figure 2 presents a variety of metrics that SIOs might use to assess the impact of their international research portfolios.

Staff members in the international office have valuable expertise to share with staff in the research office on how to approach collecting data and assessing the value associated with international research engagement, including the contributions from international partnerships, researcher mobility, and global programs and degrees. Those in the research office are encouraged to discover how the work of the international office complements their own efforts

Figure 2. Metrics for Evaluating International Research and Productivity

Personnel:

- Number and percentage of faculty traveling internationally to (a) conduct research, and (b) present research at a conference, symposium, or other academic setting

- Number and percentage of graduate and undergraduate students traveling internationally to (a) conduct research, and (b) present research at a conference, symposium, or other academic setting

Grants and Contracts:

- Number and percentage of proposals (total and those with an international collaborator)

- Number and percentage of awards (total and those with an international collaborator)

- Number and percentage of awards from an international funding source and/or award value of projects with an overseas component

Research Expenditures:

- International research expenditures (total dollars and percentage of total)

Internationally Coauthored Publications and Citations:

- Number and percentages of internationally coauthored publications

- Number of citations

- Normalized citation impact (field-weighted citation impact)

- Number of publication downloads

Patents:

- Number and percentage of coinvented patent applications

- Number and percentage of coinvented patents issued

Prestigious Prizes:

- Number of awards and prizes that are included in Association of American Universities (AAU) or Top American Research Universities (TARU) metrics

- Number of high-caliber international awards and prizes

- Dollar value of international awards and prizes received

Partnerships:

- Number of active partnerships or agreements that include an international research collaboration or project

- Number of researchers to and from (outbound and inbound) the partner university for research projects

- Research outputs (e.g., presentations, publications, funded grants, creative endeavors) from the partnership to identify research opportunities, build interdisciplinary teams, and support researchers, locally and globally.

Every SIO can attest to the personal benefits gained from shared international travel, including an individual's ability to connect with diverse peoples and his or her appreciation for different approaches to common issues. The SIO can invite the VPR on an international trip for the purpose of partnership development, fundraising and advancement, networking, or to highlight the activities of students and researchers abroad. Together, they can use the travel opportunity to reach out to alumni living and working abroad who may be able to open new doors to corporate relationships or funding streams.

Conclusion

Leadership at research institutions that have dedicated strategic plans to enhance their global profile understand that such work requires an intentional approach and investment across campus and community stakeholders, led by empowered SIOs. Central to this premise is the need for staff in the SIO's and the VPR's offices to work together to build and extend bridges across the institution. SIOs must promote strategic planning that recognizes the services needed; identifies effective ways to incentivize and reward faculty, staff, and students; and structures the data collection to accurately measure and assess progress. This undoubtedly requires focused, outcome-oriented systems, and as these commitments become normalized across the campus, stakeholders will inevitably align these institutional values in their research endeavors. This authentic and enculturating approach is essential to institutions seeking to pervasively internationalize the research enterprise.

Additional Resources

Caruson, Kiki. 2018. *International Research Partnerships*. Washington, DC: NAFSA: Association of International Educators.

McInroy, Gordon R., Catherine A. Lichten, Becky Ioppolo, Sarah Parks, and Susan Guthrie. 2018. *International Movement and Science: A Survey of Researchers by the Together Science Can Campaign*. The Wellcome Trust — Together Science Can. https://www.rand.org/pubs/research_reports/RR2690.html.

National Science Board. 2018. "Research and Development: U.S. Trends and
International Comparisons." In *Science & Engineering Indicators 2018*.
Alexandria, VA: National Science Foundation National Center for Science
and Engineering Statistics. https://nsf.gov/statistics/2018/nsb20181/report/
sections/research-and-development-u-s-trends-and-international-comparisons/
cross-national-comparisons-of-r-d-performance.

National Science Foundation. n.d. "International Science and Engineering."
Alexandria, VA: National Science Foundation. https://www.nsf.gov/dir/index.
jsp?org=OISE.

West, Charlotte. 2018. "The Rise of International Research Collaboration."
International Educator XXVII, 6:30–37. http://www.nafsa.org/_/File/_/
ie_novdec18_research.pdf.

References

Association for Public and Land-grant Universities (APLU) Commission on
International Initiatives. 2017. *Pervasive Internationalization: A Call for
Renewed Leadership*. Washington, DC: Association for Public and Land-grant
Universities. http://www.aplu.org/library/pervasive-internationalization-a-call-
for-renewed-leadership/file.

Holbrook, Karen A., and Kiki Caruson. 2017. *Globalizing University Research:
Innovation, Collaboration, and Competition*. New York, NY: Institute of
International Education.

Popowitz, Michelle, and Cristin Dorgelo. 2018. *Report on University-Led Grand
Challenges*. Los Angeles, CA: University of California-Los Angeles.

15 | Faculty Development for International Research: Michigan State University Case Study

Mary Anne Walker

As institutions increasingly invest in international research, one of the most important factors they must consider is how to best strengthen the capacity of faculty in leading their global efforts. Worldwide research networks are developed through faculty-driven collaborations that become institutionalized over time with the strategic investment of resources to support their growth. The outcomes of these research collaborations contribute to solving the global challenges of today (e.g., biodiversity loss, epidemics), with secondary benefits of enhancing institutional reputations and advancing internationalization efforts.

To support such work, senior leaders, academic administrators, and senior international officers (SIOs) must provide the resources and structures in place to support their research faculty. These considerations include identifying needs in faculty hiring, securing access to tools and technology, creating incentives for internationalization activity, and then recognizing efforts through tenure and promotions (see chapter 14). Some colleges and universities have even established academies or institutions that function to provide professional development and support for faculty engaged in global research. This chapter examines a case study from Michigan State University (MSU) that demonstrates the broader impacts of such an academy and the strategies and lessons learned that can be used to develop similarly impactful programs at other institutions.

Global Engagement: Michigan State University

Michigan State University, a land-grant university, has an extensive history of global engagement, with the first international student arriving in the 1890s. Sixty years later, intentional faculty outreach and engagement in global programming began with MSU President John Hannah (1941–1969) and his vision of facilitating human and institutional capacity development programs at the University of Jos, located in central Nigeria. Since that time, the institutional culture of MSU has strengthened its support of global research efforts, evidenced by the fact that MSU has had two presidents who served as administrators for the United States Agency for International Development: John Hannah and Peter McPherson. With the university leadership embracing and promoting this focus on global research, many early and mid-career faculty joined MSU in pursuit of their own academic interests, while factoring in the reach of MSU's global connections.

The institution soon faced a number of new challenges: How can MSU support the next generation of academics for success in a global marketplace? What will these academics need in order to grow the global footprint through teaching, research, and service to local, state, national, and global communities? How can MSU recruit and retain the faculty talent needed to prepare graduates for future success and to address tomorrow's challenges? MSU's leaders recognized that they must take strategic steps to invest in the internationalization and capacity of their faculty and students. Resultingly, MSU leadership published a monograph extending the core values inherent in MSU's land-grant mission beyond the borders of the campus, state, and nation, thus embracing a "world grant" ideal (Michigan State University 2009). This institutional commitment helped open the door to the creation of MSU's Academy for Global Engagement.

While the terms "international research" and "global research" are sometimes used interchangeably, they actually represent different concepts. International research is "Research carried out across two or more countries, often with the purpose of comparing responses between them. This might be done in order to devise strategies that work well across both or all these cultures, or to suggest local adjustments to a global strategy" (The Association for Qualitative Research 2018). Global research is research carried out independent of national borders, often by multinational networks of researchers, with the purpose of exploring global challenges (e.g., climate change), phenomena (e.g., space exploration) and trends (e.g., technology).

For examples of broad research topics that lend themselves well to both international and global research, see the United Nations's (2015) Sustainable Development Goals.

Academy for Global Engagement

In 2014, the MSU College of Agriculture & Natural Resources and the College of Engineering partnered with International Studies and Programs to create the Academy for Global Engagement (AGE) Fellowship program, which is designed to support the cultivation of future leaders in global research. The MSU College of Agriculture & Natural Resources has led global research efforts over a rich 70-year history (Horn 1985), focusing on areas such as agriculture education, food security, and natural resource management, with long-standing investments in international extension practices. Together with the College of Engineering, a key driver of science, technology, engineering, and mathematics (STEM) research, and with support from the provost and academic administrators in International Studies and Programs, the AGE was launched.

The AGE was created to empower early and mid-career faculty with the tools and skills that would enhance their capabilities as lead principal investigators in overseas research efforts. Through the AGE, faculty gain a stronger appreciation of what it means to lead teams abroad, especially in dealing with issues related to diversity and inclusiveness, science communication, and the management of logistics (e.g., people, resources, and equipment) across borders. (For more information on managing the logistics of global operations, see chapter 17.) The AGE encourages faculty to tackle grand challenges through:

- Expanding global networks via mentoring to advance international research;

- Communicating science and research ideas to diverse audiences; and

- Mapping networks and enhancing global research partnerships.

AGE APPLICATION AND PROGRAM

The AGE application is open to all tenure-stream early and mid-career faculty. There are no course buyouts. Fellows must commit to 3 hours per month in sessions that span a calendar year. The AGE leaders guiding the curriculum are uniquely trained with years of experience in global and higher education development. With each cohort, the AGE assesses the fellows' progress and tailors the modules to meet their greatest needs. The AGE provides the fellows with access to research-related campus resources, including grant writers, preaward support, graphic designers, and guidelines for managing export control. A key feature of the program is that trainers are brought in to help the fellows "pitch," or more effectively and succinctly communicate, their science to different audiences. AGE participants learn how to form global research relationships, problem solve with partners, and view scholarship through global lenses.

Benchmarking outcomes for AGE fellows include:

- Enjoy a broader array of networks through connections with mentor relationships.

- More effectively communicate their science.

- Be proficient in connecting with program officers of key corporate, foundation, and government agencies.

- Better understand market intelligence of competitive funding awards.

- More effectively connect with global innovation programs.

- Successfully administer field-based global research programs.

- Access top graduate students and share them between laboratories with mentors.

- Have a greater understanding of university support systems than peers who were hired at the same time but did not participate in the AGE Fellowship program.

- Demonstrate a higher success rate of grant returns than peers hired at the same time who did not go through the program.

MSU's AGE fellows will come to lead and expand the university's global research programs, including institutional centers and institutes abroad for the duration of their careers at MSU.

Expanding Global Networking via Mentoring

The AGE pairs each fellow with a distinguished faculty mentor from an inter-disciplinary field, thus helping early and mid-career faculty access new networks, regions, and relationships. At the launch of the program, academic affairs staff introduce the faculty mentors, distribute mentoring toolkits, and provide a conceptual framework for best practices in mentoring. An honorarium is given to each mentor to support the fellow's training (e.g., materials, conference registrations for copresentions at global conferences, meetings over dinner, etc.).

Once the fellows are paired with their mentors, they develop a plan for the year ahead and are encouraged to meet monthly, at a minimum. Together, they create a mentoring plan and revisit that plan throughout the course of the fellowship year. As the mentor brings the fellow into his or her own networks, the fellow is better positioned for success. The fellows are often able to travel globally with their mentors and become more adept at building global research relationships and adopting a global lens. This kind of professional development training anchors important promotion and tenure benchmarks. Mentors and AGE staff help the fellows to remove and navigate through obstacles to their research output, counseling the fellows on how to eliminate distractions.

Throughout the year, monthly meetings provide the fellows with new insights from different experts. At one of the monthly meetings, a panel of University Distinguished Professors—a title awarded by the MSU Board of Trustees to faculty members who are nationally recognized for their teaching, public service, and scholarly achievements—describe their individual pathways through academia and share pitfalls to be avoided. Mentoring events such as these allow the fellows to practice their communication skills with colleagues that they most likely would not otherwise be able to engage at this stage in their careers.

Communicating Science to the Public

A key goal of the AGE program is to help early and mid-career faculty diversify their sources of funding support and broaden the impact of their research. To that end, faculty members must be able to articulate the importance of their science to program officers, funding agencies, international organizations, community leaders, and program stakeholders. The AGE provides opportunities for the fellows to strengthen that skill set. For example, AGE staff bring in leaders from the MSU campus, global industry, and the nongovernmental organization community to share their expertise at monthly meetings. The AGE also invites program officers from key industry sectors, foundations, U.S. federal agencies, and international organizations for a special campus convening, with panel sessions open to the entire campus. Additionally, the fellows increase the visibility of their research through communication and branding at three key events: a campus convening of program officers, the AGE Global Research Reception anchored amid 3 days of meetings with program officers, and the Global Innovation Forum, with invited networks of stakeholders from across the state of Michigan.

To prepare for these events, the fellows practice their two-minute science pitches in front of senior faculty members and their mentors, many of whom have served as program officers during their careers. The fellows continue to improve and practice their pitches as they reach out to new networks and receive feedback. Additionally, the AGE program works with the fellows to create a one-page summary of their research that highlights research problems, approaches, and expected impacts, applications, and solutions. This activity helps to prepare the fellows for their meetings and other networking events throughout the course of the fellowship year.

Mapping Networks and Partnerships

The growth of science is rooted in developing an understanding of gaps in knowledge, which helps investigators navigate institutional partnerships and historical relationships. With guidance from their mentors, the fellows are able to map their networks to determine where gaps in knowledge reside and what kinds of partnerships may be needed to competitively advance and secure research funding. The fellows determine early in the fellowship year where they would like to build collaborations and begin outreach for partnership planning. The AGE leaders facilitate these efforts by providing an overview that advises on where current institutional network connections exist and where relationships can be complemented.

Additionally, the MSU International Data Working Group brought together stakeholders from across campus to better organize data solutions that feed decisionmaking processes of faculty and administrators. The fellows are made aware of these supportive data tools to better manage the institutional resources available to support network development. This mapping includes partner universities, international organizations, corporations, existing research relationships, and mapped institutional faculty strengths and networks that nurture the global enterprise.

The fellows and mentors travel abroad over the summer to meet with potential research partners and then travel to Washington, D.C., in the fall to meet with federal, multilateral, and private sector funding organizations. The goal is that at the end of the fellowship year, the fellow and mentor pair have well-organized submissions that result in funded research programs.

Outcomes of the AGE

The program recently celebrated its fifth year of operation and the AGE leaders, in partnership with an MSU program evaluator, have identified metrics for key performance objectives. Some of the early metrics include:

- Benchmark the research performance and impact of AGE fellows from 2014 to 2017:

  - Compare research performance and influence (impact) of AGE fellows from 2014 to 2017.

  - Cluster AGE fellows based on h-index and identify "promising researchers."

- Profile AGE fellows from 2014 to 2017 by academic output career and 10-year productivity:

  - Identify trends in research performance and impact of AGE fellows.

  - Map grant activity over the past 5 years.

  - Map the research network of AGE cohorts.

- Analyze implications of funding and next steps.

Figure 1 demonstrates some of the overall metrics that have been tracked for the AGE cohorts from 2015 to 2017.

Figure 1. Metrics Tracked for the Academy of Global Engagement Cohorts, 2015–17

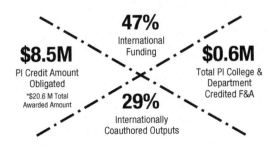

47%
International Funding

$8.5M
PI Credit Amount Obligated
*$20.6 M Total Awarded Amount

$0.6M
Total PI College & Department Credited F&A

29%
Internationally Coauthored Outputs

Source: Payumo (2017).

Figure 2. Research Performance and Academic Impact of AGE Cohorts, 2014–17

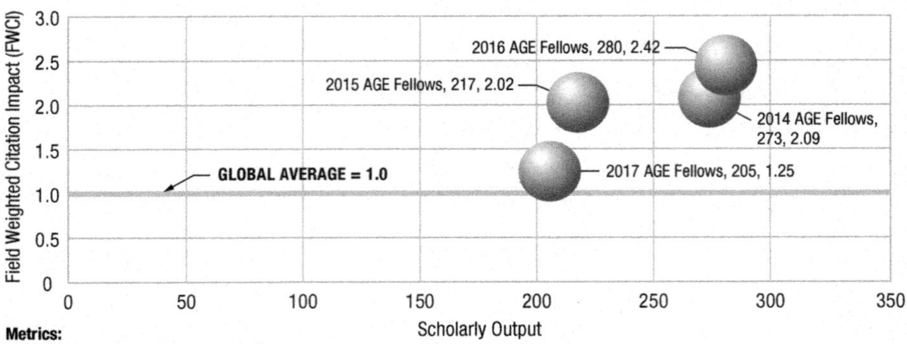

Metrics:
Scholarly output = research performance
FWCI = academic impact, global average = 1.0

Source: Payumo (2017). Based on SciVal data.

Increased Collaborations

The AGE program is producing more cross-disciplinary research as it evolves over time. The fellows are being introduced to mentors in new disciplines at an earlier stage in their career, thus complementing the existing mentoring they are receiving within their department. Through the AGE program, the fellows working between the College of Agriculture & Natural Resources and the College of Engineering are also beginning to find new areas of interest worth pursuing together. Some of the fellows share graduate students with the mentors, working between labs and bringing new innovations to the research. Figure 2 offers a visual representation of the academic impact of the AGE fellows cohorts from 2014 to 2017. AGE fellows have academic impact greater than the global average (1.0).

Many of the mentors are introducing the fellows to their own long-standing relationships with colleagues, partners, and professional organizations, helping to secure new awards for early and mid-career principal investigators more rapidly. The AGE mentor network also serves as a valuable recruitment tool for new graduate students in the fellows' labs.

Fellows' Contributions

The impact of the AGE curriculum on the fellows' professional success was initially tested to the first two cohorts (total of 19 fellows) of the five total. Findings from this impact assessment allowed the AGE leaders to retool the programming as needed and make it more relevant to the latest recruits. Early findings demonstrate that AGE fellows have successfully:

- Established new and diversified sources of funding support;

- Contributed to institutional growth in international funding (see figure 3);

- Recruited unique top students into their research programs;

- Become more competitive for global awards and competitions;

- Influenced the institution's global dialogue with partners;

- Created extensive networks and new partnerships in the research and learning process;

- Enhanced their abilities to communicate their science to wide audiences; and

- Elevated global awareness, which has impacted experiences, learning, and many other important contributions that enhance the global scholarship of teaching and learning.

Figure 3. Research Funding Received and Scholarly Output of Three AGE Cohorts After the Fellowship Program, 2015–17

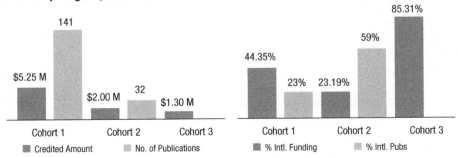

Source: Payumo (2017). Note: A study is ongoing to compare outputs of AGE faculty (participants) against a carefully assembled peer group of nonparticipant MSU researchers (control).

The positive impacts that the fellows have had on the institution and the field at large speaks to the multilayered structure of the AGE program. What began as an initiative to continue and cultivate MSU's endeavors in global research has accomplished its objective and more, especially with respect to interdisciplinary collaboration, which continues to grow in importance both domestically and globally.

Institutional Impact

The impact of the AGE on MSU's global footprint is profound. In the first 2 years alone, 19 fellows sought out 34 new partners, working together to leverage $20.6 million in research funding. These partnerships have had a significant influence on scholarship, student recruitment, and teaching and learning at MSU. Since the AGE program has been operational, the university and its faculty have received a number of National Science Foundation Faculty Early Career Development (CAREER) Awards and emerging scholar awards, and one fellow even received a prestigious U.S. Department of State Jefferson Science Fellowship, becoming the youngest person ever named to the program.

The AGE keeps the cohort size manageable by recruiting 10 fellows per year, five from the College of Agriculture & Natural Resources and five from the College of Engineering. However, by the fifth year of operation, the AGE added another fellow from the College of Natural Sciences and another fellow from The Axia Institute, one of the research centers and institutes of MSU's Eli Broad College of Business specializing in supply chain management. To date, AGE has trained 51 fellows at MSU.

The AGE program has served the institution by:

- Giving visibility to the university's global mission;

- Creating a heightened global awareness and discourse;

- Strengthening campus resources in international programming;

- Capitalizing on opportunities to leverage external resources and partnerships; and

- Serving as a force in developing global research project priorities and influencing high-level strategies to address them.

The AGE program facilitates connections and builds capacity to launch large-scale, high-impact, and high-reward research programs, providing the fellows with best practice training examples that lead to global problem-solving.

Future Directions

Based on the program's early success, AGE leaders are considering expanding access to the program so that tenure-track faculty from other schools and colleges can also apply. The leaders have even considered housing the program centrally in the faculty development unit, MSU's Academic Alliance Network, or International Studies and Programs. The AGE program is tailored to support international research, but key components of the program can benefit researchers focused on domestic issues as well.

Conclusion

The Academy for Global Engagement was conceived with the intention of strengthening the AGE fellows' abilities to work toward resolving global grand challenges on behalf of the university in the future (Hudzik 2015). The dual-impact issue of supporting global researchers and providing training and development for faculty is a priority for SIOs and senior leaders around the world. Implementing similar programs at other institutions ensures a new generation of research leaders—as the fellows turn into future mentors—who are better prepared and able to address international and global challenges through innovation, collaboration, and cross-cultural exchanges.

The Academy for Global Engagement is led and supported by a team of experts that have contributed to the program's success. I would like to acknowledge and thank: Gretchen Neisler, PhD, John Medendorp, PhD, Sara Tauqi, Jonathan Wakeman, John Bonnell, PhD, Andrew Gerard, Abby Rubley, Catherine Cunningham, Michelle Mclain, Jane Payumo, PhD, Brenna Lashbrook, Sean Lawrie, Janet Fierro, Francie Todd, Patricia Mroczek, Kathy Deshiri, Wendy Baker, Taryn Racine, John Verboncoeur, PhD, George Smith, PhD, DeAndra Beck, PhD, the International Data Working Group, the Division of Engineering Research Team, and MSU Advancement Offices.

Additional Resources

Caruson, Kiki. 2018. *International Research Partnerships*. Washington, DC: NAFSA: Association of International Educators.

Riemschneider, Bea, Science Editorial Director. 2018. *2018 Global R&D Funding Forecast. R&D Magazine*, Winter 2018.

References

Horn, Nancy E. 1985. *A Project History of Michigan State University's Participation in International Development: 1951–1985*. East Lansing, MI: Michigan State University.

Hudzik, John K., ed. 2015. *Comprehensive Internationalization: Institutional Pathways to Success*. Abingdon, Oxon, United Kingdom: Routledge.

Michigan State University. 2009. *Embracing the World Grant Ideal: Affirming the Morrill Act for a Twenty-First-Century Global Society*. East Lansing, MI: Michigan State University. http://worldgrantideal.msu.edu/.

Payumo, Jane G. 2017. "Experts Profile: Academy of Global Engagement Fellows." East Lansing, MI: Michigan State University.

United Nations. 2015. "Sustainable Development Goals." United Nations. https://www.un.org/sustainabledevelopment/sustainable-development-goals/.

PART 4

Partnerships and Outreach

16 | Strategic International Partnerships

Paulo Zagalo-Melo

International partnerships are extremely important for higher education institutions. A strategic focus in this area is a necessary response to some of the complicated issues affecting the world, including restrictions in immigration policies, instability in diplomatic relations, and the emphasis on coordinating networks of researchers around global challenges. Given the ever-changing geopolitical climate, investments in building individual and institutional international relationships will continue to be a fundamental part of strategic internationalization: "The forces now impelling internationalization have dialogue and collaboration at their core. This realization moves the exchanges and partnerships in which our institutions have long engaged to the center of any internationalization strategy" (Sutton 2010, 10). International partnerships can help to advance various institutional goals, ranging from enrollment to research to high-impact learning.

This chapter explores several topics that are fundamental to the development of strategic international partnerships. It examines institutional relationships and how these might evolve, incidentally or intentionally, into official partnerships, agreements, and contracts. The chapter explores key motivations for these partnerships and the multiple stakeholders, including senior international officers (SIOs), involved. It concludes by underlining the importance of benchmarking and assessment in the context of strategizing about international partnerships.

Structure of Relationships and Agreements

Historically, institutional partnerships developed to multiply and solidify personal relationships between faculty, administrators, students, and staff from different institutions, often through a collection of memoranda of understanding (MOUs). The sheer number of partnerships that an institution held, regardless of their actual level of activity, was once considered the primary indicator of internationalization efforts.

Today, however, the focus is centered on strategic, productive, and sustainable partnerships. Nevertheless, there seems to be a lack of consensus on what "strategic international partnership" means across higher education institutions (HEIs) around the world. For many HEIs, the word "strategic" implies that something aligns with and ultimately contributes to fulfilling the HEI's mission and goals, and "international strategic partnerships" help to advance the international dimensions of the institution's mission and goals. SIOs can help to shape international strategic partnerships by offering guidance on the scopes and aims of the different relationships in which institutions engage.

Relationships, Partnerships, Agreements, and Contracts

Strategic partnerships offer individuals and institutions the opportunity to achieve more by working together than they can achieve independently. Strategic partnerships often involve several levels of formality and commitment due to the expenditure of resources, time, and operational capacities. These levels of formality and commitment can be addressed under two typologies: (a) a division between relationships and partnerships, and (b) the differences between contracts and agreements.

Relationships and Partnerships

Understanding the distinction between informal and formal relationships is essential. Not all international relationships are partnerships, and not all partnerships are productive sources of collaboration. For instance, faculty in the department of physics may have ongoing collaborations in China without the existence of an MOU, agreement, or contract. This type of informal partnership might happen to be one of the most productive international relationships of an institution. Nevertheless, at some point, this relationship will likely require an increased level of formality for it to be continuously beneficial to the faculty and the institution. Having a formal agreement enables collaborators within the partnership to maximize the outcomes of the relationship, such as securing external funding or formalizing export control.

If an informal collaboration is working and generating the expected outcomes, it might be best not to change the nature of the relationship. However, if an agreement or contract is needed, it is the role of staff in the international office, in collaboration with other relevant units (e.g., research office, grants and contracts, legal counsel), to develop the framework to sustain an already productive partnership. The SIO should be familiar with the various forms of agreements available and select the appropriate type of agreement to nurture new partnerships or solidify existing ones (see Hoseth and Thampapillai 2018). In order to work strategically, the SIO must be informed of the origins of the relationship, keep abreast of its developments, and consider the appropriate level of formality needed with respect to the objectives and potential. These actions require discretion, perception, and purposefulness.

The SIO should collect information regarding the genesis and status of the relationship from those involved. The assessment of the relationship should include an evaluation of the initial goals, the potential for development, and the impact of a higher level of formality. During this phase, it is also important to acknowledge potential negative effects that may result from expanding the partnership. If the assessment demonstrates that it is in fact beneficial to formalize the relationship, further conversations and negotiations with present and prospective parties involved are necessary to ensure a collaborative plan is outlined through an agreement or contract.

Agreements and Contracts

The difference between agreements and contracts is a core topic of legal scholarship. An agreement results from the parties' willingness to do or not do something specific. A contract is a formal "agreement to do or not to do a specific thing" (Lewinsohn 1914, 172). The difference between agreements and contracts is "that a contract is a legally enforcible [sic] agreement" (Lewinsohn 1914, 172).

In an international education context, an agreement usually aims to prompt an institutional collaboration between the parties that has a focus (e.g., research, student or faculty exchanges) but little specificity in the outcomes of the collaboration. The MOU is the ultimate example of an agreement that has a largely undefined scope and vague goals for collaboration. Experience has shown the limited impact of largely undefined MOUs; hence, many SIOs now request greater levels of specificity in initial MOUs. When a certain level of collaboration is reached by partner institutions, there might be enough intentionality and specificity to require a contract to bind the parties to the intended processes and outcomes. The SIO can be valuable in this situation by working closely with the institution's legal counsel when a contract is required.

Legal Considerations and Export Control

International partnerships that involve sharing data and information on sensitive topics, such as defense, cybersecurity, and nuclear physics, entail undisputable concerns that can result in legal and security issues. Controlling the export of data usually includes the collaborative work of staff in the international office, the research office, and legal counsel. The SIO's leadership is important in ensuring that concerns are addressed and formalized in the contract, while confirming that the partnership's listed goals and outcomes are both realistic and achievable. All of the legal considerations around the export of data must be written into the partnership contract and reviewed and approved by both HEIs.

Strategic Reasons for Partnerships

International partnerships can be useful to HEIs in a variety of ways and for numerous reasons. These partnerships can facilitate the acquisition, expansion, and deepening of research opportunities, cross-cultural competence, education and internship abroad programs, and student, staff, and faculty exchanges (for more, see Gatewood forthcoming). Different units within a HEI may approach international partnerships for different reasons. By understanding and communicating the desired outcomes, the SIO can better establish the parameters of the partnership contract.

Complementary Strengths

Universities often choose to partner with institutions that have complementary academic or research strengths. For example, one university might be trying to build capacity for a clinical psychology and mental health program and needs trained faculty in that area. A good potential partner would be a university with a strong program in teaching, learning, and curriculum development and in clinical psychology with students seeking training and research opportunities. Such a partnership allows each institution to maximize its strengths without having to invest significant resources.

Resources

Partnerships can provide access to key resources. For example, ecology majors at one institution could be given the opportunity to participate in the partner institution's field research program in the Amazon jungle, which could result in research findings that impact the larger ecosystem. Similarly, faculty at the other institution may benefit from access to specialized equipment owned and maintained by the partner institution. Partnerships can open the doors to new and different resources and opportunities so that they are mutually beneficial to all parties.

New Collaborations

Partnerships can be between HEIs, but can also include relationships with international corporations, governments, nongovernmental organizations, primary schools, vocational schools, community colleges, business incubators, and technology and innovation research parks. (For more on community and government partnerships, see chapter 18.) Partnering with other types of organizations is important to HEIs because it expands the breadth and depth of knowledge, which can lead to the collaborative growth and success of the two entities.

Furthermore, partnerships are not necessarily "one-on-one" or bilateral; multilateralism can be conducive to synergy and expand the common or complementary ground upon which the partnership is built, thus increasing its potential for generating the expected outcomes. Connecting three or more institutions and organizations around the same objective can be advantageous because efforts are not being duplicated; in fact, such partnerships can sometimes be the only way to achieve a certain goal, such as examining a global phenomenon. When new and/or multiple partners are involved, the number of invested stakeholders likely expands as well, requiring some coordination among the SIO and staff in the SIO's and international offices.

Stakeholders

Developing and sustaining international partnerships require the motivation and effort of all participants involved in delivering the components and meeting the goals. For example, students need to be motivated to embark on an education abroad program for a specific purpose and in a specific location; faculty need to be willing to collaborate on research with their peers abroad; and administrators should understand the reasons for investing resources in any specific partnership. Buy-in from students, faculty, staff, administrators, alumni, and even local community members is essential to effectively managing international partnerships. SIOs can help to secure the necessary endorsement of the involved parties by sharing relevant information, particularly in regard to potential benefits to individuals, units, and the institution at large.

The key stakeholders for partnerships typically include faculty and students because they are the main beneficiaries of the outcomes. It is important to have representation from academic units and student organizations in the processes necessary to approve, reapprove, or end partnerships. Administrators and staff from relevant units can provide first-level recommendations that can save time and increase efficiency during these processes. For example, legal counsel representatives can provide immediate assistance in identifying potential contractual liabilities and gaps in compliance.

It can be helpful to establish a committee or formal group of stakeholders who can look at these international partnership processes. Shared responsibility in decisionmaking often results in shared support and assistance in promoting new partnerships, reviving existing partnerships, and explaining why some partnerships should be discontinued. In the end, international partnerships are created to serve the needs of specific stakeholders at home and abroad.

Partnerships that do not align with the needs and interests of the target group of stakeholders are neither strategic nor likely to be successful. However, SIOs can work with the stakeholders from the planning stages to make sure that their outcomes goals are represented and achievable through the partnerships.

Diplomacy and Protocol

It is not uncommon to hear higher education professionals refer to the SIO as the institution's "ambassador," or refer to the SIO's role as asserting academic or cultural diplomacy, which is especially relevant for partnerships. It is important for SIOs and their teams to be aware of and respect cultural differences when hosting representatives from international HEIs. Determining who to include in various meetings and their respective roles, seating arrangements, topics and the flow of conversation, exchanges of gifts, dietary restrictions, decorations, photography, and the type of document needed to substantiate an international partnership are a few examples of situations that require cross-cultural communication skills, sensitivity, and discretion.

SIOs can gather relevant information prior to meeting with international delegates—whether those meetings occur at home or abroad—and brief all representatives from the home institution who will participate in the meeting. Such briefings may include discussions of cultural norms (e.g., etiquette), sensitive topics to avoid, biographies of the delegates, roles of each representative, specific objectives for the meeting, and an overview of any prior interactions between the representatives. Unfortunately, it does not take much to set back or completely derail months of planning, so careful selection and preparation of institutional representatives is essential. SIOs can often be expected to set the example for other colleagues during these diplomatic meetings.

Benchmarking and Assessment

With the support and involvement of the key stakeholders, including the SIO, it is important to consider how the institution can set standards to seek, develop, and implement strategic international partnerships. Analyzing data, trends, and insights from peer institutions to inform the development of benchmarks and standards can be valuable and contribute to success in internationalization (Bjorklund 2018). What are other HEIs doing in terms of partnership development? Which institutions should be emulated? Where should the institution be in 5 or 10 years? Who are the international education professionals that have been recognized by their peers, and what are they doing?

Even after a strategic international partnership is established, whether it is guided by specific selection criteria or not, it is not necessarily "eternal," nor is its impact constant or even always positive. After each cycle—typically, agreements are signed for 3 to 5 years—partnerships should be reevaluated. It is important to assess the outcomes and see if all of the assets identified before entering that partnership are still valid. Another relevant question to pose at that time is whether the partnership has reached its maximum potential and is no longer needed.

There may be reasons to end an institutional partnership, for example, export control issues that led to liability problems or legal disputes, or one party stopped meeting contractual financial requirements. Early termination of a partnership requires careful diplomatic and legal considerations. It also requires engagement with key institutional stakeholders who may have developed ties to the partnership. Thus, it is important to negotiate the termination conditions and procedures with all parties involved prior to signing a formal agreement. What can be done to compensate for any losses? What efforts can be made to leave a positive view of the reasons why one or more parties discontinued the partnership? In the latter case, it is essential to build a clear narrative and a communication strategy to ensure that all relevant parties are aware of the reasons for the partnership's end. Honesty and transparency are the best policies in any relationship, especially when investments in time, energy, and resources are involved.

Conclusion

Every partnership can be important to an institution; however, not all will be strategically important, nor will they be equally important. Generally, a partnership is strategic if its objectives and outcomes are aligned with, or significantly contribute to, the strategic goals and mission of the institution.

Partnerships can be helpful to HEIs in advancing their goals in many areas, from research to student success. Partnering internationally can complement an institution's strengths and overcome its limitations by multiplying resources. It is important for SIOs to assess priorities, goals, and outcomes and exercise leadership in steering partnership development.

Additional Resources

Caruson, Kiki. 2018. *International Research Partnerships*. Washington, DC: NAFSA: Association of International Educators.

Hoseth, Chad, and Shehan Thampapillai. 2018. *International Partnership Dynamics and Types*. Washington, DC: NAFSA: Association of International Educators.

Lehigh University. 2018. "Initiating and Evaluating International Partnerships." Bethlehem, PA: Lehigh University. https://global.lehigh.edu/gpsi/initiating-evaluating-partnerships.

McGill, Patti. 2014. "Diplomacy and Education: A Changing Global Landscape." *International Higher Education* 75. https://ejournals.bc.edu/ojs/index.php/ihe/article/view/5410.

Rogers, Jenny. 2017. "The New Why of Partnerships: International Partnerships Are Expanding Their Reach and Goals." *International Educator* XXVI, 6:16–21.

Trivedi, Kalpen. 2018. *Educational Mobility Partnerships*. Washington, DC: NAFSA: Association of International Educators.

References

Bjorklund, Nancy. 2018. "Standards as Drivers of Internationalization." Doctoral dissertation, Los Angeles, CA: University of Southern California.

Gatewood, Jane, ed. Forthcoming. *NAFSA's Guide to International Partnerships: Developing Sustainable Academic Collaborations*. Washington, DC: NAFSA: Association of International Educators.

Lewinsohn, Joseph L. 1914. "Contract Distinguished from Quasi Contract." *California Law Review* 2, 3:171–190.

Sutton, Susan Buck. 2010. "Transforming Internationalization Through Partnerships." *International Educator* XIX, 1:60–66.

17 Global Operations

Dragana Nikolajevic and David L. Di Maria

The shifting landscape of global expenditures on research and development (National Science Board 2018) and the ways in which transnational challenges are studied and addressed have contributed to a steady increase in international research collaborations. Meanwhile, students' interest in international experiences, especially in global health studies and projects (Merson 2014), has resulted in a significant rise in education abroad programs. Global operations, a term that comprises these and other international activities (e.g., branch offices, dual-degree programs, faculty exchanges), often require institutions to evaluate risk considerations and ensure compliance with complex U.S. and foreign country regulations as well as university policies. Senior international officers (SIOs) are often responsible for managing their university's global operations and find that their work cuts across all divisions of the institution, from academic affairs to finance and administration to research and economic development.

This chapter gives an overview of several legal and logistical areas of consideration that SIOs and their institutions must manage, implement, and assess related to international activities. It maps the functions involved in supporting global operations and identifies opportunities for collaboration between SIOs and various administrative units to make sure that initiatives are executed effectively and responsibly.

Global Operations

Many university leaders recognize the importance of internationalization; have internationalization strategies, policies, and expertise in place; and have invested sufficient funds toward the support of their international activities. However, SIOs at some universities, especially those controlled by the state, still struggle to justify the importance of internationalization to their legislators, and, sometimes, even to their senior leadership. Global operations, unfortunately, are often in the limelight only as a result of financial, legal, or reputational losses resulting from noncompliance, inadequately assessed and managed risks, the introduction of new foreign regulations (e.g., the European Union's General Data Protection Regulation [GDPR]), or the U.S. government's attention to issues affecting national security or economic interests, such as foreign influence on U.S. universities and academic espionage. SIOs who have both the knowledge and authority to effectively manage global operations can help institutions to prepare for and address these challenges before they derail international projects and nullify institutional internationalization strategies.

Considerations of Global Operations

While some universities have created stand-alone offices to support global operations, many others rely on some form of a "functional team," made up of the SIO and staff members working in key administrative units such as human resources, legal counsel, global affairs, risk management, and research compliance. Many of the issues and risks inherent in international activities— particularly research projects that include clinical trials, technical assistance, and education and training—that are addressed and supported by these team members fall into the following categories:

- Agreements, contracts, and procurement;

- Project management;

- Legal presence abroad;

- Labor issues;

- Banking and finance;

- Research ethics and compliance; and

- Travel, health, and safety.

To ensure that each risk area of global operations is approached in a manner that is legally and institutionally compliant, SIOs and their teams must establish policies and procedures that are consistently communicated and executed.

Agreements, Contracts, and Procurement

It is standard practice for SIOs to play a leading role in the development and execution of memoranda of understanding, agreements, and contracts when there is an international partner involved. However, SIOs are not often closely involved in the procurement of services abroad for specific research projects, agreements for the use of facilities leased overseas, or even contracts with third parties when the activities do not fit within standard international education programs and services. This can be problematic because the faculty, administrators, and, sometimes, even the attorneys working on these projects are typically not thinking first and foremost about the potential international implications, such as cultural and legal differences between the home country and the country in which the partner is based or the goods and services are to be accessed. Common concerns include:

- Governing law. Which country's laws apply to the contract? Do all parties have the freedom to agree upon a governing law, or do the laws of the country in which the activities are conducted take precedence?

- Dispute resolution. Where, when, and how will disagreements be managed? Will arbitration, litigation, or mediation best serve the needs of the university from the perspective of enforceability of legal ruling in case of a dispute? Approaches to conflict resolution vary from country to country, from both legal and cultural standpoints, so it is important to consider the pros and cons of all dispute resolution mechanisms available.

- Jurisdiction. In which country will contract disputes be litigated and laws enforced? Do all parties have the freedom to agree upon jurisdiction, or does one country refuse that freedom due to issues of national or state sovereignty?

- Confidentiality. Do the laws in either country require the terms of the agreement or contract to be open or available to the public? Public colleges and universities in the United States are often subject to "sunshine laws" that may conflict with partners' expectations for confidentiality.

- Data privacy. Are both parties capable of complying with applicable data privacy regulations, such as the European Union's GDPR and the Family Educational Rights and Privacy Act (FERPA) in the United States?

- Intellectual property. What measures are in place to protect trademarks, patents, and other forms of intellectual property? For instance, do all countries adhere to international treaties and conventions, such as the Berne Convention for the Protection of Literary and Artistic Works and The Agreement on Trade-Related Aspects of Intellectual Property Rights (TRIPS)? Are all countries sufficiently committed to protecting intellectual property rights? While SIOs can use the Global Innovation Policy Center's (2018) U.S. Chamber International IP Index and the World Bank's (2018) Rankings & Ease of Doing Business Score to assess potential risks, it is important that they communicate any real concerns to their institution's technology transfer office and legal counsel prior to signing any agreement that includes intellectual property clauses.

- Agreement language and translations. What is the governing language of the agreement? Is it English, the primary language of the international partner, or bilingual? Must translations of the contract be performed by a certified translation professional, or can someone with the expertise in the exact areas of concern covered by the agreement be consulted for the accuracy of the translation? Who pays for this service? If the contract is translated to another language, does the translated version carry the same legal force as the original?

To reduce the risk of unfavorable terms entering the final partnership agreement for a global operation, it is very important for SIOs to consult with qualified internal or external legal counsel during the agreement negotiation process, and, in some cases, it may be necessary to consult with in-country legal counsel as well. On the other hand, SIOs may already know of in-country legal counsel or have contacts at a partner institution who can assist the university's legal counsel in reviewing agreements, contracts, and other legal documents where there is no conflict of interest to do so. (For more information on international partnership agreements and contracts, see chapter 16.)

Project Management

At some point during the lifespan of an international project, various academic and administrative units will need to get involved to ensure the project is a success. Such offices may include the office of research compliance, sponsored programs, procurement, finance, tax compliance, legal counsel, risk management, and information technology. While each of these units is staffed with subject matter experts who are able to explain the key considerations unique to their professional domain, it is unlikely that any one individual will be sufficiently knowledgeable about the other units to see the big picture. Moreover, some of these experts may not fully comprehend the international dimensions of the work.

Thus, international projects require special attention and specific expertise that not all of these offices are equipped to provide. Individual staff members in these offices are regularly dealing with the details of international projects, but often without proper training on the idiosyncrasies of conducting university business abroad. An SIO's unique focus on international and global engagement can help connect the dots to contribute to a more strategic understanding and treatment of international projects. Thus, the SIO does not need to be a subject matter expert in all of the administrative areas previously listed, but he or she should be knowledgeable about current and anticipated international projects, causes of concern (e.g., export control), and whom to consult when questions arise. Additionally, the SIO must be able to assist subject matter experts connect with resources related to global operations.

Legal Presence Abroad

Academic programs, projects, and activities abroad vary greatly in terms of scope, location, and duration. These may range from a single visit for an international conference to a multiyear engagement requiring staff, vendors, space, and equipment. While the rationale and modality for structuring a university's operations abroad must always be evaluated on a case-by-case basis, there are two basic questions that must first be considered: (1) How will the structure advance the university's agenda? (2) What is the "business" threshold in that country that would require legal registration? Answering the first question often requires the SIO to closely consult with internal stakeholders across the institution. For the second question, given that activities abroad are subject to laws and regulations of the host country, the SIO may have to seek out answers from qualified legal counsel knowledgeable in the laws of the host country.

Compliance with the U.S. Foreign Corrupt Practice Act (FCPA) is especially important for the SIO to bear in mind when going through the process of registering an office in another country. While the FCPA allows for the payment of legitimate fees, it explicitly prohibits "any offer, payment, promise to pay, or authorization of the payment of money or anything of value to any person, while knowing that all or a portion of such money or thing of value will be offered, given or promised, directly or indirectly, to a foreign official to influence the foreign official in his or her official capacity, induce the foreign official to do or omit to do an act in violation of his or her lawful duty, or to secure any improper advantage in order to assist in obtaining or retaining business for or with, or directing business to, any person" (The United States Department of Justice 2017). In order to distinguish between legitimate and illegitimate payments, it is important to comply with institutional purchasing policies and processes and to document in detail each payment for goods or services.

After the type of operational or legal structure is determined and established, setting up programs and activities in the host country will likely require substantial involvement on the part of the SIO. For instance, the SIO may be asked to serve as the primary liaison to in-country legal counsel, supervise local staff, or perform program assessment. Additionally, the SIO may have an ex-officio appointment to an internal or external board charged with oversight of any special purpose vehicles created for the purposes of registering legal presence in the host country. For a legal discussion of this topic, see Ferreira (2013).

Labor Issues

The complexities of employing faculty, staff, and contractors overseas—whether they are U.S. nationals, local workforce members, or third-country nationals—can expose universities to certain liabilities, especially in relation to taxation, compensation and benefits, and termination. Knowledge of local labor laws is essential, and the university's legal counsel, human resources (HR) officers, and staff in related administrative units (e.g., research compliance and risk management) should be consulted to establish and enforce appropriate procedures prior to starting any project that may require hiring abroad, for both salaried employees and independent contractors.

The tasks involved often require working closely with in-country legal counsel and government offices to make sure that the correct forms are completed, permissions are received, and payments are made. Alternatively, some institutions contract for services with staffing agencies, accounting firms, and other entities based in the host country to better manage the legal and logistical complexities of hiring abroad. SIOs, in serving as the university's point of contact for international partners, can often leverage their contacts, such as their counterparts at local universities, in the host country to assist in finding credible resources to make the international employment process run more smoothly.

VISAS AND WORK PERMITS

Before hiring, it is important to work with legal counsel and HR firms that are knowledgeable about the host country's laws, bureaucratic systems, and cultural norms. These partners can help determine the proper classification of each staff member, the foreign country visa category most appropriate for each person's intended activities, and the work permit requirements. Depending on the country, work permits can be difficult to obtain and take a long time to process, which may delay the start date of any activities and could also impact budgets. Ideally, SIOs should be aware of the general timelines of activities and projects abroad to best manage the necessary preparations in advance.

Banking and Finance

There are three major categories of financial transactions involved in supporting global operations: (a) currency exchange (and how fluctuations affect budgeting); (b) international payments; and (c) banking. It is important for the SIO to coordinate with the university's finance office to protect larger funds from currency fluctuations and seek solutions for international banking needs in a specific country. The university finance office can partner with large financial institutions and, more recently, with financial technology companies for payments needed to maintain the university's international activities.

The SIO should be familiar with all applicable institutional policies, procedures, and resources that can help or hinder international initiatives. The SIO can then work with the pertinent administrators to raise awareness of any problems and liabilities and to develop solutions. For instance, an institution may have in place an overly frugal policy on meal reimbursements and per diem applied to faculty leading short-term programs abroad, acting as visiting scholars, conducting research, or presenting at international conferences. While a $10 limit for lunch may be sufficient in the small town or rural state in which the university is based, this is usually not enough to cover expenses in high-cost cities and countries. Faculty and staff who have to use their personal funds and end up losing money while traveling abroad on university business will eventually grow discouraged and may wish to avoid engaging in future international endeavors. To address this issue, many universities grant exceptions to the standard per diem rate for international travel by either reimbursing the full cost of the meal when a receipt is provided (this can also be problematic because receipts may not be available or may be written in another language) or an amount equal to the U.S. Department of State's determination of foreign per diem rates by location (U.S. Department of State Office of Allowances n.d.).

Other financial considerations that SIOs should be aware of include cybersecurity, the Foreign Account Tax Compliance Act, the U.S. Office of Foreign

Assets Control screening, tax treaties, and safety considerations for employees carrying cash. It would be beneficial to SIOs to work closely with their finance office, controllers, accounts payable unit, procurement, and export controls office to anticipate the risks inherent in certain international financial transactions and set up the most appropriate systems for their needs that are in compliance with home and host country laws.

Research Ethics and Compliance

One of the most common types of global operations that institutions fund and facilitate is research projects abroad, which comprise some unique challenges and considerations. Any research that involves humans or animals needs to be reviewed and approved by the respective university review boards. For example, Institutional Review Boards (IRBs) that protect the rights and welfare of human subjects participating in research activities must verify that the same ethical and regulatory standards are applied to research conducted abroad as they are to domestic research. Proposed protections must be appropriate for the setting in which the research will be conducted, more specifically, based on the: (a) nature of the proposed research; (b) level of risk; and (c) local research context. IRB review of research abroad also takes into account the local culture, tradition, and languages, as well as the current political and social climate. In addition, researchers must comply with the relevant laws protecting human subjects in the host country.

For research that involves animals, the approval process is both more straightforward and more complex. Investigators must usually receive approval from the university's Institutional Animal Care and Use Committee (IACUC) on research projects involving animals abroad. Additionally, federal regulations require that all research funded by the U.S. Department of Health and Human Services be conducted only at assured institutions that have provided a Statement of Compliance with the Office of Laboratory Animal Welfare. Universities generally find compliance with requirements for post-approval monitoring of animal research abroad and for inspections of the international animal research facilities to be the most challenging.

Finding an in-country partner in order to ensure understanding of the local context and regulations, and for obtaining approval from the appropriate authorities abroad, can be crucial for the success of a project. SIOs may consider looking into whether their existing in-country networks may be in the position to assist the IACUCs. SIOs may also be valuable assets for IRBs in assessments of local research contexts and, sometimes, even in finding an international research partner.

LOGISTICS

International research conducted in remote field locations requires institutional risk assessment and planning to safeguard not only the welfare of the research subjects, but also the safety of the researchers and students and any equipment transported to the location. Team collaboration, mentoring relationships, field research techniques, the provision of adequate equipment (e.g., satellite phone) suitable for use in remote locations, contingency safety planning, etc., all require close engagement and coordination between multiple academic and administrative units, as well as with the international partners. For such logistically complex projects, it is crucial that SIOs are included right from the project planning phase.

When research involves bringing specimens into the United States, sometimes, material transfer specialists working in the technology transfer (intellectual property) office and legal counsel office will need to be consulted to ensure adherence to the partnership agreements and international and in-country laws restricting certain types of activities. Finally, there are several international treaties that protect endangered species and biodiversity, and while the United States is not a signatory to all of them, any violations or negligent behavior on the part of university personnel could present a

There are several international treaties protecting endangered species and biodiversity that must be considered when engaging in certain research projects abroad.

- Convention on Biological Diversity (CBD) www.cbd.int/
- Convention on International Trade in Endangered Species of Wild Fauna and Flora (CITES) www.cites.org/
- International Treaty on Plant Genetic Resource for Food and Agriculture (ITPGRFA) www.fao.org/plant-treaty/en/
- Nagoya Protocol on Access to Genetic Resources and the Fair and Equitable Sharing of Benefits Arising from their Utilization (ABS) to the Convention on Biological Diversity www.cbd.int/abs/about/default.shtml/

reputational risk to the institution and may result in complex amnesty efforts with which SIOs may eventually get embroiled.

EXPORT CONTROLS

In an effort to advance and protect economic, foreign policy, and national security interests, governments often control the export or transfer of sensitive equipment, information, services, software, technology, and other controlled items. In the United States, "export controls" is the term used to describe the various federal laws and regulations that govern these restrictions. Nearly all research universities have an office charged with assisting university stakeholders in understanding the restrictions and applying for relevant export licenses from the U.S. Departments of Commerce, State, Treasury, or other government agencies. The export regulations cover not only tangible items (e.g., equipment and software), but also the release of certain critical technologies, information, and services to foreign nationals, both inside the United States (i.e., deemed exports) and outside the country. When a project involves international activities, such as exporting equipment or providing foreign visitors with access to certain facilities, it is prudent to involve the export controls office for a review of the project. While few SIOs are expected to be experts on export controls, SIOs, especially those serving at research intensive institutions, should maintain familiarity with basic principles, critical concerns, and the latest resources. One key resource is the Export Compliance Dashboard (2019), which can be downloaded from the Export Compliance Training Institute.

Travel, Health, and Safety

All students, faculty, staff, and others participating in global operations must be informed of any health, safety, and security concerns relevant to the regions they are visiting. Many institutions require travelers to complete an international travel registry in advance of their trip, and an international travel committee on campus reviews the location, dates, and purpose of the trip. Individuals traveling to locations that have been flagged with government travel warnings, such as the U.S. Department of State's Travel

Advisories and the Centers for Disease Control and Prevention's Travel Alerts, may be required to receive special training, sign a waiver of liability, take additional precautions, or they may have their travel request denied altogether. Trips with an extended duration (e.g., 6 months or more) may raise questions about the need to register legal presence or possible tax implications. Finally, the committee may inform the traveler of any permits or licenses required to conduct the proposed activities. This may include authorization from the host country's government to conduct research or access certain locations.

Aside from the students, faculty, and staff who take trips abroad on university business, there may be employees who reside abroad to manage in-country global operations, such as directing an education abroad center or working at a branch campus. Generally, the benefits that foreign-based faculty and staff receive depend on the allowable costs covered under the funding model supporting their stay abroad. It is important for SIOs to make sure that this second group of participants is not forgotten by administrators when it is time to renew insurance policies or update procedures.

TRAVEL TOOLS

Universities can greatly assist in the planning process by developing easily accessible online and off-line tools and support services to travelers, such as country guidelines and password-protected sites to house personal documents (e.g., copies of passports, visas, and insurance cards) and other important information. Many universities provide such tools on their global operations websites. SIOs can help develop and disseminate the material.

HEALTH TOOLS

Travelers appreciate planning tools that take into account the type of activities in which they will be engaged during their time abroad. These include reminders to get necessary vaccines, information about health insurance coverage while abroad, and considerations (e.g., tips for preventing certain diseases) pertinent to their travel destination. However, there are several health-related issues, such as mental health, sexual harassment, and managing existing medical conditions, that often get neglected during pre-travel preparations. Resulting incidents can seriously affect an international project, so it is important for institutions to develop and make accessible resources that address these issues before, during, and after a trip. SIOs can work with the university risk management team to help shape relevant pre-travel tools and procedures.

SAFETY TOOLS

When travelers' safety is in question, SIOs are often pulled in to work with the university crisis management team to respond quickly and effectively to situations, while maintaining compliance with institution, national, and international laws. (For more on risk and crisis management, see chapter 3.) Travelers should have the safety considerations of their destinations assessed prior to their trips and, especially for high-risk countries, detailed plans for protecting their safety. An understanding of the local context and travelers' resources while in-country is essential for their safety. SIOs should remain aware of important health and safety protocol, both at the university and abroad, to mitigate the risk factors and help secure the well-being of university faculty, staff, and students.

From the development of contracts to the health and safety of participants abroad, SIOs are involved in helping institutions manage the risks, challenges, and considerations involved with different types of global operations. By building close working relationships with key stakeholders on campus and partners off campus, SIOs can ensure that international initiatives are productive and sustainable.

Case Study: University of California

While the university leadership's commitment to effective global operations is crucial, at institutions where that commitment is less than explicit, SIOs can still make a great impact by identifying and focusing on the low-hanging fruit. This section of the chapter reviews the University of California as a case study.

University of California Global Operations

For the last several years, the University of California Office of the President (UCOP), which is the system headquarters of the University of California, has been coordinating a unique "grassroots" approach to providing support to global operations efforts at the system-wide level. Through a gap analysis, which included interviews with staff in the offices that support international activities across the UC system, needs were identified along with immediate opportunities to strengthen global operations without significant financial or structural investment. These low-hanging fruit consisted of a website, listserv, functional support team, and annual system-wide meetings on global operations.

WEBSITE

One of the low-cost, high-impact global operations activities at UC was the development of a website for UC Global Operations (UCGO) (www.ucgo. org), which supports UC faculty, staff, and students engaged in international activities. UCGO, the brainchild of several UC campuses, was developed by UCOP's Research Policy Analysis and Coordination unit and UCOP's Ethics, Compliance and Audit Services unit, in consultation with various offices and resources across the UC system.

UCGO's website is an ever-evolving portal that directs users to information and support services on their campus that center on specific areas of concern. UCGO serves as a clearinghouse for guidance on the most frequently asked questions, concerns, and issues around international activities, and it provides or links to various tools developed at UC or by other institutions. As such, UCGO touches on all the issues discussed in this chapter and can serve as a tool for navigating through common global operations concerns even for SIOs outside the UC system.

LISTSERV

The UC International Research Listserv disseminates information on international research to different categories of research stakeholders at UC. The majority of the listserv members are UC system-wide staff who support international research in various ways, including contracts and grants officers, risk managers, health and safety officers, faculty, department chairs, vice presidents for research, etc. The listserv was created to provide an additional and direct way for hundreds of UC staff, and some faculty, to communicate, enabling them to share announcements, questions, requests, etc., in real time when existing channels of communications may not be sufficient. The listserv is often used to quickly generate responses to calls for comments on proposed legislations and rules, quick polling, and the exchange of practices.

FUNCTIONAL SUPPORT TEAM

At UCOP, the "functional team" is not a formal unit, but a network of staff who collaborate when international issues arise. Team members are located in the offices of legal counsel, controllers, finance, risk management, and research compliance, to name a few. In many of the large academic systems such as UC, support for international activities is frequently provided in a siloed manner, with support staff and units rarely aware of each other's involvement or the full spectrum of issues that their approach to a project, partnership, or initiative might raise down the line. However, with a team comprised of stakeholders from different units, procedures and actions can be more cohesive and effective. The inclusion of the SIO in such a team further strengthens the university's global operations and internationalization efforts overall.

GLOBAL OPERATIONS ANNUAL MEETINGS

Another effective strategy has been to organize an annual, system-wide "Global Operations" meeting where the staff members who support the UC campuses' international activities have an opportunity to meet colleagues from other campuses, share their practices, learn from each other, and even elevate some of their concerns for system-wide attention. Over time, these meetings have garnered an impressive level of interest, both on campuses and at UCOP. Compared with the first year, attendance at the third annual meeting, which took place in the summer of 2018, tripled.

Conclusion

It is important to keep in mind that a focus on just the low-hanging fruit has at least one serious limitation. After all the low-hanging fruit have been "picked," in order to sustain the momentum that the enthusiastic staff and faculty have created, institutions will eventually have to start investing in global operations at a more structural and financially invested level. SIOs who understand and are engaged with different global operations issues are in a unique position to guide their university's leadership to make informed decisions on the next steps toward internationalization.

SIOs have one of the most complex roles at a university. Yet, the variations in their scope of responsibilities are usually determined by the extent of the university's commitment to internationalization, the reporting lines, allocated budgets, and whether SIOs work in siloed environments or are in position to break them. Collaboration is a two-way relationship. All of the offices that support global operations affect the university's internationalization efforts. In turn, SIOs and their offices are in a position to provide their unique expertise, insights, and resources to these support offices and direct the global operations chain for the benefit of the overall institution. Establishing strong collaboration between SIOs, the university's office of research, and other administrative units is the first step in building a global operations infrastructure to support the university's internationalization efforts.

Additional Resources

Ferreira, William F. 2011. "Going Global: Legal Trends in University International Programs." NACAU CLE Workshop: The Global University. April 29, 2011. https://www.hoganlovells.com/~/media/hogan-lovells/pdf/publication/nacua_pdf.pdf.

Ferreira, Bill. 2014. "International Projects: Reflections from Counsel." *NCURA Magazine* March/April 2014:20–21. https://www.hoganlovells.com/~/media/hogan-lovells/pdf/publication/ferreirareflections_pdf.pdf.

Hoseth, Chad, and Shehan Thampapillai. 2018. *International Partnership Dynamics and Types*. Washington, DC: NAFSA: Association of International Educators.

United Nations Educational, Scientific and Cultural Organization (UNESCO). 2017. "International Scientific Collaboration Has Become a Must, Says Report." June 1, 2017. http://www.unesco.org/new/en/natural-sciences/ science-technology/single-view-sc-policy/news/international_scientific_ collaboration_has_become_a_must_sa/.

United States Patent and Trademark Office. 2009. "Trade Related Aspects of IP Rights." United States Patent and Trademark Office. https://www.uspto.gov/ patents-getting-started/international-protection/office-policy-and-external- affairs-trips-trade.

University of Washington Global Operations Support. 2016. *International Projects Start-Up Guide*. Seattle, WA: University of Washington Global Operations Support. https://finance.uw.edu/globalsupport/sites/default/files/IPAG%20 4.14_0.pdf.

World Intellectual Property Organization. n.d. "Berne Convention for the Protection of Literary and Artistic Works." Geneva, Switzerland: World Intellectual Property Organization. https://www.wipo.int/treaties/en/ip/berne/.

References

Export Compliance Training Institute. 2019. "Export Compliance Dashboard." Harrisonburg, VA: Export Compliance Institute. https://www. learnexportcompliance.com/tools/export-compliance-dashboard/.

Ferreira, William. 2013. "Key Operational Risks in International Ventures: What University Lawyers Need to Tell Their CFOs." NACUA 2013 Annual Conference. https://www.hoganlovells.com/~/media/hogan-lovells/pdf/ publication/legal-status-and-corporate-structure-issues--04262013pdf_pdf.pdf.

Global Innovation Policy Center. 2018. "U.S. Chamber International IP Index." Washington, DC: U.S. Chamber of Commerce Global Innovation Policy Center. https://www.theglobalipcenter.com/ipindex2018/.

Merson, Michael H. 2014. "University Engagement in Global Health." *New England Journal of Medicine* 370:1676–1678. https://www.nejm.org/doi/ full/10.1056/NEJMp1401124.

National Science Board. 2018. *Science & Engineering Indicators 2018*. Alexandria, VA: National Science Foundation National Center for Science and Engineering Statistics. https://nsf.gov/statistics/2018/nsb20181/.

The United States Department of Justice. 2017. "Foreign Corrupt Practices Act." Washington, DC: The United States Department of Justice. https://www. justice.gov/criminal-fraud/foreign-corrupt-practices-act.

U.S. Department of State Office of Allowances. n.d. "Foreign Per Diem Rates by Location DSSR 925." Washington, DC: U.S. Department of State Office of Allowances. https://aoprals.state.gov/web920/per_diem.asp.

The World Bank. 2018. "Rankings & Ease of Doing Business Score." Washington, DC: World Bank Group. http://www.doingbusiness.org/en/rankings.

18 | Community and Government Partnerships: Salisbury University Case Study

Brian N. Stiegler

Senior international officers (SIOs) play important roles in the global engagement of their local, regional, and state communities. Particularly at higher education institutions (HEIs) located in small cities, towns, and rural communities, where opportunities for significant international engagement may be more limited, the leadership of SIOs in government and public affairs can be of value to both the campus and the larger community. This chapter examines the dynamics of relationships between SIOs and government and public affairs representatives and the benefits of collaboration. It takes a focused look at HEIs with international sister city and sister state partnerships, using Salisbury University as a case study.

Institution-Government Dynamics

Some HEIs, large and small, public and private, are located in capital cities and have many natural ties to state governments and political power. In such cases where HEIs are geographically close to state legislatures and governors, the contact between SIOs and government officials may occur more readily due to regular exchanges of information, overlapping personal contacts, and similar or shared goals for the community. SIOs in these contexts should take full advantage of their close working relationships to enhance internationalization efforts on campus through established public and government programs.

It is also worth examining HEIs that are not located close to the halls of political power. In secondary and tertiary cities, small towns, and rural areas, HEIs ranging from community colleges to regional liberal arts colleges to public comprehensive regional universities possess different opportunities to contribute to the internationalization of their local communities by connecting their campus-based international strategies to local priorities, resources, and concerns. The global learning that SIOs are charged to advance and promote on campus will also directly affect the surrounding community, as globally literate graduates emerge as citizens and members of the workforce in secondary cities, small towns, and rural communities across the United States. Salisbury University offers a prime example of how an institution's internationalization initiatives and outcomes can extend and enhance ties to the community.

Case Study: Salisbury University

Salisbury University is a public regional comprehensive university and one of the 12 higher education institutional members of the University System of Maryland. The university is located 100 miles from the state capital, Annapolis, Maryland. Its host city, Salisbury, is situated in a rural area east of the Chesapeake Bay, with a population of just over 30,000. Despite its relatively modest size, Salisbury University's international engagement efforts make it a key global actor in the region. The past two five-year comprehensive internationalization strategic plans have identified sister city and sister state relationships as instruments to strengthen comprehensive internationalization on campus and global partnerships in the local and state communities (Salisbury University 2009, 2014).

Sister Cities International

Sister Cities International traces its roots to the people-to-people public diplomacy efforts of the Eisenhower administration in the 1950s in the United States. Today, there are Sister Cities organizations in 46 states, with only Louisiana, Mississippi, North Dakota, and Wyoming having yet to establish organizations (Sister Cities International 2018). Within those 46 states, there are 500 communities engaged in 2,000 partnerships around the world (Sister Cities International 2018). The 500 communities include large cities, small cities, towns, and sister state relationships. All of the partnerships subscribe to

Sister Cities International's organizing principle: "Connect globally. Thrive locally" (Sister Cities International 2018).

Salisbury University and the University of Tartu

One of Salisbury University's most successful efforts to connect globally and thrive locally involves the sister state relationship between Maryland and Estonia, and the corresponding sister city partnership between Salisbury, Maryland, and Tartu, Estonia. Salisbury University made a major delegation visit to the University of Tartu in 2009, led by Salisbury University's SIO and several deans and key members of the faculty. The result of the visit was a memorandum of understanding (MOU) for a bilateral exchange program. (For more on MOUs and partnerships, see chapter 16.) Since signing the agreement, dozens of undergraduate students have participated in mobility programs between the universities; multiple Salisbury University faculty members have visited Estonia, including one on a Fulbright Scholar fellowship; and Salisbury University has hosted an Estonian Fulbright Scholar. This global partnership has borne great fruit for both Salisbury University and its local community.

COMMUNITY BENEFITS

Because of the sister city and sister state relationships between Salisbury University and the University of Tartu, there have been larger community-wide dividends. Salisbury University hosted two of the last three Estonian ambassadors to North America on its campus for visiting public lectures, which were well attended by members of the regional community. The Estonian embassy has proven to be particularly interested in supporting the people-to-people exchanges that happen with sister city and sister state relationships. Embassies of many other nations share such enthusiasm for sister city activities because they can inspire international friendships, economic development, and soft diplomacy outside of major global cities and among communities where the embassies often have few other resources and contacts. SIOs should strive to maintain contact with officials of embassies and consulates of nations representing the sister city and sister state partnerships of their communities.

When a university's global engagement strategy supports community-based priorities and needs, foreign embassies may be more likely to engage with that institution. This is because community-aligned international initiatives not only provide access to academic programs and research, but also serve to promote public diplomacy, cultural exchange, and the establishment of economic ties. SIOs should be familiar with their state's major exports and imports, top trade partners, and related international initiatives. Additionally, SIOs should establish close relationships with state offices of international trade, chambers of commerce, economic development offices, international business leaders, and other globally engaged organizations within their community. It is then possible to identify the embassies with which to engage, either independently or collaboratively with local community partners.

Depending on the goals for the interaction and how the embassy is staffed, the SIO may interact with educational attachés, cultural attachés, military attachés, or even an ambassador. Regardless of the point of contact, the SIO should have a clear idea of how the university's offerings in teaching, research, and engagement can help to compliment the interests, needs, and priorities of the nation represented by the diplomatic staff. With strategic guidance from the SIO, the institution can establish beneficial partnerships with embassies and serve as a global gateway for the local community.

COMMUNITY PARTNERS

Sister City committees can be useful allies to SIOs in establishing bridges from campus-based internationalization efforts to the local community. These committees are generally comprised of members of local Rotary clubs and the local Chamber of Commerce, along with other community leaders who typically have extensive networks. For example, Salisbury University collaborated with the community-based Sister City committee to invite a local choir to sing several songs in Estonian for a performance on campus during one of the Estonian ambassador's visits. It provided a unique opportunity for a "town-gown" global collaboration, the "town" being the local community and the "gown" representing the academic community. Members of Sister City committees can also serve as volunteers for other events, demonstrating good will toward foreign cultures and peoples. These individuals can be very helpful to SIOs looking for local community partnerships. Even if the SIO cannot attend every meeting, getting on the email list and attending even a few meetings each year can lead to increased engagement and collaboration, locally and globally.

Another key stakeholder for these sister city relationships are the mayors of cities and towns who have connections throughout the community. Following the development of the sister city relationship with Tartu, Salisbury University established an annual welcome meeting for all international students with the mayor of Salisbury. The students and mayor participate in a 30-minute question and answer session at the start of the school year to discuss cultural differences, city governance, and other issues of interest. Members of the Sister City committee often join these meetings, which are held in the chambers of the city council. The SIO always joins in this event to represent the university. This welcome meeting has been repeated for many years under different mayoral administrations, and it all began because of the sister city relationship.

Maryland and Anhui

Another important sister city relationship included in Salisbury University's comprehensive internationalization strategic plan is with Anhui Province, Maryland's sister state in China. The Anhui-Maryland sister state partnership originated in the years immediately following President Nixon's historic visit to China in 1972. When Salisbury University first began collaborating with Anhui Province on higher education exchange in 2009, the sister state partnership was already 29 years in the making.

By building a new academic partnership with a sister state, educational initiatives by Salisbury University were more enriching to the larger community in ways that a partnership not based in a sister state would be able to accomplish. Because of Anhui Province's position as a sister state, leaders in business, government, and arts and culture across the state of Maryland have pursued an array of actions and activities designed to strengthen relationships between Maryland and Anhui. Any success in a university-based international education initiative would become part of the existing fabric of partnership between the two regions. A global success for Salisbury University in Anhui Province would contribute to something larger at the state level.

The Anhui-Maryland sister state partnership has grown in depth since the SIO led a large delegation with the provost and numerous deans to Anhui Province in 2009. Today, there are now more students from Anhui Province studying at Salisbury University than any other HEI in Maryland. Salisbury University has become a leader in the sister state partnership by pursuing its own educational strategies with Chinese universities in Anhui Province. For example, in May 2017, Salisbury University cosponsored a dinner in the World Trade Center building in Baltimore, Maryland, in honor of a sister state-organized delegation visit by the Communist Party secretary of Anhui Province. The formal reception was cosponsored by the city of Salisbury's largest corporate resident, Perdue Farms, Inc. The world-famous chicken company, which was founded and remains headquartered in the city of Salisbury, operates a plant in Anhui Province. Perdue Farms has also pursued a strategy to expand its business in collaboration with the sister state. The keynote speeches of the night belonged to the chief executive officer of Perdue Farms, Jim Perdue, and two Salisbury University students, one from Anhui Province and one from Maryland. The university's comprehensive internationalization strategy achieved a larger impact because its initiatives aligned with existing sister state partnerships.

As in the case with the partnership with Tartu, Estonia, the SIO at Salisbury University faced challenges in securing support from some campus constituents for a new initiative in Anhui Province, China. Anhui Province is not as well known as the megacities of Shanghai, Beijing, Guangzhou, or Hong Kong. Similarly, some campus constituents doubted whether Estonia was a wise place to build a partnership instead of better known European destinations. SIOs should be prepared to defend the larger strategy of connecting university international activities to statewide and community-wide international initiatives. For example, enrollment management leaders might resist the notion of developing a new global partnership outside a densely populated metropolitan area just because a sister city relationship may be based in a smaller foreign market. Academic departments might also advocate for new partnerships at locations where faculty have existing research interests, not where their city and mayor have established relationships through a sister city relationship. SIOs need to consider all of these competing interests, especially at institutions in smaller cities and towns or more rural communities.

Government Relationships

In the state of Maryland, the sister city and sister state partnerships are loosely organized under the supervision of the Office of the Secretary of State. In other states, sister city and sister state partnerships may be organized under a lieutenant governor. But, in general, states often seek to grow their sister city and sister state partnerships as part of their business development efforts at the state level.

Salisbury University's efforts to build international collaborations with sister cities and sister states have put the university in constant communication with the secretary of state. When the Maryland secretary of state traveled to Anhui Province several years ago, a Salisbury University representative traveled with the delegation and helped facilitate engagements in the province based on the university's educational network. In a similar trip to Dubai, United Arab Emirates, the Salisbury University SIO was part of the secretary of state's business development delegation and used the visit to recruit new students. SIOs should consider how sister city and sister state initiatives can lead to new internationalization opportunities by connecting the university to state and local governments in substantive ways. There are numerous reasons why developing new campus-based global partnerships in collaboration with off-campus governmental or community-based priorities can benefit the HEI in the long term.

State Consortia

The U.S. International Education Study State Consortia initiative began in 1999 as an effort to promote closer collaboration between the global engagement efforts of HEIs and their respective states. The initiative receives support from the U.S. Department of Commerce, U.S. Commercial Service, International Trade Administration, and various other federal, state, and local agencies. At the time of writing this chapter, there are active consortia in 30 states (U.S. Department of Commerce 2018), which appear darkened in figure 1. Additional consortia exist in two cities (Pittsburgh and Philadelphia, Pennsylvania) and one unincorporated U.S. territory (Puerto Rico) (Study Alabama 2018).

Figure 1. Map of U.S. International Education Study State Consortia

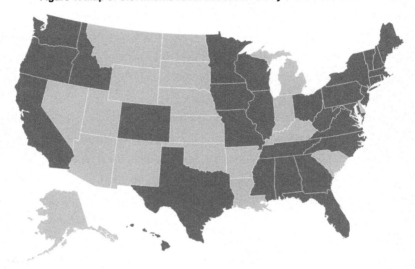

The state of Maryland established its study state consortium in 2017. Founded as an independent nonprofit organization with members representing public and private HEIs, intensive English programs, and related organizations, the Maryland International Education Consortium (MIEC) markets Maryland as a study destination for international students, while also promoting statewide collaboration on international initiatives. MIEC plays an important role in fostering support for international education among academic, government, and other community leaders in the state. For example, through the work of MIEC, Governor Larry Hogan proclaimed that April 26 be designated Maryland International Education Day (Study Maryland 2018).

SIOs should be knowledgeable about and supportive of the international education consortium in their state. Consortia support local and regional economic development missions and provide a venue for SIOs to connect their campus internationalization efforts with larger issues. In many states, consortium members work closely alongside representatives of the governor's office, the U.S. Department of Commerce, district export councils, chambers of commerce, city economic development offices, international corporations, state tourism boards, and other key stakeholders with whom SIOs might otherwise have little interaction. These connections serve to advance statewide dialogue on international issues, promote resource sharing, and help frame campus internationalization efforts in ways that are most relevant to local communities.

Conclusion

Colleges and universities across the country embed a commitment to their local communities within their missions. SIOs have to balance the many priorities and competing interests of different constituencies on campus as they lead their institution's internationalization efforts. SIOs should not fail to consider off-campus government, civic, and community-based leaders among those constituencies. By connecting with international strategies in the larger community, SIOs are positioning their institution to serve their mission to their community, strengthening town-gown activities, building relationships with off-campus leaders in government and business, and helping to foster global competencies not just at their institution but also in their community.

Additional Resources

American Association of State Colleges and Universities. 2015. *Strategic Plan 2015–2020*. Washington, DC: American Association of State Colleges and Universities. http://www.aascu.org/strategic-plan/VisionandMission/.

Griffin, Jermaine, Craig T. Cobaine, Mark Schaub, and Brian N. Stiegler. 2018. "Internationalization at U.S. Public Comprehensive Universities: Three Case Studies." *AIEA Occasional Paper*. October 2018. https://aiea.memberclicks.net/assets/docs/OccasionalPapers/10.2018_Griffin__Cobane_Schaub_Stiegler_Occasional%20Paper.pdf.

Kacenga, George. 2019. "On the Rise: State Consortia." *International Educator* XXVIII, 1:40–43.

Kiehl, William P. 2008. *Global Intentions, Local Results: How Colleges Can Create International Communities*. Scotts Valley, CA: CreateSpace.

Maryland Secretary of State. n.d. "Maryland Sister States Program." Annapolis, MD: Maryland.gov. https://sos.maryland.gov/International/Pages/MSSP.aspx.

Sister Cities International. 2018. *2018 Annual Report & Membership Directory*. Washington, DC: Sister Cities International. https://user-2221582232.cld. bz/2018-Annual-Report-and-Membership-Directory.

Stiegler, Brian N. 2017. "On Being Provincial and Global: International Education at American Comprehensive Regional Universities." *Higher Education Today*. May 18, 2017. https://www.higheredtoday.org/2017/05/18/provincial-global-international-education-american-comprehensive-regional-universities/.

Study Maryland. n.d. "Study Maryland." Study Maryland. https://www.studymarylandorg/.

West, Charlotte. 2012. *Engaging Stakeholders in Internationalization: Strategies for Collaboration*. Washington, DC: NAFSA: Association of International Educators.

References

Salisbury University. 2009. *Comprehensive Internationalization Strategic Plan 2009–2014*. Salisbury, MD: Salisbury University. https://www.salisbury.edu/administration/academic-affairs/center-for-international-education/_files/International%20Education%20Strategic%20Plan.pdf.

Salisbury University. 2014. *Comprehensive Internationalization Strategic Plan 2014–18*. Salisbury, MD: Salisbury University.

Sister City International. 2018. "About Sister Cities International." Washington, DC: Sister Cities International. https://sistercities.org/about-us/.

Study Alabama. 2017. "US International Education Study State Consortia." Study Alabama. https://studyalabama.us/economic-reach/usstudystate/.

Study Maryland. 2018. "Maryland International Education Day." Study Maryland. https://www.studymaryland.org/maryland-international-education-day.

U.S. Department of Commerce. 2018. "U.S. International Education Consortia." Washington, DC: U.S. Department of Commerce. https://2016.export.gov/industry/education/eg_main_022048.asp.

19 | Engagement of International Students with Host Communities: A Case Study of St. Cloud State University

Shahzad Ahmad

The changing terrains of higher education, population demographics, technology, workforce development needs, economics, and geopolitics have had a direct effect on international student enrollment trends at colleges and universities around the world. Presidents, provosts, and others have increasingly looked to senior international officers (SIOs) to guide institutional efforts that address the needs, goals, and interests of international students. While much attention is placed on the recruitment of international students, it is equally important to develop high-impact practices, programs, and other initiatives that advance their academic success, cultural adjustment, and social integration. Using St. Cloud State University as a case study, this chapter discusses how intentional approaches to campus and community programming can lead to international students' development and engagement and enrich host communities simultaneously.

International Student Support

As global competition for the world's best and brightest students increases, it is imperative for colleges and universities to implement strategic initiatives that give international students the support, tools, and resources that they need to have positive, productive educational experiences. Institutions must prepare international students for successful transition to the host institution and provide opportunities for them to build substantive connections to the host community.

A review examining nearly 4 decades of published research on international student support services suggests that international students experience three primary types of needs: (a) universal needs shared by all students; (b) needs arising from their unique international status; and (c) culturally specific needs (Chalmers 1976; Di Maria 2012; Furnham and Bochner 1986). The primary responsibility for the delivery of customized academic, cultural, legal, and social support services for international students most often falls under the purview of SIOs (Kwai 2017). While the work is usually led by a specialized team of advisers within an international student and scholar services (ISSS) unit, partnership with academic, student affairs, and administrative units, as well as student organizations and community organizations, is essential for success.

Academic administrators, faculty, and advisers at universities and in ISSS offices must be cognizant of the cultural differences that exist between the students' home countries and their new host countries and the effect these variances may have on interpersonal interactions and student success. Furthermore, SIOs and ISSS staff should recognize that certain needs generally remain constant within particular groups, such as cultural or religious restrictions on consumption of beef, pork, or other meats, while additional needs, such as avoidance of certain foods due to personal allergies, will differ across individuals. SIOs and ISSS staff must not only take into account students' countries of origin, but also the effect that the host institution and community play on their success or struggles. Because of this, it is suggested that recruitment and retention efforts be multifaceted with varying levels of support throughout the transition process.

In order to promote academic success, institutions must keep students engaged throughout the different stages of an international student's academic and immigration lifecycle (Andrade 2009). Examples of such activities and support services include pre- and post-arrival orientation, cultural and academic advising, social activities and events, student organization support, and collaboration with the community through cross-cultural sharing activities. St. Cloud State University offers examples of some of the structures and programs that institutions can offer to assist international students in developing ties on and off campus.

Case Study: St. Cloud State University

St. Cloud State University (SCSU) is a mid-size public institution located in central Minnesota. SCSU has a long history of international engagement and currently enrolls more than 1,400 international students representing 90 countries. The winner of a 2013 NAFSA Senator Paul Simon Award for Campus Internationalization, SCSU employs highly innovative and impactful strategies to assist international students and advance internationalization at home (Feighner 2013).

SCSU's Center for International Studies (CIS), an administrative unit led by the SIO and home to the ISSS team, coordinates opportunities for international students and scholars to engage with the St. Cloud community. In order to fully serve and advocate for international students and scholars, the CIS staff routinely evaluate processes and implement new programs. Below is a discussion of some of the most popular and beneficial offerings, which may serve as inspiration for other institutions.

Prearrival Orientation

Since the process of gaining cultural familiarity should begin before students arrive on campus, it is useful to create orientations for international students that prepare them for arrival to the university and host community. These orientations can be in person or through virtual means. While it would be ideal for all students to receive an in-person prearrival orientation, budget constraints make this unfeasible, and so it is often helpful to utilize cost-effective technology solutions.

Over the past 3 years, SCSU has enhanced its traditional international student orientation program to include an online prearrival component offered in collaboration with the international admissions unit. Delivered as a webinar, the orientation provides students with important information in a more dynamic format than email communication alone. It has the added benefit of acquainting international students with key staff members before their arrival to the United States, which supports yield efforts as well as ensures students feel connected with key contacts at SCSU before they even leave their home country. Students may ask questions or share concerns that can be individually addressed by qualified staff, thus increasing their comfort levels and connections to the institution.

In addition to the online orientation, the SIO and other administrators offer in-country orientations for groups of international students in targeted countries. For example, SCSU has a large Nepalese student population, so every year, the SIO and one staff member travel to Nepal to provide an in-country prearrival orientation. This trip allows the staff to prepare a large group of students for their transition to the United States and the St. Cloud community through a strategic cost-benefit analysis of targeting a location (e.g., Nepal) with significant student representation. At the same time, the SIO uses these opportunities to meet with international partners and strengthen relationships with local institutions and organizations that support study abroad and exchanges.

On-Site Orientation

Prearrival orientations are a small, albeit important, part of the comprehensive orientation program. The bulk of orienting students to the campus community happens after students arrive on campus. This includes acclimating students to the university, university community, and greater campus community through tours that introduce them to support centers on campus, including those designed specifically for international students and those that serve all students. On-campus orientation is a great opportunity for the SIO and staff to collaborate with other campus units to fully illustrate the cohesive campus culture.

SCSU's on-campus orientation revolves around the partnership between CIS and the Advising and Student Transitions Office, allowing the creation of a hybrid orientation geared toward international students that is integrated into Huskies First Four Days, the campus-wide orientation program. By merging the international student and campus-wide orientations together, international students receive the specific information (e.g., immigration documents, communication, holidays) they need in relation to their immigration status (see chapter 10) and cultural adjustment, as well as general academic information such as academic honesty policies, class participation expectations, and graduation requirements—all while participating in a shared experience with other students. These early interactions with their peers can help international students establish more personal links to the institution.

After classes begin, orientation at SCSU continues via a required one-credit administrative orientation course that focuses on academic policies, processes, and resources available to international students. All new undergraduate international students must also enroll in a two-credit orientation course during their first semester that centers on cultural adjustment issues and gives students the space to share their experiences, voice concerns, and ask questions about U.S. culture and the greater campus community. Because SCSU offers banded tuition, these courses do not increase costs for the students.

Throughout the students' time at St. Cloud State, orientation programming continues in less formal ways. For instance, the ISSS team offers a workshop series throughout the semester that provides both just-in-case and just-in-time information to help international students feel less dependent on staff and more empowered to address opportunities and challenges faced during their stay. SCSU's unique combination of required, elective, formal, and informal orientation activities engage the international students in different ways, at different times, and on different levels in hopes of connecting with each student in a way that resonates. As international students get more comfortable with the academic and social environments on campus, they often are more eager to participate in other cultural sharing activities.

Academic and Cultural Sharing Scholarship

SCSU further prioritizes international students' academic success and sociocultural adjustment by encouraging positive study habits and community engagement through the use of scholarships and awards. As a member of the Minnesota State Colleges and Universities system, SCSU is permitted to provide international students with a nearly 50 percent discount on tuition (Minnesota State 2018). This discount is administered in the form of the Academic & Cultural Sharing Scholarship (ACSS), an effective recruitment and retention tool that makes SCSU's degree programs more accessible to international students from a broader range of socioeconomic backgrounds.

Eligibility requirements for the ACSS include:

- Attend and check in at orientation upon arrival to the university. Students do not have to apply for the first semester, but they must attend orientation to be initially eligible for the scholarship. Thus, orientation attendance rates are generally very high.

- Maintain a 2.5 cumulative GPA as an undergraduate student, or a 3.0 cumulative GPA as a graduate student.

- Maintain legal F-1 or J-1 status.

- Complete two cultural sharing activities every semester. In order to be accepted for the purposes of the scholarships, the activities must be preapproved by the CIS staff.

- Verify completion of cultural sharing activities each semester by completing an online form.

The integration of academic and cultural sharing activities serves to ensure that students engage in behaviors that not only promote academic success, but also facilitate cultural adjustment and social integration within the host community. These activities also help to advance internationalization on the campus and in the local community. Examples of typical activities students can partake in include:

- Cultural night volunteer. SCSU has very active and vibrant multicultural and international communities. Most weekends during the academic year, student organizations host cultural nights where students can showcase aspects of their culture through fashion shows, dinners featuring traditional foods, performances, and theatrical acts designed to educate others about culturally significant beliefs, ceremonies, traditions, and histories. These events often attract hundreds of attendees from both the campus and surrounding community.

- Department of Campus Involvement (DCI) volunteer. The Center for International Studies partners with the Department of Campus

Involvement to enlist international students as volunteers for campus events hosted and sponsored through the DCI. The DCI organizes six large-scale events each year, including family weekend and the Husky Spirit Challenge, a weeklong competition among student groups. International students can use the opportunity to make friends, show off their individual skills and talents, and learn more about their SCSU peers.

- Student organization position. St. Cloud State strongly encourages student leadership by allowing a position, whether elected or appointed, on any registered student organization's executive board to count as an ACSS cultural sharing activity. By taking on leadership positions, international students can see the more tangible outcomes of their presence and perspectives on campus and expand their personal networks exponentially.

- On-campus employment. On-campus employment positions such as office assistants, support staff, tutors, desk workers, and orientation assistants provide viable cultural exchange experiences. Even employment in areas such as food service can have a cultural sharing effect as international students learn about U.S. cuisine while they enjoy cultural exchanges with their peers and customers.

- Global Friends experience. The Center for International Studies teams up with a community-based student organization, Global Friends, to provide international students with cultural enrichment experiences. International students and St. Cloud area community members gather together for activities such as boating, ice fishing, camping, hayrides, biking, and sharing dinner in a Minnesotan's home. These activities offer active learning moments outside of the academic environment.

As a result of the Academic & Cultural Sharing Scholarship, SCSU and the surrounding community are greatly enriched by the depth of student engagement, the volume of cultural exchanges, and the diversity of cultural sharing activities. The ACSS has helped international students to build social networks in the United States through their support of and engagement with the local community. These experiences serve to provide international students with a sense of belonging within Minnesota, while those in the community have an opportunity to learn from, engage with, and befriend international students. Table 1 provides a snapshot of the impact of these cultural sharing activities.

Table 1. International Student Participation in Cultural Sharing Activities

Fiscal Year	# of Students Participated	# of Cultural Sharing Activities Logged	# of Hours* Logged	# of Different Volunteer Opportunities Logged
FY18	835 (Fall 2017) 851 (Spring 2018)	3,174	6,348	46
FY17	783 (Fall 2016) 767 (Spring 2017)	3,118	6,236	47
FY16	586 (Fall 2015) 853 (Spring 2016)	2,332	4,664	38

*2 hours minimum commitment for each activity.
Source: Data provided by St. Cloud State University Center for International Studies.

Over the last 3 years, the number of students who have volunteered through the ACSS have ranged each semester from 580 to 860 students, with the total of number of activities ranging from 2,300 to 3,200 each year. The accumulated hours of these cultural sharing activities have varied between 4,600 and 6,350 hours each academic year. The types of activities that students engage in varied between 35 and 50 different categories. Cultural sharing activities not only create a space for international students to express their culture, but also an opportunity for international students to engage with each other, allowing for the creation of diverse networks within the international student community.

The success of the ACSS helps maintain and grow SCSU's international student population. It also allows the university to remain cognizant of the quality of the international student experience, while enriching the overall culture of the university and greater campus community through deliberate and constructed efforts.

Global Living Communities

Another approach to encouraging cultural exchange and learning between domestic and international students is to be intentional about the housing assignments of international students. Assigning domestic and international students to globally themed living and learning communities serves to promote cross-cultural friendships and global learning among all students. However, care must be taken to ensure substantive cross-cultural interactions, given that much of the research on friendship patterns of international students indicates that meaningful relationships with domestic students can be difficult to achieve (Di Maria 2012).

To this end, SCSU created the Global Living Community within Lawrence Hall, which pairs 50 domestic students with 50 international students. The offices of the SIO and CIS staff are also located in Lawrence Hall, providing easy access to support services and opportunities to participate in shared programming.

The Global Living Community is an ideal home for both international and domestic students who are interested in improving their foreign language aptitudes, developing their intercultural communication skills, and expanding their knowledge of international affairs. Thus, this international living and learning community serves an important role in advancing internationalization and promoting global learning. SIOs should work collaboratively with faculty and residential life staff to design and support such programs. While the establishment and maintenance of international living and learning communities may require SIOs to allocate additional financial and staff resources to ensure success, the impact they have on students often includes a greater sense of social support compared with other residential communities, greater appreciation for diversity, and increased interest in study abroad (Freeman et al. 2012; O'Neal Kelley 2009).

These and other strategic initiatives implemented by SIOs and partnering units on campus help to create a welcoming environment for international students. SIOs can also team up with organizations in the community (e.g., libraries, museums, cultural centers, language banks, etc.) to find other ways for internationals students to learn and share through cross-cultural dialogues that promote understanding. These opportunities support international students' academic success, cultural adjustment, and contributions to the campus culture and identity.

Conclusion

Support structures need to be in place to assist and orient international students to the campus community. How these structures are implemented and enacted will vary from institution to institution, depending on the unique campus communities present at each individual institution. However, certain elements are often present at most colleges and universities, including pre- and post-arrival orientations, recruitment and retention techniques specifically aimed at international students, academic support initiatives that utilize existing structures as well as ones designed specifically for international students, and unique ways to engage and involve international students with the campus community. This area can be easily overlooked and is often the first to be cut in times of budget constraints. Thus, SIOs must ensure that programs designed to support international student success are maintained.

Additional Resources

Choudaha, Rahul, and Paul Schulmann. 2014. *Bridging the Gap: Recruitment and Retention to Improve International Student Experiences*. Washington, DC: NAFSA: Association of International Educators.

Rubin, Kyna. 2014. "Retaining International Students." *International Educator* XXIII, 5:30–37. https://www.nafsa.org/_/File/_/ie_sepoct14_retaining.pdf.

References

Andrade, Maureen S., and Normal W. Evans. 2009. *International Students: Strengthening a Critical Resource*. Plymouth, United Kingdom: Rowman & Littlefield Education.

Chalmers, Paul. 1976. "The Professionalization of the Foreign Student Advisor." *NAFSA Newsletter*, 12–14.

Di Maria, David. 2012. "Factors Affecting Students Affairs Administrators' Views of Campus Services for International Students at Five Public Universities in Ohio." Doctoral dissertation. University of Minnesota.

Feighner, Michael. 2013. "Celebrating the Best of Internationalization." *NAFSA Blog*. November 19, 2013. http://www.nafsa.org/2013/11/19/celebrating-the-best-of-internationalization/.

Freeman, Michael, Nathanial Lynch, Mark Leech, and Sylvain Chabra. 2012. "Creating an Intentional, Interdepartmental International Living Learning Community." Presented at the NAFSA Bi-Regional Conference, Puerto Rico. https://www.nafsa.org/_/File/_/regbi/creating_intentional_inter.pdf.

Furnham, Adrian, and Stephen Bochner. 1986. *Culture Shock: Psychological Reactions to Unfamiliar Environments*. London, United Kingdom: Methuen.

Kelley, Caitlin O'Neal. "Building an Intentional, Interdepartmental International Living Learning Community: The Case of Holcombe Hall." Capstone Collection. 1237. https://digitalcollections.sit.edu/capstones/1237/.

Kwai, C. K. 2017. "The SIO Profile: A Preliminary Analysis of the Survey on Senior International Education Officers, Their Institutions and Offices." Durham, NC: Association of International Education Administrators. https://www.aieaworld.org/assets/docs/Surveys/final-2017%20executive%20summary_sio%20profile%20survey.pdf.

Minnesota State. 2018. "2.2 State Residency." St. Paul, MN: Minnesota State. http://www.minnstate.edu/board/policy/202.html.

20 | International Alumni Engagement

Jaishankar Raman

International students and scholars make significant contributions to higher education institutions in the areas of research, publications, and the sharing of new perspectives and experiences. International students also provide significant financial benefits. NAFSA: Association of International Educators (2018b) reports that during the 2017–18 academic year, international students and their families supported more than 455,000 jobs and contributed $39 billion dollars to the U.S. economy.

While much of the institutional focus is on the support and services provided to international students while they are in the United States (see chapters 10 and 19), there has been increased attention placed on the valuable role that alumni can play. An important question on the minds of many senior international officers (SIOs) is how to cultivate and maintain active relationships with these international students and scholars once they graduate and return home. This chapter highlights some of the issues related to working with international alumni and offers strategies for engagement.

The SIO Role

In 2018, NAFSA sent a survey to 1,697 individuals who attended the NAFSA International Education Leadership Knowledge Community workshops and the NAFSA Symposium on Leadership from 2010 to 2018, asking these SIOs and leaders to list the hot trends that are priorities to them and their institutions (NAFSA 2018a). While 16 specific areas were identified, ranging from education abroad (9 percent) to transnational education (2 percent), the engagement of international alumni did not make it onto the list (NAFSA 2018a). Yet, it is vital for an institution's internationalization strategy to have a robust alumni engagement plan. And SIOs are uniquely positioned to spearhead the work because they are involved in all aspects of international students' experiences on campus, starting from recruitment to graduation. As a member of the institution's senior leadership team, the SIO can work with the alumni office and the advancement office, which typically handles fundraising efforts, to create an effective and coordinated platform for engaging international alumni.

Alumni Engagement

The first step in developing a clear strategy for fostering ongoing relationships with international alumni is to understand the goals for such an effort. The purposes of the engagement will vary from institution to institution. The goal may be to maintain contact and share university-related news, enlist alumni in helping with the recruitment of new students from their country, provide networking opportunities for other alumni (both U.S. and international), inspire alumni to make donations to their alma mater, or all of the above.

Once the goals of these relationships are determined, more targeted strategies can be employed by members of the SIO's office, in partnership with staff from the alumni and advancement offices, for engaging different alumni populations. Such strategies may include encouraging alumni to post internship, grant, and work opportunities for students and other alumni; submitting news items for the alumni magazine; participating in local alumni activities; starting a new alumni chapter; and mentoring a current student.

Recruitment Efforts

International students often describe their U.S. college education as a transformative experience and recall fond memories of their time on campus (Wilkie 2015). It is important to create an academically enriching and socially welcoming campus climate because students who have a positive experience are more likely to tell their friends and family about the institution, providing good word-of-mouth momentum (Loo, Mixell, and DeProto 2018). These alumni can be valuable and influential brand ambassadors of the university when speaking with and recruiting students.

Prospective students, and their families, appreciate hearing from alumni who are from their own nationality and are familiar with their culture, educational system, and language. International alumni can share stories of their personal experiences, answer questions, and provide guidance and insights, all in their native language. Alumni can also call on their local connections to create partnerships with local high schools, recruitment agencies, and other entities to reach new audiences of prospective students.

Enlisting alumni to assist with recruitment efforts can be an effective, low-cost strategy. In fact, in times of declining student interest, alumni can even help to inspire confidence among prospective students and mitigate their fears. However, universities must have clear guidelines for alumni engagement to ensure that roles and expectations are defined in advance. For instance, it should be made clear to alumni and prospective students that admissions decisions are outside the purview of alumni; specific questions regarding admission should be directed to the appropriate admissions officer.

To facilitate the more general discussions that alumni can have with prospective students, managers in the International Student and Scholar Services (ISSS), International Enrollment Management (IEM), or alumni units can share information, brochures, and other marketing material that highlight the university's latest internationalization initiatives and global activities. By having regular communications and exchanges with alumni about the current curricular and cocurricular programming, ISSS and IEM staff can make sure that the information is being communicated in a way that is accurate and consistent with the university's standards.

Networking Opportunities

Using the international alumni database as a transnational networking tool is a win-win opportunity for all involved. Alumni can serve as resources or support figures for students and faculty who are going abroad. They can offer local recommendations on maximizing the experience and provide assistance if needed. Universities can also enlist the help of their alumni in creating internships and job opportunities for current students. Alumni may be able to facilitate virtual interviews, set up mentoring or shadowing sessions, and provide in-country insights on navigating the institutional, regional, and national systems. Alumni could potentially help current or recent graduates get their foot in the job marketplace in their home city or country by connecting them to important contacts and local groups and organizations.

Much of this communication and networking occurs transnationally via email, videoconferencing, and social media platforms. Thus, it is important for the SIO's office to have a strong digital presence and updated online network. At Valparaiso University, for example, international office staff members encourage and help all current international students open and maintain a functioning LinkedIn account. This professional social media platform may be more accepted in certain countries and allows for both one-on-one exchanges and larger discussion groups. Staff members of the SIO's office can create a LinkedIn group specifically for international alumni of the university and send out communications all at once, saving time and effort. These online exchanges build connections between the alumni and the institution, as well as between alumni across the world.

Fundraising Purposes

The alumni database can also be used to help secure funds for various university initiatives. This aspect of the alumni relationship is nuanced depending on the country in which the alumni live. There are important cultural differences between how fundraising is approached and appropriated within the United States versus in other countries. For example, in some countries, there may not be a historical precedence or cultural norm of philanthropy, so more lengthy discussions and information may be involved when reaching out to these alumni. Care must be taken on how topics related to finances are brought up by different offices.

One effective strategy is to remind international alumni of the positive experiences they enjoyed during their academic careers. By making the cause more personal, the alumni may be more inspired to donate and provide those same opportunities for future generations of students. Conversely, if certain alumni experienced challenges in relation to a lack of funds at the time, they may be motivated to set up a scholarship to prevent students from having to experience the same struggles.

It is important for the SIO to work with staff in the alumni and advancement offices to determine the most appropriate strategy to use and to avoid mis- or over-communication with potential donors. Through this collaborative approach, the units can share in the costs, efforts, and benefits for the good of the overall institution.

Challenges of Alumni Engagement

While the benefits to engaging international alumni are numerous, the path to getting there can sometimes be slow. One of the most challenging aspects is developing and maintaining a database of international alumni contacts. Often, institutions have not made a strong effort to collect and update the contact information for international alumni due, in part, to the difficulty in gathering such data from other countries given the different privacy laws (e.g., General Data Protection Regulation in Europe) and a higher likelihood of having incorrect information.

However, universities that are interested in international alumni engagement should start working on compiling alumni information from a variety of sources. The most common location for such information is either in the ISSS office or with some of the more popular professors on campus who have continued to stay in touch with their students. For many institutions, it is difficult to access older student records that are in paper form or in a system that did not transfer over to the new enterprise system being used. To help resolve this issue, some institutions have invested funding to hire student assistants to pull alumni contact information together.

Social Media

Social media is a useful tool for finding data on alumni. For example, at Valparaiso University, as part of a preliminary exercise, staff members in the alumni office gathered the contact information for more than 900 students through Facebook. However, it is important to note that social media does have its limitations since people use a variety of platforms (e.g., Line, WeChat, WhatsApp, Viber, etc.). Additionally, some social media platforms are not easily accessible in certain countries, such as Facebook and Google in China. Universities need to ensure that the SIO's, alumni, and advancement offices are not only aware of such alternative platforms, but staff members use them effectively and appropriately.

If one of the objectives of creating an international alumni database is to provide campus updates and information, then sending printed material over-seas can become cost prohibitive. Social media, however, allows for a more effective use of university resources and provides more options for sending customizable information. The only caveat is to make sure that the electronic information sent over is accessible; for example, some videos and website links cannot easily be retrieved in certain countries in Asia. Some institutions may benefit from having a staff member who specializes in social media and is able to maintain multiple accounts across platforms and disseminate targeted information to alumni channels.

Reaching out to alumni with relevant content in a timely manner will require some financial investment. However, the instant and sharable nature of social media and other electronic campaigns can often keep the alumni far more engaged when compared with the traditional print material that many universities are still using. The online modes of engagement allow SIOs to combine alumni activities with recruitment efforts by providing an oppor-tunity for sharing alumni success with prospective applicants. The ability to connect stories to faces and reach audiences around the world with the touch of a button can make efforts toward alumni engagement much more efficient and successful.

Conclusion

International students have a transformative impact on college campuses and globally. It is important to maintain these connections long after students leave the campus and return to their home country. Cultivating meaningful relationships with international alumni needs to be a high priority for all SIOs and their institutions. A comprehensive internationalization strategy should thus include a robust alumni engagement program. The benefits of connecting with international alumni can enhance the university brand, recruit new students, and create a wider global network of influence.

Additional Resources

Conroy, Philip, and Sandra Rincon. 2012. "International Alumni Matter." *EAIE Forum* Spring 2012:29–31. https://www.nafsa.org/uploadedFiles/Chez_NAFSA/Find_Resources/Internationalizing_Higher_Education/International%20Alumni%20Matter%20EAIE%20article.pdf.

Dobson, Gretchen. 2011. *Being Global: Making the Case for International Alumni Relations*. Washington, DC: CASE.

Dobson, Gretchen. 2015. "Staying Global: How International Alumni Relations Advances the Agenda." *EAIE blog*. September 3, 2015. https://www.eaie.org/blog/staying-global-how-international-alumni-relations-advances-the-agenda.html.

Funaki, Julia, Brian Flahaven, Joanna Grama, Mark McConahay, Mary Chapin, Tracy Locklin, Caroline Donovan White, and Joann Ng Hartmann. 2018. *Implications of the General Data Protection Regulation: An Interassociation Guide*. American Association of Collegiate Registrars and Admissions Officers, Council for Advancement and Support of Education, EDUCAUSE, Indiana University-Bloomington, National Student Clearinghouse, and NAFSA: Association of International Educators. https://www.aacrao.org/signature-initiatives/trending-topics/gdpr/gdpr-interassociational-guide/.

Wilkie, Dana. 2015. "A Remarkable Resource—International Alumni." *International Educator* XXIV, 3:77–72.

References

Loo, Bryce, Jeremy Mixell, and Marcella Pitcher DeProto. 2018. "Understanding and Enhancing Student Experience, for IEM Professionals." Presented at the 2018 NAFSA Region XII Conference, Monterey, CA. https://www.nafsa.org/uploadedFiles/NAFSA_Dojo/Connect_and_Network/Regions/Region_XII/Districts/Northern/Understanding%20and%20Enhancing%20Student%20Experience%20for%20IEM%20Professionals_NAFSA%20Northern%20District%202018_FINAL.pdf.

NAFSA: Association of International Educators. 2018a. "2018 Hot Trends for International Education Leaders." Washington, DC: NAFSA: Association of

International Educators. https://www.nafsa.org/uploadedFiles/NAFSA_Dojo/ Professional_Resources/Browse_by_Interest/Internationalizing_Higher_ Education/Network_Resources/International_Education_Leadership/ sio_hot_trends.pdf.

NAFSA: Association of International Educators. 2018b. "NAFSA International Student Economic Value Tool." Washington, DC: NAFSA: Association of International Educators. https://www.nafsa.org/economic.

Wilkie, Dana. 2015. "International Enrollment." *International Educator* XXIV, 3:70–72.

Appendix A | The SIO's Checklist for Mapping Immigration Services

Ravi Shankar and Jim Hammerschmidt

At some institutions, the SIO serves as the principle designated school official (PDSO), responsible officer (RO), and campus authority on all immigration-related matters. In other instances, the international student and scholar advising office may not even report to the SIO (see chapter 10). Whether or not immigration services falls directly under their purview, SIOs should familiarize themselves with the nonimmigrant and immigrant visa categories supported by their institution and know the roles various internal and external stakeholders play in serving these individuals. Such knowledge is essential because it informs multiple aspects of internationalization, including terms of exchange agreements, the feasibility of research projects, and admissions policies.

The simple checklist below is designed to assist SIOs who do not have prior experience dealing with immigration issues.

1. Meet with a representative from the office of institutional research to determine how the institution codes and tracks international constituents for official reporting purposes. Also ask for a report showing the institution's international constituents, including students, scholars, and employees, by country and visa category. Do not be surprised if there are gaps or discrepancies.

2. Based on the report received from institutional research, review the categories of nonimmigrant and immigrant visas that the institution supports either formally or informally (see table 1).

Table 1. U.S. Nonimmigration Visa Categories at U.S. Higher Education Institutions

Visa Category	Description
F-1 Visa	International students in the United States who are pursuing an educational objective (e.g., certificate, bachelor's degree, master's degree, doctoral degree)
M-1 Visa	International students studying at approved U.S. vocational schools (e.g., information technology school, aviation school)
J-1 Visa	Exchange visitors from a range of categories, including professor, scholar, trainee, intern, and more

Source: U.S. Department of State (n.d.); U.S. Citizenship and Immigration Services (2018a, 2018b).

3. Review the information contained on the U.S. Department of State's Study in the States website (studyinthestates.dhs.gov/schools) or, if the SIO has direct oversight of immigration services, complete the Student and Exchange Visitor Program's Training for Designated School Officials (egov.ice.gov/exec/training/login.asp).

4. Determine who serves as the institution's PDSO, RO, and subject matter expert (SME) on filing employment-based immigration petitions.

5. Meet with the institution's PDSO to review the following:

   - Form I-17;

   - Recertification scorecard;

   - SEVIS batch system, if applicable;

   - Report obtained from institutional research;

   - Categories of student visas for which the institution issues visa documents;

   - Programs for which student visas are not supported;

   - Minimum requirements, including financial and English-language proficiency, for international students to obtain a Form I-20;

   - Employment, registration, practical training, and other policies pertaining to international students;

   - International student orientation;

- Current challenges and ways the SIO can be helpful; and

- If the PDSO is also responsible for J-1 immigration advising services, then discuss the topics listed above for J-1 exchange visitors as well.

6. Meet with the institution's RO to review the following:

    - J-1 annual report;

    - Current process faculty must follow to host international scholars;

    - Departments that host the most international scholars;

    - Typical activities of international scholars;

    - Orientation for exchange visitors; and

    - Current challenges and ways the SIO can be helpful.

7. Meet with the institution's employment-based immigration SME to review the following:

    - Employment-based visa categories sponsored by the institution;

    - Types of positions sponsored by the institution;

    - Role of internal and outside legal counsel;

    - Which units pay for employer expenses associated with immigration petition sponsorship; and

    - Current challenges and ways the SIO can be helpful.

        - Identify how other international constituents are served. Such groups include international visitors, undocumented students, Deferred Action for Childhood Arrivals, legal permanent residents, and dual citizens.
        - Determine which units have the authority to create and enforce institutional policies and procedures related to international constituents.

- If immigration advising services are provided across multiple units, assess to what extent efforts are coordinated and interpretations are aligned.
- Assess the current caseload of immigration advisers to advisees in relation to comparable institutions.
- Advocate on behalf of staff for access to basic tools, resources (e.g., NAFSA's Advisers Manual) and regular training to perform their duties effectively.

References

U.S. Citizenship and Immigration Services. 2018a. "Students and Exchange Visitors." Washington, DC: U.S. Citizenship and Immigration Services. https://www.uscis.gov/working-united-states/students-and-exchange-visitors.

U.S. Citizenship and Immigration Services. 2018b. "Students and Employment." Washington, DC: U.S. Citizenship and Immigration Services. https://www.uscis.gov/working-united-states/students-and-exchange-visitors/students-and-employment.

U.S. Department of State. n.d. "Student Visa." Washington, DC: U.S. Department of State. https://travel.state.gov/content/travel/en/us-visas/study/student-visa.html.

Appendix B | **Resources for Senior International Officers**

Gonzalo R. Bruce

Senior international officers (SIOs) enter the profession from many different academic and professional backgrounds. In many cases, SIOs received training in a specific academic discipline and served in faculty roles before taking on administrative responsibilities in international education. Some SIOs "fell into the profession" and have faced a steep learning curve as they navigate their new administrative responsibilities. However, in recent years, an increasing number of SIOs are joining the profession with formal training in international education or higher education administration, as more and more universities are offering academic programs and advanced degrees in the field.

This appendix aims to give an overview of key resources that SIOs may find helpful in their quest for leadership development in the international education field. The nature of the field is dynamic and constantly changing. For this reason, this section does not intend to, nor can it, provide an exhaustive list of resources. Any exclusion of resources was not intentional, and inclusion in this book does not imply endorsement of any kind. An online appendix (shop. nafsa.org/detail.aspx?id=2090) lists additional print and digital resources that may be of interest and use to SIOs.

Professional Associations and Conferences

Professional associations present SIOs with significant professional development and networking opportunities. Some associations serve to address the more general aspects of international education, while others respond to specific niches or regional foci. Below is a list of only a few of the international,

national, and regional associations that provide resources and networking opportunities.

American International Recruitment Council (AIRC) – www.airc-education.org

SIOs with responsibilities in international enrollment management will benefit from AIRC's resources and services. AIRC is a membership-based organization created to safeguard the interests of international students and enrolling institutions through the promotion of ethical, standards-based international recruitment strategies. It is the only professional association focused solely on issues relating to international student recruitment, and it serves members from higher education institutions, pathway program providers, certified student recruitment agencies, and secondary schools. AIRC facilitates learning through its annual conference, webinars, trainings and workshops, and comprehensive list of resources that includes contract models, budgets, and international enrollment strategies.

Association of International Education Administrators (AIEA) – www.aieaworld.org

AIEA is a U.S.-based professional association with a mission to serve primarily SIOs. AIEA holds an annual conference that is a meeting opportunity for SIOs to discuss pressing topics related to college and university internationalization. The AIEA Senior Advisers Program connects seasoned and established international education leaders with professionals who recently joined the field. In addition, AIEA serves new SIOs (professionals with fewer than 5 years in their current role) through the SIO Academy. AIEA also supports Thematic Forums, which are small-scaled conferences organized by SIOs to explore specific topics in the field. AIEA's website contains a list of international education organizations and a schedule of international education conferences worldwide. Finally, AIEA administers a listserv used by its members to share information about difficult issues pertaining to managing campus internationalization and understanding best practices across the member institutions.

Diversity Abroad Network – www.diversitynetwork.org

The Diversity Abroad Network provides resources on student diversity and inclusion in education abroad. Diversity Abroad is the leading professional consortium of educational institutions, government agencies, and for-profit and nonprofit organizations dedicated to advancing good practices to increase access, achieve equitable diversity, and foster inclusive excellence in global education. A member-driven organization, Diversity Abroad members support the organization's mission to advance research, develop effective advising tools, and offer learning and development opportunities that are essential to creating equitable access to global education. Salient among the resources available to SIOs are the Access, Inclusion, Diversity, & Equity Roadmap and the Diversity & Inclusion Resource Center. Two particularly relevant learning opportunities coordinated by Diversity Abroad are the annual Diversity Abroad Conference and the Global Institute for Inclusive Leadership.

European Association of International Educators (EAIE) – www.eaie.org

EAIE is dedicated to developing knowledge, expertise, research, and networking opportunities in higher education internationalization with a European focus. A member-led association, EAIE equips academic and nonacademic professionals with best practices and solutions to internationalization challenges. EAIE holds Europe's largest international education conference, attended by international education professionals from all over the world. In addition to the annual conference, the EAIE Academy aims to equip SIOs with knowledge, tactics, and innovative tools in credential evaluation, marketing and recruitment, management, intercultural communication, student services, and policy and strategy. Finally, EAIE's website contains useful links to research and trends in international education, conference publications, and access to selected articles from its member magazine, *Forum.*

The Forum on Education Abroad – forumea.org

For international education leaders who are responsible for study abroad and global learning opportunities, The Forum is a resource for developing and implementing standards of good practice for education abroad, supporting research initiatives, and finding educational programs. The Forum is a member-based organization comprised of U.S. colleges and universities, overseas institutions, consortia, agencies, provider organizations, and foundations. Particularly relevant to SIOs is the resource page that contains standards of good practice, assessment resources, and research and publications. The organization holds two annual meetings, one in the United States and the other in Europe. Additionally, The Forum hosts workshops on study abroad standards that touch on student selection, student learning, emergency response and protocols, and preparation and return support, among other topics. It also offers a Competency Credentials Program that is designed for new and experienced education abroad professionals.

NAFSA: Association of International Educators – www.nafsa.org

NAFSA is the premier professional association for international educators worldwide. NAFSA provides critical services and resources in all of the administrative areas pertaining to international education. SIOs rely on NAFSA for professional development, networking, advocacy, information on the latest trends and events impacting international education, and more. Specific to SIOs, NAFSA's International Education Leadership Knowledge Community (IEL KC) supports senior international officers and internationalization leaders in their efforts to implement a vision and build commitment for comprehensive internationalization at their institutions. The IEL KC facilitates opportunities for engagement between SIOs through an online discussion forum and makes available the latest publications on pressing issues facing SIOs. Finally, the IEL KC manages the Symposium on Leadership, a signature program designed for SIOs during the NAFSA Annual Conference & Expo.

NAFSA members and nonmembers can take advantage of different professional development opportunities, including the e-Learning Courses and e-Learning Seminars. Renowned professionals lead these interactive sessions built on the latest research and their own professional experiences. NAFSA organizes the annual Management Development Program, a comprehensive training program for international education professionals who aim to become effective managers in international education, develop expert skills in the field, and participate in a learning space between peers and trainers. NAFSA collaborates with the American Association of State Colleges and Universities to deliver the Institute for Senior International Officers, which is discussed in further detail below.

NAFSA's Annual Conference & Expo is the largest international education conference in the world, with more than 350 exhibitors representing every aspect of international education, including academic institutions, pathway providers, third-party providers, consulting firms, and insurance companies. The NAFSA Annual Conference & Expo serves as a unique networking opportunity for international educators and partners around the world. NAFSA also produces Regional Conferences in 11 geographical regions across the United States each year.

In addition to its *International Educator* magazine, NAFSA publishes books, articles, and other resources for the field of international higher education. NAFSA's website features pivotal publications for SIOs that cover all areas in international education, including international education leadership, education abroad, international student recruitment, English as a second language, international student success, and the management of international offices, among others. A particularly influential publication for SIOs, for example, is John K. Hudzik's *Comprehensive Internationalization: From Concept to Action* (2011), which was updated in 2018 as *Comprehensive and Strategic Internationalization: Lessons Learned and Future Prospects.*

University Associations and Affiliations

SIOs can benefit from exploring the university affiliations that may or may not already exist at their institutions. This section describes a few university-wide associations and affiliations with globally focused programs, which provide resources and direction to assist SIOs in advancing internationalization strategies, programs, and activities.

American Association of State Colleges and Universities (AASCU) International Program – www.aascu.org/Programs/InternationalPrograms

AASCU is a member-based organization serving public colleges and universities. While AASCU deals with broader issues of public higher education, its International Programs division contributes key resources for SIOs. For example, the Institute for Senior International Officers is an AASCU/NAFSA collaboration designed for new SIOs working on AASCU member campuses. The Institute introduces SIOs to skills and knowledge essential to leading internationalization at a public comprehensive college or university. AASCU also offers opportunities to advance internationalization through faculty-development opportunities in China and Japan. AASCU's China Initiatives are well established both in the United States and in China and present opportunities for SIOs to develop knowledge related to international enrollment management, faculty development, and education abroad. Among these initiatives is the Sino-American CHEPD 1+2+1 Program, a dual-degree program recognized by the Chinese Ministry of Education as a Program of Excellence, which is managed by AASCU in coordination with the China-based Center for International Educational Exchange.

American Council on Education (ACE) Center for Internationalization and Global Engagement – www.acenet.edu/news-room/Pages/Center-for-Internationalization-and-Global-Engagement.aspx

ACE is a membership organization that represents nearly 1,700 college and university presidents. ACE's Center for Internationalization and Global Engagement (CIGE) promotes the advancement of internationalization for its member colleges and universities. Among the resources that CIGE provides to SIOs is the *Mapping Internationalization on U.S. Campuses* study, which is conducted every 5 years to assess the current state of internationalization at U.S. colleges and universities (Helms and Brajkovic 2017). CIGE organizes the Internationalization Laboratory, a two-year, cohort-based program that imparts customized (i.e., university-specific) guidance and insight to help colleges and universities achieve their internationalization goals. Additionally, ACE's Institute for Leading Internationalization is designed to support SIOs with comprehensive internationalization efforts at their institutions. CIGE's website contains the Internationalization Toolkit, a useful page of resources for campus internationalization, including policies, programs, surveys, and information from other institutions.

Association of American Colleges & Universities (AAC&U) Global Learning – www.aacu.org/resources/global-learning

AAC&U is a U.S. membership-based organization that comprises 1,400 institutions committed to liberal education and includes accredited public and private colleges, community colleges, research universities, and comprehensive universities of every type and size. AAC&U aims to increase capacity to help undergraduate students engage in diversity and develop stronger understandings of the common aspects among peoples, cultures, nations, and regions. The association's website lists useful resources on the topic of global learning, including campus models and case studies and publications on global learning definitions and service learning in global settings. Additionally, AAC&U coordinates General Education for a Global Century, a curriculum and faculty development project sponsored by Shared Futures: Global Learning and Social Responsibility initiative and the Liberal Education and America's Promise initiative.

Association of Public and Land-grant Universities (APLU) International Programs – www.aplu.org/projects-and-initiatives/international-programs

APLU is a North American organization serving 238 public research universities, land-grant institutions, and state university systems from Canada, Mexico, and the United States. APLU's (2017) *Pervasive Internationalization: A Call for Renewed Leadership* report is an influential publication targeting university leadership and their mandate to internationalize U.S. campuses. For SIOs who serve at institutions invested in international development projects, APLU acts as a link between the university community, the U.S. Agency for International Development, and the Board for International Food and Agricultural Development. In addition, APLU houses the Knowledge Center on Higher Education for Advancing Development through Higher Education, which is intended to foster knowledge and support engagement and partnerships with higher education institutions in developing countries, while strengthening capacity to address socioeconomic development challenges. Finally, APLU's Commission on International Initiatives promotes a comprehensive internationalization agenda for senior leadership aiming at integrating international dimensions into the learning, discovery, and engagement missions of its member institutions.

Community Colleges for International Development (CCID) – www.ccidinc.org

SIOs at community colleges may appreciate the contributions of CCID. It engages and empowers an international association of community, technical, and vocational institutions to create globally engaged learning environments. CCID's membership base is mostly from the United States, although a growing number of international colleges are joining the network. The association offers many resources on its website, including a login-protected internationalization toolkit and discussion board. CCID organizes global familiarization trips and an annual conference.

Institute of International Education (IIE) – www.iie.org

IIE develops important resources for many international education professionals. Its membership-based program, IIENetwork, grants access to exclusive research data, a weekly newsletter, the *IIENetworker* magazine, and services delivered through IIE's 18 offices and affiliates around the world. IIE receives funding from the U.S. Department of State to administer flagship programs, one of which is the Fulbright Program. Fulbright awards grants for U.S. citizens to go abroad to study, teach, and conduct research and for non-U.S. citizens to come to the United States for academic work. IIE also administers programs focused on higher education capacity building and partnership development.

Through its grant funding, IIE does much to address the issue of displaced students and scholars at risk. Its Platform for Education in Emergencies Response, the Scholar Rescue Fund, the Artist Protection Fund, and the Emergency Student Fund help provide resources, funding, and guidance to students from countries of crisis and the SIOs who work with these populations. Every year, IIE produces the *Open Doors* report, which is discussed below.

Formal Education and Credentials

There is not a single path or academic trajectory that SIOs must follow that leads to international education leadership roles and responsibilities. In fact, the multiple perspectives and backgrounds of SIOs help to make international education a rich and dynamic field (Deardorff et al. 2012).

A growing number of higher education institutions have developed advanced degrees and graduate programs to prepare the next generation of SIOs (Dessoff 2006). These include master's and doctoral degree programs as well as graduate certificate programs focused on international education administration. The presence of these advanced studies in international/comparative education and intercultural relations/communications demonstrates the growing value of formal education as a way to enter the profession and reflects the consolidation of international education as a profession. For SIOs seeking to advance their career in the field, several U.S. and international universities offer doctoral degree (PhD and EdD) programs in higher education administration, comparative and international education, international education development, and educational policy and leadership.

To support new SIOs in their job search and acquired roles, as well as established SIOs in meeting changing priorities and responsibilities, NAFSA developed the *NAFSA International Education Professional Competencies* (2015). This resource includes critical competencies that international education professionals must demonstrate in each of the major areas in the field, including comprehensive internationalization, education abroad, international enrollment management, and international student and scholar services. In addition, the publication addresses cross-cutting competencies, or "shared skills, knowledge, and competencies needed across all international education domains" (NAFSA 2015, iv).

Suggested Scholarship and Publications

This section does not intend to provide an exhaustive list of publications, but rather highlights a few publications for SIOs to consider as they face new challenges in their roles.

Books

- John K. Hudzik's edited volume *Comprehensive Internationalization: Institutional Pathways to Success* (2015) explores practices and approaches to comprehensive internationalization, with case studies drawn from U.S. and overseas institutions.

- *Leading Internationalization: A Handbook for International Education Leaders* (2018), edited by Darla K. Deardorff and Harvey Charles, is a useful resource for SIOs. With contributions from several active SIOs, the book gives context to the role of SIO. It addresses issues related to the SIO's leadership and expertise in areas such as curriculum, enrollment management, assessment, and risk management. This resource stands out from others because it covers essential skills and qualities for leading effective internationalization strategies, among which are entrepreneurship, communication, data analysis, and ethical perspectives.

- *NAFSA's Guide to International Partnerships: Developing Sustainable Academic Collaborations* (forthcoming), edited by Jane Gatewood, delves into the parameters of international partnerships, identifying sound practices for the cultivation of partnerships that foster deep, rich, and sustainable connections internationally.

- *The SAGE Handbook of International Higher Education* (2012) is a comprehensive edited tome from Darla K. Deardorff, Hans de Wit, John D. Heyl, and Tony Adams written for SIOs, examining contextual and historical frameworks, strategic dimensions, internationalization at home, internationalization abroad, and the future of international higher education.

- John D. Heyl and Fiona Hunter published the second edition of *The Senior International Officer as Change Agent* in 2019. The book examines the role of SIOs amid the turbulent global context, their role within their institutions as change agents, and practical dimensions on shaping an internationalization plan and stewarding the internationalization process.

Journals and Magazines

- *Frontiers: The Interdisciplinary Journal of Study Abroad* (frontiersjournal.org) is a peer-reviewed publication that disseminates the latest research on education abroad.

- *International Educator* (www.nafsa.org/ie) is NAFSA's bimonthly magazine that includes briefings on current topics as well as columns focused on international education leadership and other areas of interest to SIOs.

- *International Higher Education* (ejournals.bc.edu/ojs/index.php/ ihe/index) compiles articles from scholars and administrators on issues pertaining to higher education globally, including campus internationalization.

- *Journal of International Students* (jistudents.org) is a peer-reviewed quarterly publication that focuses on issues related to international student affairs.

- *Journal of Studies in International Education* (journals.sagepub.com/ home/jsi) is a peer-reviewed publication that contains the latest scholarship on all facets of the internationalization of higher education.

Online Resources

- IIE's *Open Door* data (www.iie.org/Research-and-Insights/Open-Doors) is an online and paper-based resource for SIOs interested in understanding trends in international enrollment management and study abroad. The U.S. Department of State funds the *Open Door* data.

- NAFSA's International Student Economic Value Tool (www.nafsa. org/economic) is an important tool for SIOs who face the need to demonstrate and articulate the economic impact of international students in the United States, their state, and their campus.

- US Journal for International Enrollment Management (www.usjournal.com/fairs/) is an online directory of international student recruitment tours and events.

References

Association of Public and Land-grant Universities (APLU). 2017. *Pervasive Internationalization: A Call for Renewed Leadership.* Washington, DC: Association of Public and Land-grant Universities. http://www.aplu.org/library/pervasive-internationalization-a-call-for-renewed-leadership/file.

Deardorff, Darla K., and Harvey Charles, ed. 2018. *Leading Internationalization: A Handbook for International Education Leaders.* Sterling, VA: Stylus Publishing.

Deardorff, Darla K., Hans de Wit, John D. Heyl, and Tony Adams, eds. 2012. *The SAGE Handbook of International Higher Education.* Thousand Oaks, CA: Sage Publications.

Dessoff, Alan. 2006. "A Key to Your Career? Master's Degrees." *International Educator* XV, 1:36–43.

Helms, Robin Matross, and Lucia Brajkovic. 2017. *Mapping Internationalization on U.S. Campuses: 2017 Edition.* Washington, DC: American Council on Education.

Heyl, John D. 2007. *The Senior International Officer (SIO) as Change Agent.* Durham, NC: Association of International Education Administrators.

Heyl, John D., and Fiona J. Hunter. 2019. *The Senior International Officer as Change Agent, Second Edition.* Durham, NC: Association of International Education Administrators.

Hudzik, John K. 2011. *Comprehensive Internationalization: From Concept to Action.* Washington, DC: NAFSA: Association of International Educators.

Hudzik, John K. 2015. *Comprehensive Internationalization: Institutional Pathways to Success.* Abingdon, Oxford, United Kingdom: Routledge.

Hudzik, John K., ed. 2018. *Comprehensive and Strategic Internationalization: Lessons Learned and Future Prospects.* Washington, DC: NAFSA: Association of International Educators.

NAFSA: Association of International Educators. 2015. *NAFSA International Education Professional Competencies.* Washington, DC: NAFSA: Association of International Educators. http://www.nafsa.org/competencies.

About the Authors

Shahzad Ahmad is associate vice president for the Center for International Studies and Multicultural Student Services at St. Cloud State University. In his position with Multicultural Student Services, Ahmad focuses on academic and personal support and development of all students, particularly students of color, and works to enhance education abroad opportunities for both domestic and international students. With the Center for International Studies, Ahmad provides leadership on recruitment and admission of international students, as well as developing opportunities for students to study abroad. Ahmad holds a BA in biomedical sciences and an MS in international economics from St. Cloud State University.

Lance R. Askildson, PhD, serves as vice provost and chief international officer at Kennesaw State University, where he also holds a tenured faculty appointment in applied linguistics. Previously, Askildson was the assistant provost and founding director of the Center for the Study of Languages and Cultures at the University of Notre Dame. He is a board member for the Assessment and Evaluation Language Resource Center at Georgetown University, a trustee of the Center for the Advanced Study of International Education, and chairman of the Atlanta-based training center for the United Nations Institute for Training and Research.

Director international at the University of Auckland, **Brett Berquist** leads the international office at New Zealand's largest international education provider.

Berquist has more than 25 years' experience in Asia, Europe, and the United States as academic staff and administrator leading international recruitment strategy, transnational education, English as a second language provision, campus-wide internationalization strategy, credit mobility, and international partnerships. He has presented and published on these themes, and he serves in leadership roles in a number of international education organizations. Currently, he chairs the Forum of International Managers and Directors of Universities New Zealand.

Roger Brindley, EdD, is vice president for USF World at the University of South Florida, overseeing global research, international student mobility, study abroad, and international student success on campus. USF World promotes global curriculum development, resulting in broader cultural understandings, sustainable and substantive multidisciplinary global partnerships, and globally focused faculty research designed to create applied solutions at this preeminent research university. Brindley currently serves on the Board of the Association of Public and Land-grant Universities Commission on International Initiatives. He is a full professor in education and served as the dean of education at USF from 2016 to 2018. Brindley received an EdD from the University of Georgia.

Gonzalo R. Bruce, PhD, is assistant provost for global education and senior international officer at Boise State University. Bruce has been in international education for more than 17 years, serving universities in Chile and the United States. He completed his PhD in higher education administration at The Ohio State University, where his dissertation research focused on institutional design and internationalization of U.S. research universities. He received his master's degree from the Graduate School of International Public Affairs at the University of Pittsburgh. Bruce is a Fulbright alum and has served as a U.S. Department of State guest lecturer in Latin America.

Kiki Caruson, PhD, is the assistant vice president for research, innovation, and global affairs for the University of South Florida (USF) System. In this capacity, she provides leadership regarding the university's global engagement strategy, including student international mobility, global programming, international research services, and partnership development. Caruson manages the USF Global Discovery Hub and was the recipient of the inaugural Society for Research Administrators International's Big Ideas Award, which funded the development of an online Global Research Toolkit. Caruson received her bachelor's degree from Smith College, her master's degree from Johns Hopkins University, and her doctoral degree from the University of Georgia.

Geraldine de Berly, PhD, vice president for academic affairs at Springfield Technical Community College in Massachusetts, is responsible for all academic matters at the institution. Previously, she was vice provost for continuing and professional education at University of Massachusetts-Amherst and, for many years, she was at Syracuse University as senior associate dean and director of the English Language Institute. de Berly holds a PhD in educational administration from New Mexico State University, an MA in applied linguistics from the University of Essex in England, and an AB in political science from Stanford University.

Erich Dietrich, PhD, is assistant vice president for global programs at New York University (NYU) and associate dean of global affairs for the NYU Steinhardt School of Culture, Education, and Human Development. He oversees international partnerships, study abroad, curricular internationalization, and international student recruitment strategy. He was chair of NAFSA's International Education Leadership Knowledge Community in 2018 and served on the 2019 Diversity Abroad Conference Committee. An expert on affirmative action in higher education in Brazil, Dietrich regularly teaches graduate courses in international education and higher education at NYU. He holds a PhD in history and received a Fulbright International Education Award to India in 2016.

David L. Di Maria is associate vice provost for international education at the University of Maryland-Baltimore County. As senior international officer, he leads internationalization strategy while overseeing a diverse portfolio of programs, projects, and initiatives supporting the international dimensions of teaching, research, and service. Di Maria earned a doctorate from the University of Minnesota, where he studied internationalization from a P–16 perspective. Di Maria holds leadership positions within the American Council on Education's Commission on Internationalization and Global Engagement, Association of Public and Land-grant Universities's Commission on International Initiatives, and NAFSA: Association of International Educators's International Education Leadership Knowledge Community. He is also a former president of the American International Recruitment Council.

Jim Hammerschmidt, PhD, is the associate vice provost for global engagement and the executive director of the Office of International Services at the University of Illinois-Chicago (UIC). Hammerschmidt and his staff provide immigration-related services to more than 5,000 international students, scholars, physicians, and staff at UIC. Hammerschmidt is an active member of NAFSA and currently serves as chair of NAFSA's Healthcare Institute Interest Group. Hammerschmidt has served as past chair of NAFSA's International Education Leadership Knowledge Community and chair of NAFSA's Regulatory Ombudspersons Subcommittee.

Heather Housley is director of international student and scholar services at Georgia State University in Atlanta, where she has worked with international students and scholars since 1997. A two-time Fulbright award recipient and former chair of NAFSA Region VII, Housley holds a bachelor's degree from the University of Tennessee-Knoxville and a master's degree in student affairs and higher education from The Ohio State University. She has been honored with Region VII's International Excellence Award and the Award of Excellence from NAFSA's Knowledge Community for International Student and Scholar Services.

Victoria Jones, PhD, is the chief global affairs officer at the University of California-Irvine. She previously led international relations at Seattle University, the University of Texas-San Antonio School of Business, and in Brazil at Escola de Administação de Empresas de São Paulo da Fundação Getulio Vargas. Jones teaches and conducts research in international marketing and management. Her degrees are from Cornell University, the University of Pennsylvania Annenberg School, and the University of Southern California.

Jeet Joshee, PhD, is associate vice president for international education and global engagement and dean of the College of Professional and International Education at California State University-Long Beach. As the chief international officer of the university, he advises the president and provost on international education policies and priorities and advances the university's global mission by establishing strategic international partnerships and creating engagement opportunities for students, faculty, and staff. Joshee served as president of the American International Recruitment Council in 2018. He earned his doctoral and master's degrees in international development education from University of Massachusetts-Amherst.

George F. Kacenga, PhD, is the executive director of the Office of Global Engagement at Purdue University-Northwest, where he leads the strategic efforts to extend global programs and initiatives, including international admissions, immigration services, education abroad, and the English language program. Kacenga is an award-winning scholar and administrator, having received the Sepmeyer Research Grant, Marjorie Peace Lenn Research Award, and Fulbright Korea Administrator Award. Kacenga received his PhD in social and comparative analysis in education from the University of Pittsburgh, analyzing changes in foreign credential evaluation strategies related to international student enrollment trends.

Jun Liu is vice president and vice provost for global affairs, dean of international academic programs and services, and professor of linguistics at Stony Brook University. Liu received the 2015 Governor's Award for International Programs of the Year for Georgia State University and the 2018 NAFSA Simon Award for Campus Internationalization for Stony Brook University. Liu is a past president of TESOL and a former board member of the Association of International Education Administrators.

Jesse Lutabingwa, PhD, is associate vice chancellor for international education and development and professor of public administration at Appalachian State University. He holds a PhD in public administration from Jackson State University, where his dissertation focused on the role of nongovernmental organizations in the policymaking process in Tanzania. Lutabingwa received a master's degree in international development management from the School for International Training and a bachelor's degree in business administration and economics with a political science minor from Wartburg College. He has been a NAFSA member since 1992 and has served in leadership positions at the national and regional levels.

Dru Marshall, PhD, has served as the provost and vice president academic at the University of Calgary since 2011. She is currently chair of the U15 Group of Canadian Research Universities Provosts and is the only non-American executive committee member on the Association of Public and Land-grant Universities's Council on Academic Affairs.

Cheryl Matherly, PhD, is vice president and vice provost for international affairs at Lehigh University. She previously served as vice provost for global education for the University of Tulsa. Matherly is president of the Association of International Education Administrators (AIEA) and coauthor of the AIEA's "Standards of Professional Practice for International Education Leaders and Senior International Officers." She often writes on international education and employability. Matherly is the recipient of two Fulbright grants for international education administrators. She earned her doctorate from the University of Houston.

Dragana Nikolajevic is a research policy and international relations manager at the University of California Office of the President (UCOP), where she facilitates internationalization efforts for the University of California system. She completed her master of public administration and international development at Maxwell School, Syracuse University. Prior to her work at UCOP, Nikolajevic helped establish the Consortium of Universities for Global Health, and she worked for UNDP in Serbia and for Central European University in Budapest,

Hungary. She coauthored articles on intercultural education in Europe and on Serbia's democratization efforts for *Nations in Transit 2010*.

Anthony L. Pinder, PhD, is the associate vice president of academic affairs for internationalization and global engagement at Emerson College. He manages Emerson College's European Center at Kasteel Well, The Netherlands; Global BFA in Paris, France; international institutional partnerships/agreements; education abroad; the Curriculum Internationalization Studio; international student affairs; English language learning; and faculty-led Global Pathway Programs. A graduate of the Institutes for Higher Education at Harvard University, Pinder holds a doctorate in educational leadership and higher education administration from Clark Atlanta University, an MA in international economics and Latin American studies from Johns Hopkins University, and a BA in finance from Morehouse College.

Jaishankar Raman, PhD, is the assistant provost for international affairs at Valparaiso University in Indiana. He is also an associate professor of economics and currently teaches a graduate seminar. Raman completed his doctoral degree in economics from the University of Notre Dame and has a master's in economics from Fordham University. He received his bachelor of arts degree from the University of Mumbai in India. Raman is president of the Indiana Academy of the Social Sciences and the regional outreach coordinator for NAFSA's International Enrollment Management Knowledge Community.

Janaka Y. Ruwanpura is the vice provost international and a professor in civil engineering at the University of Calgary. Prior, he served as the director and Canada research chair in project management. Ruwanpura has been recognized for outstanding academic, research, and administrative leadership with many local, national, and international awards. He led the University of Calgary to win prestigious awards for internationalization and produced new models and tools to enhance internationalization such as the International Partnership Assessment Rating Index (IPARI) and seven-point model of Recipe for Success. He is a professional engineer and a professional quantity surveyor in Canada.

Ravi Shankar is the director of the International Office at Northwestern University, where he directs the work of 11 professionals who serve an international population of nearly 7,000 students, faculty, research scholars, and dependents. He has been in the field of international education for more than 20 years and has worked in various types of institutions. Shankar currently serves as the president and chair of the Board of Directors for NAFSA. He completed his undergraduate degree at the University of Delhi and earned his MA in English literature at University of Mysore in India. He completed a MS in management and organizational development at the United States International University in Nairobi.

Brian N. Stiegler, PhD, currently serves as assistant provost for international education at Salisbury University and has served as the director of the Janet Dudley-Eshbach Center for International Education since 2006. His current duties include the supervision of education abroad programming, international student and scholar services, the English Language Institute, and global partnerships. Stiegler has served on multiple international education leadership boards in the United States, including the American Council on Education's Commission on Internationalization and Global Engagement and the Benjamin A. Gilman International Scholarship National Advisory Committee. He earned his PhD in Spanish language and Latin American literature at the Pennsylvania State University.

Mary Anne Walker is the director of global STEM engineering programs at Michigan State University (MSU). In 2017, she was selected by DAAD to grow research cooperation with U.S. and Canadian academic leaders. Walker led MSU Global's research and development and created the first international research office at MSU in 2000. Walker joined MSU after serving with the United States Agency for International Development in eastern Europe. Her graduate work was in U.S. foreign policy at Tufts University Fletcher School of Law and Diplomacy and in international law at American University School of International Service.

Paulo Zagalo-Melo, PhD, is associate provost for global education, serving as the senior international officer of Western Michigan University. Previously, Zagalo-Melo served as associate provost for global century education at the University of Montana and held senior leadership positions at the Luso-American Foundation and Fulbright Portugal. Zagalo-Melo is vice chair of the Association of International Education Administrators (AIEA)'s Policy and Advocacy Committee and was a 2015–16 AIEA Presidential Fellow. He has a master of public administration degree from Harvard University and a PhD in political science from the Catholic University of Portugal.